VISUAL QUICKSTART GUIDE

QUICKTIME PRO 4

Judith Stern
Robert Lettieri

 Peachpit Press

Visual QuickStart Guide
QuickTime Pro 4
Judith Stern
Robert Lettieri

Peachpit Press
1249 Eighth Street
Berkeley, CA 94710
(510) 524-2178
(510) 524-2221 (fax)

Find us on the World Wide Web at: http://www.peachpit.com

Peachpit Press is a division of Addison Wesley Longman

Copyright © 1999 by Judith Stern and Robert Lettieri

Editor: Clifford Colby
Production Coordinator: Amy Changar
Copy Editor: Jill Simonsen
Compositor: Owen Wolfson
Indexer: Rebecca Plunket

ISBN: 0-201-35469-1

0 9 8 7 6 5 4 3

Printed and bound in the United States of America

 Printed on recycled paper

Dedication

To the memory of Louis Lettieri, who was always a teacher.

Acknowledgements

As always, we first need to thank the people who created QuickTime, for without them this book wouldn't exist. The QuickTime team consists of many amazing people, but we are especially grateful to Peter Hoddie, Eric Carlson, Mike Dodd, Ian Ritchie, Kathy Stevens, Mitchell Weinstock, Charles Wiltgen, Tim Monroe, and Brandee Allen for all the information and support they've provided us while writing this book.

In addition, thanks to Darren Giles, Brian Greenstone, Brent Burgess, Susan Kitchens, Greg Paschall, Brandon Muramatsu, and Tom Sicurella for answering miscellaneous technical questions. We also thank Marvin Stern, Lois Stern, David Schwartz, and Tom Baer for testing steps.

Many thanks go to our editor, Cliff Colby, and copy editor, Jill Simonsen, who edited this edition; as well as to Simon Hayes, Bill Cassel, and Charles Wiltgen, who edited our previous QuickTime VQS. Thanks also to Marjorie Baer, Victor Gavenda, Amy Changar, Owen Wolfson, and others at Peachpit who've been responsible for making this project a reality.

On the personal front, thanks to Sam (who thinks all parents "go to work upstairs" at night time), and to her "village," especially those who were there to care for her while we were writing—Betsy and Garrett, Phil and Judy, Brandon, Phil and Karen, Annma, Grandma and Grandpa, and the wonderful teachers at Monteverde School.

About the Authors

Judith Stern is an instructional multimedia specialist. Her background includes corporate training, expert systems development, educational research, and multimedia development. She works for the Instructional Technology Program at the University of California at Berkeley, where she provides support and training to faculty and staff developing instructional multimedia software; she's also a software designer and multimedia consultant for the Computer as Learning Partner Project and the Web-Based Integrated Science Environment project, both of which are NSF-funded educational research projects.

Robert Lettieri is a computer consultant, specializing in graphics and multimedia technologies. At the University of California at Berkeley, he is the multimedia specialist for NEEDS, A Digital Library for Engineering Education. He has been experimenting and working with digital and analog video for more than 12 years. He has taught many people how to use graphics and desktop publishing software, both individually and in training workshops.

Together, Stern and Lettieri are the authors of several books and articles on multimedia. They also coauthor The Little QuickTime Page (www.bmug.org/quicktime/), a weekly news Web page. In addition, they do freelance consulting and training as well as multimedia production work and have been involved in many aspects of the development of various Web, CD-ROM, and kiosk projects. They can be reached at jandr@ccnet.com.

TABLE OF CONTENTS

INTRODUCTION

Welcome to the *QuickTime Pro 4: Visual QuickStart Guide.*

In this book you'll learn how to use QuickTime, QuickTime Player Pro, and a few other tools—remarkable yet inexpensive pieces of technology that have become standards in the multimedia industry.

We've been QuickTime users since its introduction in 1991 and completed our first book about the technology in 1992. We wrote that book, and have continued to write and teach about the topic, because QuickTime is such an elegant technology: It's easy for beginners to understand and use, yet it provides tremendous power and flexibility as you learn more about it.

With the introduction of QuickTime 4 this year, the technology has become accessible to an even wider variety of users. Plus, it's more powerful than ever.

A Visual QuickStart Guide, with its emphasis on clear, illustrated, step-by-step instructions, provides a perfect forum for us to share our enthusiasm for QuickTime and QuickTime Player.

Whether you're new to the world of QuickTime or a seasoned veteran, we think you'll find this book a good learning and reference tool.

What Are QuickTime and QuickTime Player?

Unlike most pieces of software you might buy a book about, QuickTime isn't an application but rather an *enabling technology*: If it's installed on your system, it enables many other programs to provide important multimedia features.

QuickTime enables other software to handle multimedia data (for example, video, audio, and animation) gracefully and simply. It allows media to be viewed, edited, combined, transformed, and manipulated in whatever way an artist, teacher, communicator, business person, video professional, or kid sees fit.

QuickTime Player is one of the many programs that derives its power from QuickTime. The Player, however, is not just any old tool. Called MoviePlayer until the introduction of QuickTime 4, QuickTime Player occupies a special place in the QuickTime world. Written by the creators of QuickTime, it was originally used for internal testing: If a feature was added to QuickTime, MoviePlayer was enhanced so that the QuickTime engineers could test and demonstrate that feature.

Over the years MoviePlayer (now QuickTime Player) has evolved into a powerful tool for playing, editing, and preparing movies for distribution. However, a lot of its functionality isn't immediately obvious—after all, the engineers knew where to find what they needed. This book will explain how you can gain access to all of those features.

Figure i.1 A standard QuickTime movie can be viewed much like a videotape using controls at the bottom of the window.

Figure i.2 A QuickTime VR movie is one in which a viewer clicks and drags in the movie window to explore a space or object.

Figure i.3 An interactive movie has clickable objects (like buttons) that cause changes in the movie.

Anatomy of a QuickTime Movie

A QuickTime *movie* is the container that holds multimedia data. The movie may be a standard time-based movie (**Figure i.1**), which is typically played in a linear fashion (though it can also be accessed randomly). Or it may be a QuickTime VR movie (**Figure i.2**), which provides an immersive spatial environment in which users can move around in spaces or view objects from different angles by dragging and clicking in the movie image. The movie can even have interactive buttons and other elements, resembling a multimedia application more than a traditional QuickTime movie (**Figure i.3**).

Regardless of whether it's linear or spatial, noninteractive or interactive, a QuickTime movie is a container that can potentially hold many types of multimedia data. Most people associate QuickTime with video and audio, but there's also text, MIDI music, and animation (2D and 3D).

QuickTime stores different types of media separately in what are called *tracks*. Although you don't need to know about this underlying architecture to view QuickTime movies, it helps to be aware of the different track types if you want to understand and tap QuickTime's power and flexibility.

A *video track*—which generally consists of an image or sequence of images—is the standard track for holding visual data in QuickTime movies. Each image in a track is usually composed of pixels, or individual squares of color. (However, see the sidebar "Of Pixels and Vectors.")

A *sound track* is the standard track for holding digitized audio.

A *music track* contains what is essentially a musical score—information about a sequence of musical notes that QuickTime can play back. It's analogous to MIDI (Musical Instrument Digital Interface), a standard in the electronic music industry. The storage space taken up by music-track data is very small compared with digitized sound.

A *text track* holds only text. Because tracks in a movie are synchronized, the text track provides a way to caption a movie, index it, or even include URLs that can cause a Web page to download at a specific point in playback. Text tracks are also searchable; viewers can search for key words to find precise points in the movie.

A *3D track* holds 3D data, which includes geometric definitions of objects as well as descriptions of the objects' surfaces (including texture and lighting). A 3D track works in conjunction with the *tween track*, which defines an object's motion. (The term *tween* comes from the animation world, where the key frames are created first and then the in-between frames are generated.)

A *sprite track* contains graphic objects, or sprites, which can be pixel-based, vector-based, or even contain 3D data. Animated sprites are stored only once in a movie file, and the path they follow across the screen is specified separately. (Sprite track files are much smaller than most video tracks, which require new sets of pixels to be stored whenever an object changes positions in a scene.) Some sprites have associated actions and can act as interactive buttons; these are referred to as *wired* sprites. Sprites can be both animated and wired.

Some additional track types include *MPEG tracks* and *Flash tracks*, which are created when an MPEG (Moving Picture Experts Group) file or a Flash file is opened with a QuickTime tool. (See "QuickTime Compared to Other Technologies," later in this chapter for more about MPEG. Flash is an interactive

Of Pixels and Vectors

Computer graphics come in two basic types: *bitmap* (or pixel-based) and *vector*.

The pixels in a bitmap image are a predetermined size. If you resize a bitmap image, you just stretch the pixels, causing the image to become fuzzy.

Vector images are composed of lines and curves, which are mathematically defined. When you stretch a vector image, the computer recalculates the image so that it retains its resolution. In addition, because it's much more efficient to represent images mathematically, vector images require less disk space than bitmap images.

Most QuickTime video tracks and sprites in sprite tracks are composed of bitmap images. However, QuickTime video tracks or sprites can contain vector-based images (also called *curve media*) as well. In fact, many Web developers are starting to go this route because it allows them to create smaller files. QuickTime can now handle Flash, Macromedia's vector-based format.

vector-based animation format widely used on the Web.)

A single QuickTime movie can have lots of tracks—a mix of different track types or multiple tracks of the same type.

One of the great things about QuickTime is that it knows when to keep its tracks tightly linked and when to let them stand alone. When someone plays a QuickTime movie, the tracks play together, at the same time, synchronously. When it's time to edit, however, you can treat the movie as a unified piece or you can make alterations to individual tracks. There may even be instances during playback when you need to turn one track off and another on—QuickTime can handle this, too.

Streaming Tracks

New to QuickTime 4 is the ability to do true streaming—or *RTSP (Real Time Streaming Protocol) streaming*—over the Internet. However, only certain types of tracks can be streamed in this way; these include video, audio, text, and music. When you prepare a movie to be streamed, a special *hint track* is created for each of the streamable tracks. Hint tracks tell a video server how to send movie data over the network. When a movie is viewed as it's being streamed, it contains a single *streaming track* (rather than its original tracks), which contains all of the streamed data.

ANATOMY OF A QUICKTIME MOVIE

QuickTime Compared with Other Technologies

If you compare QuickTime with most other multimedia or video technologies, you'll find that QuickTime offers much more to many more people. Not only can QuickTime movies hold video, audio, music, text, 3D and sprite animation, QuickTime can also import files in many formats (currently more than 30, see the sidebar on this page); none of the other technologies can integrate as many media types. It works as well on the Internet as it does for CD-ROM and kiosks and provides an integrated solution for both Mac OS and Windows 95/98 and NT. Programmers can use QuickTime on multiple platforms without having to rewrite their code. They can also use QuickTime's standard user interface elements for common functions as well as extend QuickTime with their own features without having to worry about the basics. This means that users get better tools faster.

Take, for example, AVI files—the file type for Microsoft's Video for Windows technology. Unlike QuickTime files, AVI files can only contain video and audio. Video for Windows has always been considered inferior to QuickTime—even Microsoft chose QuickTime over Video for Windows for such products as its best-selling Encarta. (In fact, Microsoft no longer supports Video for Windows.) For several years Microsoft promised a more robust replacement technology called ActiveMovie, but that product was never fully released (only the playback portion saw the light of day). The company then integrated ActiveMovie with its DirectX technology, calling the result DirectShow, but this technology is neither cross-platform nor mature enough where good end-user tools are being developed (as in the QuickTime world).

File Formats That QuickTime Can Handle	
◆ 3DMF	◆ MPEG-1 (Mac OS only)
◆ AIFF	
◆ Animated GIF	◆ MPEG-1 Layer 3 audio (MP 3)
◆ AU	
◆ Audio CD (Mac OS only)	◆ Photoshop
	◆ PICS
◆ AVI	◆ PICT
◆ BMP	◆ PNG
◆ DV	◆ QuickDraw GX
◆ FlashPix	◆ QuickTime Image File
◆ FLC/FLI	
◆ GIF	◆ SGI
◆ JPEG/JFIF	◆ Sound Designer II
◆ KAR (Karaoke)	
◆ MacPaint	◆ System 7 Sound
◆ Macromedia Flash	◆ Targa Image File
◆ MIDI	◆ Text
◆ MPEG Layer 1 & 2 audio (Mac OS only)	◆ TIFF
	◆ WAV

QUICKTIME COMPARED WITH OTHER TECHNOLOGIES

Another video format you may be familiar with is MPEG, a high-quality format used for years by multimedia professionals. Until recently, however, MPEG was difficult and expensive to create and could only play back on computers with special MPEG decoding hardware. So, it was less useful as a technology for the masses. Now, however, MPEG encoding software has come down in price from tens of thousands of dollars; hardware encoding options run in the thousands of dollars; and slower software encoding options run in the hundreds of dollars or are even sometimes free. In addition, today's faster processors mean that more computers are now powerful enough to play back MPEG in software without extra hardware. However, many more computers can handle QuickTime. What's more, the current incarnations of MPEG (MPEG-1 and MPEG-2) are restricted to just video and audio. MPEG-4, which should be available in a few years, will be based on QuickTime's file format. (In case you're wondering, there's no MPEG-3; there's an audio format called MP-3, but it's a variant of MPEG-1.)

QuickTime also holds its own among the newer technologies (such as RealMedia and Windows Media) being used to stream video and audio over the Internet. Previously, these technologies held certain advantages because they offered "true" streaming. (See Chapter 16 for a discussion of different types of streaming.) Now, however, QuickTime 4 can handle true streaming as well. Plus, it's the most widely used video technology on the World Wide Web.

In the realm of immersive technologies, several developers offer products similar to QuickTime VR. Companies such as IPIX and Live Picture offer their own competing versions of immersive spatial technologies; however, these don't offer the full range of capabilities and smooth integration provided by the complete QuickTime architecture.

AVI and MPEG Playback

One important thing to remember about QuickTime is that it can be used to open, play back, and edit AVI files. On the Mac, QuickTime can open and play MPEG-1 files as well.

QUICKTIME COMPARED WITH OTHER TECHNOLOGIES

The World of QuickTime

As we've mentioned, many products either are based on QuickTime or support it in some fashion. Although we can't begin to cover them all here, it helps to know what categories of tools are out there. We mention a few specific tools here; however, such references aren't necessarily endorsements.

Tools for capturing QuickTime video and audio

Many tools exist for capturing audio and video from videotape, audiotape, or even a live video signal. Generally you use these tools in conjunction with hardware inside your computer. This hardware may come with its own software to do the QuickTime capture. Most often, however, the tool of choice for QuickTime capture is Adobe Premiere, which includes a capture feature even though it is primarily an editing tool.

Tools for generating QuickTime tracks

You can also create QuickTime movies using standard media creation tools. For example, many animation tools export their data as QuickTime video tracks, and a few can also export data as QuickTime sprite tracks. Macromedia Director is the most well-known tool in this category. When tools don't create QuickTime tracks, they often export in a format that a QuickTime tool (such as QuickTime Player) can open or import.

Tools for editing QuickTime video and audio

Once you have a QuickTime track, you can use QuickTime Player (or any other editor that supports the track type) to combine and edit tracks to create something completely new. The tool you are most likely to have heard of is Adobe Premiere. This general-purpose video editing and effects tool lets you do things that QuickTime Player can't, such as adding transitions between scenes. On the other hand, most video editing tools only handle a subset of the full range of QuickTime tracks, whereas QuickTime Player supports them all.

Tools for compressing and optimizing QuickTime movies

Once you have composed your movie, you must prepare it for delivery over a network or on CD-ROM or hard disk. In particular, video and audio need to be compressed. You can use QuickTime Player, Premiere, or another editing tool for basic compression. Other tools are used exclusively for compression and optimization; one of these, Media Cleaner Pro, is generally considered to produce the best-looking movies.

Tools for integrating QuickTime movies with other media

Macromedia Director (which we mentioned as a tool that creates animations) is also well known as a multimedia authoring tool and allows users to assemble sophisticated interactive presentations that contain many types of media. The QuickTime file format can be included in and controlled from a Director presentation. Other authoring tools, such as Apple HyperCard, Asymetrix ToolBook, and Tribeworks iShell, also support QuickTime in this way. In addition, simpler presentation tools such as Microsoft PowerPoint let you include QuickTime movies in a presentation. QuickTime movies can also be embedded in Web pages; most Web browsers and many Web-page creation tools offer QuickTime support. Even such tools as word processors and spreadsheets often allow you to include QuickTime movies in their documents.

THE WORLD OF QUICKTIME

Tools for streaming QuickTime movies over the Internet

You'll prepare movies for streaming using the compression tools mentioned above. However, to do true, or RTSP, streaming, you must have an RTSP streaming server. Currently the only shipping RTSP streaming server for QuickTime comes as part of the Mac OS X Server. If you want to do live streaming, you'll also need an application that can capture and stream the video. In most cases you'll use a live streaming application in conjunction with an RTSP server; one of these is Sorenson Broadcaster.

What's New in QuickTime 4?

The most radical and publicized change in this version of QuickTime is the ability to do true streaming. (We go into more detail about this in Chapter 16.)

Also new to this version is QuickTime Player, which replaces MoviePlayer. Sporting a different look than its predecessor, QuickTime Player also offers some new features, including a way to bookmark favorite movies, a way to open movies found on the Internet, the ability to create chapter lists (points in the movie that viewers can quickly jump to), and more audio controls and displays. In addition, Windows users can now access some features that were previously available only for the Mac OS, such as music track playback through external MIDI devices and drag-and-drop editing. (You'll find information about all of these additions, as well as others, beginning in Chapter 3.)

QuickTime itself also has some new features, which can be accessed from a variety of tools. New and updated compressors improve your ability to compress movies for distribution over the Internet. And new import and export capabilities allow QuickTime to import MP3, Flash, and FlashPix files, as well as export any movie as an AVI file, a FLC file, or a sequence of still images in a large variety of formats. In addition, QuickTime can be used to export movies so they are ready for streaming (see Chapter 16).

QuickTime now uses a new installer that lets you download only those components you need. (See next chapter.)

Other improvements include new options for embedding movies on Web pages (see Chapter 17), hyperlinks in text tracks (see Chapter 17), new video filters (see Chapter 15), and some performance improvements, particularly for QuickTime VR movies.

QuickTime on Windows and Mac OS Computers

QuickTime 3 was the first fully cross-platform release of the program. Although you could play back QuickTime movies on Windows computers in earlier versions, you couldn't create or edit them.

Now, you can have virtually the same experience on either platform.

In this book we use screen shots from the Mac and Windows platforms interchangeably because just about all of the menus and dialog boxes contain the same content on both platforms.

When keys, names of screen elements, or procedures differ between the two platforms, we note both options—for example, "Press the Option key (Mac OS) or the Alt and Ctrl keys (Windows) to..."

In the few cases where a feature is available on only one platform, or where the sequence of steps to follow is significantly different, we'll label the section as "Mac OS Only" or "Windows Only."

What You'll Find in this Book

Now that you have some idea what QuickTime and QuickTime Player are, you're ready to move on to Chapter 1. Here we'll show you how to get up and running with these pieces of software.

Beginning with Chapter 1, this book is divided into three parts: Chapters 1 through 5 show you how you can view QuickTime movies *without* changing them. Chapters 6 through 14 detail the vast array of techniques for editing movies, including manipulating tracks independently. And Chapters 15 through 18 examine movie distribution, with an emphasis on Web delivery.

If you're new to QuickTime, you'll probably want to use this book as a primer: Go through it from beginning to end, making sure to work through all the step-by-step instructions. As in all Visual QuickStart Guides, we've used lots of screen shots to illustrate instructions and speed learning.

Even if you're already familiar with QuickTime or QuickTime Player, you should still find this book a useful reference. You can look up specific tasks in the Table of Contents (or Index). And in some cases, the screen shots may be all you need to successfully accomplish what you set out to do.

As you use this book, we hope you'll come to enjoy QuickTime and QuickTime Player as much as we do. There's a lot to learn, so let's get going.

Staying Up to Date

While everything in this book was accurate at the time of its writing, QuickTime is not standing still. If you really want to keep abreast of changes in QuickTime, QuickTime Player, or other related technologies, we suggest you visit our Web site, Judy and Robert's Little QuickTime Page, at http://www.bmug.org/quicktime/. We will also post updates to this book at http://peachpit.com/vqs/quicktime/.

WHAT YOU'LL FIND IN THIS BOOK

QuickTime Basics

Before you can begin learning how to use QuickTime and QuickTime Player, you must have working versions of the software on your computer.

Let's start by stating that QuickTime Player is included in the QuickTime package; so any reference to QuickTime in this chapter implicitly includes QuickTime Player.

Because QuickTime is a standard for delivering multimedia, it may already be installed on your computer as part of the installation process for another multimedia program. We'll show you how to determine whether you have QuickTime and, if so, which version you have.

One key point to remember is that there's a free Standard edition of QuickTime as well as a $30 Pro edition. We'll explain why you'll want the latter.

After going over the software and hardware required to run QuickTime 4, we'll show you how to get and install the Standard edition and then upgrade to the Pro edition by obtaining and entering a registration number.

We'll end this chapter with a few miscellaneous topics—how to always make sure you have the latest version of QuickTime, where to find sample movies, and what to expect in terms of QuickTime's various interfaces.

Differences Between the Pro and Standard Editions

The Pro and Standard editions of the QuickTime system software are essentially the same. What *is* different is the QuickTime Player tool.

The name *Player* is really only appropriate for the version that comes with the Standard edition: You use it to play movies, and that's about it.

When you upgrade to QuickTime Pro, QuickTime Player gains a tremendous amount of functionality, becoming much more than just a "player." Many more menu items appear, providing a slew of additional features. Plus, you gain the ability to import from and export to other media formats as well as to prepare QuickTime movies for Internet playback. Editing features also become available, allowing you to merge movies, add media, alter the movie's components, and save new creations. There are even some new playback features, such as the ability to play full-screen movies.

Upgrading to the Pro version also enhances the other software that is part of the QuickTime package. The PictureViewer application, which is used to view still images, gains the ability to save, import, and export still-image files. And the QuickTime Plugin, which is used to view QuickTime movies on Web pages, allows you to easily save to your hard drive most movies that you would find on a Web page.

In short, you can't do most of what's in this book unless you've upgraded to the Pro version. We won't even bother to indicate the Pro-only features because the Pro version is needed to do just about everything covered here.

Figure 1.1 QuickTime Settings icon in the Mac Control Panels folder.

Figure 1.2 QuickTime icon in the Windows Control Panel folder.

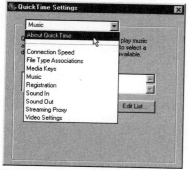

Figure 1.3 Choose About QuickTime in the QuickTime Settings (Mac OS) or QuickTime (Windows) control panel.

QuickTime version number

Figure 1.4 The About QuickTime panel shows which version of QuickTime you have if you have version 3.0 or later.

Checking for QuickTime 4

To take advantage of this book's instructions, you'll want to have QuickTime 4. Since there's a possibility that you may already have it, we'll show you how to first check for it here. If you don't have it, you'll need to get it; we'll explain how later in this chapter.

To see if you already have QuickTime 4:

1. Open your Control Panel(s) folder and look for a QuickTime Settings icon (Mac OS, **Figure 1.1**) or a QuickTime icon (Windows, **Figure 1.2**).

   If the icon is not there, you don't have QuickTime 4; you need to get it.

2. Double-click the QuickTime Settings or QuickTime icon to open the QuickTime Settings control panel.

3. If the pop-up menu at the top of the window is not already set to About QuickTime, click it and choose About QuickTime (**Figure 1.3**).

   Text below the pop-up menu will indicate which version of QuickTime is installed (**Figure 1.4**). If the version number is 4.0 or greater, you have QuickTime 4, though you may still need to upgrade to the Pro edition.

✔ Tips

- On the Mac, if About QuickTime is not one of the choices presented by the pop-up menu in the QuickTime Settings control panel, you probably have QuickTime 2.5. You need to get QuickTime 4.

- On a Windows computer, if you see only a QuickTime 32 or QuickTime 16 icon in the Control Panel window, you have a version of QuickTime earlier than 3. You need to get QuickTime 4.

Checking for the Pro Edition

If you know that you have QuickTime 4, you'll want to determine whether you have the Standard edition (in which case you'll want to upgrade) or the Pro edition.

To see if you have QuickTime Pro:

1. If it's not already open, open the QuickTime Settings control panel (Mac OS) or the QuickTime control panel (Windows).

2. From the pop-up menu choose Registration (**Figure 1.5**).

3. Determine which edition you have:

   If the QuickTime line reads Standard Edition (**Figure 1.6**), you don't have the Pro edition.

   If the QuickTime line reads Pro Player Edition (**Figure 1.7**), you do have the Pro edition.

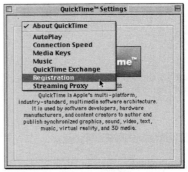

Figure 1.5 Choose Registration in the QuickTime Settings (Mac OS) or QuickTime (Windows) control panel.

Figure 1.6 The Registration panel looks like this when you have only the Standard edition of QuickTime 4.

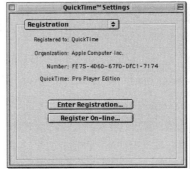

Figure 1.7 The Registration panel looks like this when you have QuickTime 4 Pro.

Hardware and Software Requirements

QuickTime has very few software and hardware requirements.

Mac OS requirements:

◆ Mac OS version 7.1 or higher.

◆ Any 68020, 68030, 68040 or PowerPC-based computer.

◆ 16 MB of RAM for PowerPC–based computers or 8 MB of RAM for 680x0-based computers.

Windows requirements:

◆ Windows 95 or 98 or Windows NT 4.0 (or higher).

◆ Any 486DX-based computer running at 66 MHz or faster, any Pentium-based computer, or any MPC2-compliant PC.

◆ 16 MB of RAM.

◆ SoundBlaster-compatible sound card. Direct X version 3.0 or higher (recommended for best performance).

✔ Tips

■ On a Mac, you'll need a PowerPC processor if you want to play RTSP streaming movies; to access QuickTime's 3D, effects, DV, or MPEG capabilities, or if you want to compress or play back movies using the Web compressors of choice: QDesign for audio and Sorenson Video for video.

■ On a Windows computer, a Pentium processor is recommended for accessing effects as well as DV and 3D capabilities, if you wish to use Sorenson Video or QDesign compressors. In addition, get the latest DirectDraw and DirectSound drivers for your video and audio cards (recommended for best performance).

Obtaining and Installing QuickTime 4

If you don't have QuickTime 4, you'll need to get it: You can download an installer from Apple's QuickTime Web site, which you can then run on your computer.

To get the QuickTime 4 installer:

◆ Using a Web browser, go to Apple's QuickTime Web site, http://www.apple.com/quicktime/ (**Figure 1.8**), and follow the instructions for downloading QuickTime 4 for free.

A file called QuickTimeInstaller (Windows) or QuickTime Installer (Mac OS) will be downloaded to your computer.

To install QuickTime 4 on a Windows computer:

1. Quit all open programs.

2. Locate the file called QuickTimeInstaller and double-click to open it.

3. On the first screen, click Next.

   At this point, you'll be told to quit other programs before proceeding; since you already did this in Step 1, click Next.

4. On the Software License Agreement screen, read the license agreement and (assuming you agree) click the Agree button. (If you disagree with the license agreement, installation will be halted.)

5. On the Choose Destination Location screen, if you're not happy with the default destination directory listed, use the Browse button or type in a destination directory. Click Next when you are finished.

6. On the Choose Installation Type screen (**Figure 1.9**), select the Custom button and click Next.

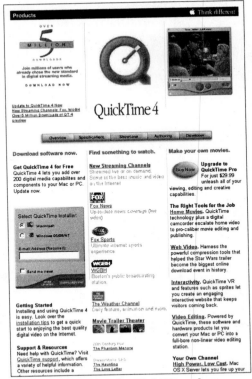

Figure 1.8 You can download QuickTime 4 from Apple's QuickTime Web site.

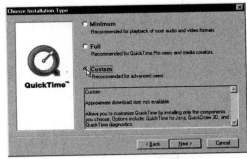

Figure 1.9 To get all the QuickTime components, select Custom.

Figure 1.10 Click Select All to select all components simultaneously.

Figure 1.11 Specify where to place the QuickTime Plugin; we suggest installing it for all listed browsers.

Figure 1.12 Choose your connection speed (you can change it later).

We're going to have you install all QuickTime components because you'll need most of them to use this book.

7. On the Select Components screen, click Select All, so all the checkboxes are selected, and then click Next (**Figure 1.10**).

8. On the Select Program Folder screen, choose a Program folder name (by leaving the default name of QuickTime, typing a new name, or choosing an existing folder) and then click Next.

9. On the QuickTime Plugin Options screen (**Figure 1.11**), specify where you want to place the QuickTime Plugin for Web browsers. (We recommend installing it for all listed browsers.) Then click Next.

10. On the Connection Speed screen (**Figure 1.12**)—which you won't see if QuickTime already knows your connection speed; skip to the next step if this is the case—select the speed of your Internet connection. Then click Next.

If you're unsure of the correct setting, take a guess; you can easily change this later. If you select one of the three slowest speeds, the Allow Multiple Simultaneous Streams checkbox becomes available. Leave it as is; you can easily change this later as well. (See "Using the QuickTime Settings Control Panel" in Appendix B for details on changing all the settings on this screen.)

continues on next page

OBTAINING AND INSTALLING QUICKTIME 4

11. On the Enter Registration screen (**Figure 1.13**), enter your Pro info if you have it. (This info may appear automatically if you previously upgraded to the Pro edition for QuickTime 3.) Then click Next.

If you don't have your Pro info, don't worry. The next section describes how to get it and enter it at a later point.

12. The next screen you'll see will tell you that the Installer is about to download data.

If you're behind a firewall—which is likely if you work for a large corporation—you may need to check Use HTTP Proxy, and enter necessary data. (Talk to your network administrator for help with this.) Click Next.

A new screen appears to monitor your downloading progress. Eventually a Setup dialog box appears, and finally a Finished screen.

13. On the Finished screen, check "Yes, I want to view the QuickTime README file," "Yes, I want to view the Sample Movie," or neither or both. Then click Close.

To install QuickTime 4 on a Mac:

1. Locate and double-click the QuickTime Installer file to open it.

2. On the Welcome screen, click Continue.

3. On the License screen, read the license agreement and (assuming you agree) click the Agree button. (If you disagree with the license agreement, installation will be halted.)

4. On the Choose Installation Type screen (**Figure 1.14**), select the Custom button and click Continue.

We're going to have you install all QuickTime components because you will need most of them to use this book.

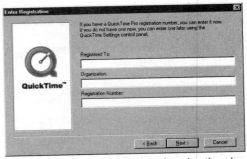

Figure 1.13 Type your Pro info if you have it; otherwise you'll enter it later.

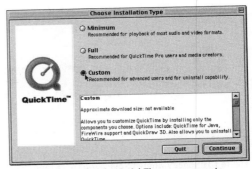

Figure 1.14 To get all the QuickTime components, select Custom.

QuickTime for Windows Before QuickTime 3

The pre-3.0 versions of QuickTime for Windows (QuickTime 32 or QuickTime 16) can coexist with QuickTime 4. In fact, they may even be necessary for some older applications, games, or other software. The QuickTime 4 installer will not remove pre-QuickTime 3 versions of QuickTime for Windows, and neither should you.

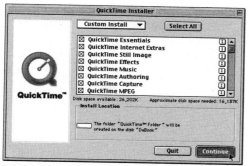

Figure 1.15 Click Select All to select all of the components simultaneously.

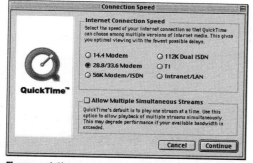

Figure 1.16 Choose your connection speed (you can change it later).

Figure 1.17 Type your Pro info if you have it; otherwise you'll enter it later.

5. On the next screen, click Select All so all the checkboxes are selected and then click Continue (**Figure 1.15**).

6. On the Connection Speed screen (**Figure 1.16**)—which you won't see if QuickTime already knows your connection speed; skip to the next step if this is the case—select the speed of your Internet connection. Then click Continue.

If you're unsure of the correct setting, take a guess; you can easily change this later. If you select one of the three slowest speeds, the Allow Multiple Simultaneous Streams checkbox becomes available. Leave it as is; you can easily change this later as well. (See "Using the QuickTime Settings Control Panel" in Appendix B for details on changing all the settings on this screen.)

7. On the Registration screen (**Figure 1.17**)—which you won't see if QuickTime already knows your Pro info—enter your Pro info, if you have it. Then click Continue.

If you don't have your Pro info, don't worry. The next section describes how to get it and enter it at a later point.

8. The next screen you'll see will tell you that the Installer is about to download data.

If you're behind a firewall—which is likely if you work for a large corporation—you may need to check Use Web Proxy, and enter necessary data. (Talk to your network administrator for help with this.) Click Continue.

A new screen appears to monitor your downloading progress. Eventually you'll encounter a screen that tells you your QuickTime components are being updated.

continues on next page

OBTAINING AND INSTALLING QUICKTIME 4

9. When you see a dialog box telling you that Installation was successful, click the Restart button.

Your computer restarts; when it finishes the startup process, QuickTime 4 is installed.

✔ Tips

■ You may also be able to get QuickTime 4 on CD-ROM—either on a multimedia title or bundled with other video software. In addition, you may be able to obtain a QuickTime CD-ROM directly from Apple by calling (888) 295-0648. (As we write this, the CD-ROM isn't available, but Apple promises it will be. When you call you'll probably reach a voice-mail system that gives you the option of purchasing "an unlock code for QuickTime"; this is the choice you want. You'll speak with a live operator. You will probably be able to order either a CD-ROM with only QuickTime 4 for either platform or a CD-ROM with QuickTime 4 and a registration number to upgrade to the Pro version.)

■ If you're doing the installation for someone else (for example, someone who may only be interested in playing movies), you may want to choose a different installation type.

What If You Don't Install Everything?

The full QuickTime package is composed of a large number of files, each with a particular function (thus the different installation options).

If you try to open a file that requires any of the missing components for playback, a dialog box will tell you what you need and and will offer to go get the missing components. If you have an active Internet connection, you can click the Do It Now button to get QuickTime to retrieve whatever is necessary to view the movie,

On the other hand, if you're missing editing components, you'll notice that certain menu choices are simply missing. To remedy this problem, you'll need to run the QuickTime Updater. See "Getting QuickTime Updates and Missing Components" later in this chapter.

Figure 1.18 Click the Upgrade Now button in the Get QuickTime Pro movie to automatically go to the Upgrade to QuickTime 4 Pro page.

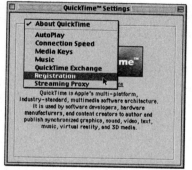

Figure 1.19 Choose Registration in the QuickTime Settings (Mac OS) or QuickTime (Windows) control panel.

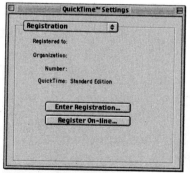

Figure 1.20 Click the Register On-line button to go to the Upgrade to QuickTime 4 Pro page; click the Enter Registration button once you have your registration information.

Upgrading to QuickTime 4 Pro

Unless you already have the Pro edition of QuickTime 4, you will need to upgrade to it after installing QuickTime 4. Go to the Upgrade to QuickTime 4 Pro page at Apple's Web site (as described below) and follow the instructions. You will need to provide a credit card number to pay the $29.99 upgrade fee. You will receive a registration code, also called an *unlock code,* which you will need to enter to "unlock" the Pro features.

To reach the Upgrade to QuickTime Pro Web page:

◆ Enter the URL https://apple-order1.apple.com/ qtupgrade/index.html directly into your Web browser.

or

When you see the window advertising the Pro version (**Figure 1.18**), click the Upgrade Now button. (This advertisement appears automatically the first time QuickTime Player is run if you haven't already upgraded to Pro.)

or

1. Open the QuickTime Settings control panel(Mac OS) or the QuickTime control panel (Windows).

2. From the pop-up menu choose Registration (**Figure 1.19**).

3. In the Registration panel (**Figure 1.20**) click the Register On-line button.

To enter your registration code:

1. Open the QuickTime Settings control panel (Mac OS) or the QuickTime control panel (Windows) and from the pop-up menu choose Registration (**Figure 1.19**).

2. In the Registration panel (**Figure 1.20**), click the Enter Registration button.

3. In the dialog box that appears (**Figure 1.21**), enter your registration information.

   Be sure to enter your name and organization exactly as you did on the Web site, or your registration number won't match. (If you can't remember how you typed the name, it's a good bet that it matches what's on your credit card.)

✔ Tips

- If you don't have Internet access or you're uncomfortable with purchasing over the Internet, you can call (888) 295-0648 to upgrade.

- Another way to get the Pro edition is to purchase a tool that comes with QuickTime 4 Pro, such as Terran's Media Cleaner Pro, Electrifier's Electrifier Pro, or Totally Hip's LiveStage. A QuickTime Pro serial number and registration name will be included with the software; you'll have to follow the directions above to enter this registration information.

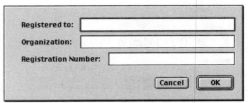

Figure 1.21 Enter the registration information provided by Apple.

Did You Upgrade to Pro for QuickTime 3?

If you upgraded to the Pro edition of QuickTime 3, you should automatically be running the Pro edition of QuickTime 4 (once it's installed), so you don't have to pay $30 again. The same registration info works, and you shouldn't need to reenter it.

Figure 1.22
From QuickTime Player's Help menu , choose Check for Updates.

Getting QuickTime Updates and Missing Components

Apple has made it easy to make sure you always have the most current version of QuickTime.

Once you have obtained QuickTime 4, you have several ways to check for and download updates. When in QuickTime Player, you can ask QuickTime to check for updates to any components you already have. An application called QuickTime Updater will do the same thing; this tool will also allow you to get components that you don't have installed.

To check for updates in QuickTime Player:

◆ From the Help menu, choose Check for QuickTime Updates (**Figure 1.22**).

If you have an Internet connection, you'll be informed of updates. If there are updates, an Update button will appear; clicking it opens the Updater application.

To update QuickTime using QuickTime Updater:

1. Open the application QuickTime Updater: On Windows, you'll find QuickTime Updater in the QuickTime folder, which is in the Program Files folder (unless you specified a different location when you installed QuickTime 4). You can also use the Start menu (choose Programs, then QuickTime, then QuickTime Updater).
On the Mac OS, you'll find QuickTime Updater in the QuickTime Folder at the top level of your hard drive. (If QuickTime 4 came as part of a Macintosh operating system, it may be in the QuickTime Folder within the Applications folder.)

continues on next page

GETTING UPDATES AND MISSING COMPONENTS

2. On the first screen of the Updater (**Figure 1.23**) click Continue.

If the Updater determines you have components that need updating or that you are missing components it will tell you this on the next screen (**Figure 1.24**).

3. Click Update Now.

Any components that need updating will be downloaded and installed.

✔ Tips

■ When QuickTime Updater tells you that there are updates available, you can click the Custom button if you want to pick and choose which components to install; then click Update Now on this screen (**Figure 1.25**).

■ QuickTime will also automatically check for updates, about once a week. However, it only will check for updates if you've just viewed a movie over the Internet; this way it knows that you have an active Internet connection and won't try and dial in when that's not necessarily what you want to happen. If it finds that there are updates available it will notify you and let you choose to download the updates. If you don't want to be automatically notified of updates, choose Check for QuickTime Updates in QuickTime Player's Help menu and then check "Don't notify me of updates."

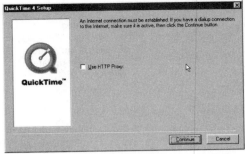

Figure 1.23 You can also use the QuickTime Updater application.

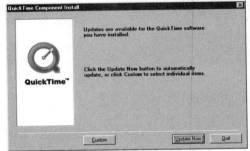

Figure 1.24 If the Updater determines that you have files that need updating; click Update Now to get the updates. Click Custom to see which updates are available or to get missing components.

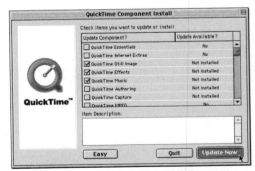

Figure 1.25 Choose which components you want by clicking the checkboxes.

To get missing components using QuickTime Updater:

1. Follow Steps 1 and 2 above.

2. On the screen that tells you whether your QuickTime software is up to date or whether you are missing components (**Figure 1.24**), click Custom.

   A screen appears listing all of the QuickTime component packages. (Each package consists of one or more files.) Only the items listed as Not Installed are missing from your system. You can click on the text of any line to get a description of that item in the field at the bottom of the window.

3. Select the item or items you'd like to install.

   You must click directly on the checkbox to the left of an item name to select it (**Figure 1.25**).

4. Click Update Now.

5. The missing components will be downloaded and installed.

Finding Sample Movies

If you're trying to learn everything you can about QuickTime, you may want to know where to find various sample movies. We recommend going to Apple's QuickTime Web site (http://www.apple.com/quicktime/) and clicking the Showcase button. You'll be taken to a page that has links to lots of categories of movies.

You can, of course, also use a search engine. For example, if you go to HotBot (http://www.hotbot.com/), you can do an Advanced Search for file extensions of .mov. (We got 40,000 matches when we looked for .mov.)

If that seems like too many choices to weed through, you might want to try Yahoo's Computers/Multimedia/Video section (http://www.yahoo.com/Computers_and_Internet/Multimedia/Video/).

Figure 1.26 The pre-QuickTime 4 standard controller was used to control movies on the Web, in many applications, and in MoviePlayer, the precursor to the QuickTime Player.

Figure 1.27 QuickTime 4's standard controller, though more modern-looking, provides the same functionality as the older controller.

Figure 1.28 QuickTime Player's user interface is quite different than that of the standard controller.

Figure 1.29 The VR controller is used in many places where QuickTime VR movies are viewed, including Web pages and the QuickTime Player.

About the QuickTime Interfaces

Before the introduction of QuickTime 4, QuickTime users interacted with QuickTime movies using a single set of controls, called the *standard controller* (**Figure 1.26**). Whether in MoviePlayer (the precursor to QuickTime Player), on Web pages, or in a variety of other applications, this controller was the standard.

Things are a bit different now. The QuickTime 4 version of the standard controller has some cosmetic changes (compare **Figure 1.26** with **Figure 1.27**). But the major change is that the movie playing and editing tool that comes with QuickTime no longer uses the standard controller; QuickTime Player has a completely different set of controls (**Figure 1.28**).

The story for QuickTime VR movies is somewhat simpler—at least for now. A single set of standard controls (**Figure 1.29**) is used by QuickTime Player, on Web pages, and in most applications that open QuickTime VR movies. (We anticipate that Apple will eventually make some changes in the QuickTime VR controls.)

In the next chapter, we'll cover the controls in the standard controller. In Chapters 3 and 4 we'll cover the QuickTime Player and its controls for playing linear movies. In Chapter 5, we'll cover the QuickTime VR controller.

THE QUICKTIME STANDARD CONTROLLER

2

When you view movies embedded on a Web page, you'll often see a bar with various buttons beneath the movies. This is the QuickTime standard controller, which is also used by many QuickTime applications (though not QuickTime Player).

This controller gives you a way to play and pause a movie as well as methods to step through a movie frame by frame, to speed or slow playback, to access different points in the movie quickly and efficiently, and to adjust its audio volume.

In this chapter we'll show you how to use all the buttons on the standard controller as well as a few hidden tricks that can help you control movies in a variety of ways.

Playing and Pausing Movies

The most common thing you'll do with movies is play them. When you've heard or seen enough, however, you'll want to stop (or pause) the movie. There are a number of ways of doing either.

To play a movie:

◆ Click the Play button, located on the left side of the controller and marked with a triangle (**Figure 2.1**).

or

Press the Return key (Mac OS) or Enter key (Windows).

or

Press the Spacebar.

or

Double-click the movie image.

or

Hold down the Command key (Mac) or the Ctrl key (Windows) and click the right Step button or press the right arrow key.

When the movie is playing, the Play button is replaced by the Pause button, marked with two vertical bars (**Figure 2.2**).

Play button

Figure 2.1 Click the Play button to start playing a paused movie.

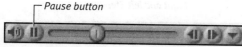

Pause button

Figure 2.2 When a movie starts playing, the Play button is replaced by a Pause button. Click the Pause button to pause a playing movie.

To pause a movie:

◆ Click the Pause button, located on the left side of the controller and marked with two vertical bars (**Figure 2.2**).

or

Press the Return key (Mac OS) or Enter key (Windows).

or

Press the Spacebar.

or

Click the movie image.

To play a movie backward:

◆ Hold down the Command key (Mac) or the Ctrl key (Windows) and click the left Step button or press the left arrow key.

or

Hold down the Shift key and double-click the movie image.

PLAYING AND PAUSING MOVIES

Stepping Through a Movie Frame by Frame

Most QuickTime movies are composed of a sequence of individual images, or *frames*. You can step through a QuickTime movie frame by frame if want to view each image on its own.

To step through a movie frame by frame:

◆ Click the right Step button to move forward a frame and the left Step button to move back a frame. (The Step buttons are located on the right side of the controller and look like a triangle and vertical bar pointing right and a vertical bar and triangle pointing left; see **Figure 2.3.**)

or

Press the right or left arrow keys.

✔ Tip

■ Some QuickTime movies, such as those containing only audio or 3D data, are not made up of frames, so the Step buttons do not work as described above. In 3D movies, the Step buttons advance the movie by a few fractions of a second. In audio-only movies, the Step buttons move you in quarter-second increments.

Right and left Step buttons

Figure 2.3 The right Step button moves you one frame forward, and the left Step button moves you one frame back.

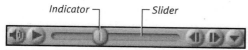

Indicator — — Slider

Figure 2.4 The oval indicator marks your current location in the movie; the slider represents the entire duration of the movie.

Figure 2.5 Moving the indicator changes where you are in the movie. For example, if you move the indicator halfway across the slider, you'll be taken to the halfway point in the movie.

Randomly Accessing Points in a Movie

You can quickly move to any point in a movie without having to play it or step through it frame by frame. (Unlike a videotape you have random access to a QuickTime movie!)

As a movie plays, an oval indicator moves in the area to the right of the Play/Pause button. That area comprises a slider, which represents the entire length of the movie. The indicator marks your current location in the movie (**Figure 2.4**).

To quickly move to any point in a movie:

◆ Drag the indicator to the right or left.

You'll see the movie image change as you drag the indicator. When you release the mouse button, the movie remains at the point in time represented by the location of the indicator (**Figure 2.5**).

or

Click directly in the slider.

The indicator jumps to the location you clicked.

To jump to the beginning of a movie:

◆ Hold down the Option key (Mac OS) or the Ctrl and Alt keys (Windows) while clicking the left Step button.

The indicator jumps to the beginning of the slider.

To jump to the end of a movie:

◆ Hold down the Option key (Mac OS) or Ctrl and Alt keys (Windows) while clicking the right Step button.

The indicator jumps to the end of the slider.

Changing the Audio Level

You may want to adjust your movie's audio level.

To change the audio level:

1. Click and hold down the button with the speaker icon located at the far left of the controller. This is the Volume Control button (**Figure 2.6**).

   A vertical slider pops up to the left of the button (**Figure 2.7**).

2. As you continue to hold down your mouse button, slide the pointer up or down to move the slider indicator up or down.

   As you slide up or down, the number of lines emanating from the speaker changes.

   Moving the indicator up increases the volume, and moving it down decreases the volume.

   When you play the movie, the volume of the audio will be correspondingly louder or softer.

To mute the audio:

◆ Hold down the Ctrl and Alt keys (Windows) or the Option key (Mac OS), and click the Volume Control button.

To return the audio to the volume at which it was set before muting:

◆ Hold down the Ctrl and Alt keys (Windows) or the Option key (Mac), and click the Volume Control button again.

✔ Tip

■ If you don't see a Volume Control button in the movie controller (**Figure 2.8**), the movie does not contain audio.

Volume Control button

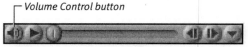

Figure 2.6 Use the Volume Control button to adjust the audio volume of a movie.

Figure 2.7 Click and hold down the Volume Control button until the image that looks like a thermometer appears; then slide the cursor up to increase the volume or down to decrease the volume.

Figure 2.8 If there's no Volume Control button, the movie doesn't include audio.

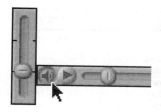

Figure 2.9 When you hold down the Shift key while clicking the Volume Control button, you'll see two black horizontal lines.

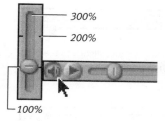

300%

200%

100%

Figure 2.10 You can then set the volume to up to 300 percent of the normal maximum volume.

Overdriving Audio

If you've set the volume of a movie as high as it can go, but it's still not loud enough, never fear: You can overdrive the audio in a QuickTime movie, increasing the actual sound above the normal maximum sound level.

To overdrive a movie's audio:

1. Hold down the Shift key while you click the Volume Control button.

   The area in which you can move the indicator is now dissected by two black horizontal lines (**Figure 2.9**).

2. Drag the indicator anywhere above the lower black line.

   When you play the movie, the audio level will be higher than the previous audio level.

   The lower of the two black lines represents the normal maximum volume. The higher line represents double the normal maximum volume. The top of the area in which you can move the indicator represents three times the normal maximum volume (**Figure 2.10**).

✔ Tip

- Overdriving the audio will likely reduce the acoustical quality of the sound and generally create some distortion.

Varying a Movie's Playback Rate

You can play a QuickTime movie in fast or slow motion, forward or backward using a hidden interface element.

To vary a movie's playback rate:

1. Hold down the Control key (Mac OS) or Alt key (Windows) while you click either Step button.

   The Step buttons will disappear, and you'll find your pointer atop a tiny white indicator that sits on a gray horizontal bar (**Figure 2.11**).

2. Move your pointer right or left.

   The indicator moves and the movie plays at different rates:

   When the indicator is moved all the way to the right, the movie plays at 2-1/2 times normal playback speed.

   When the indicator is three-quarters of the way to the right, the movie plays at normal speed.

   When the indicator is just slightly to the right of center (**Figure 2.12**), the movie plays in slow motion.

   When the indicator is in the middle, the movie is paused.

   When the indicator is just slightly to the left of center, the movie plays backward in slow motion.

   When the indicator is all the way to the left (**Figure 2.13**), the movie plays backward at 2-1/2 times normal speed.

Figure 2.11 If you hold down the Control key (Mac OS) or Alt key (Windows) while clicking on either Step button, a tiny indicator and sliding area appear. Move the indicator all the way to the right to play the movie at two and a half 2-1/2 times normal playback speed.

Figure 2.12 Move the indicator just slightly to the right of center for slow-motion playback.

Figure 2.13 Move the indicator to the left of center for backward play.

VARYING A MOVIE'S PLAYBACK RATE

Chapter List button ⌐

Figure 2.14 The Chapter List button only appears for some movies.

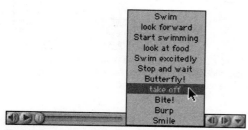

Figure 2.15 To jump to a chapter, click and hold down the Chapter List button and select the chapter.

Using Chapter Lists

In some movies, you'll see an extra element in the movie controller: an area between the slider and the Step buttons that contains text (**Figure 2.14**). Called the Chapter List button, it provides a way to jump quickly to designated points in the movie, called *chapters*.

To jump to a chapter:

1. Click and hold down the Chapter List button (**Figure 2.15**).

2. Select the chapter to which you'd like to jump.

   The indicator jumps to the beginning of the portion of the movie represented by the chapter you selected.

Saving Movies on the Web

When you view a movie on a Web page, you may decide that you'd like to save a copy of the movie to your hard drive. This copy can later be opened in QuickTime Player or any other application that can open and play QuickTime movies.

To save a QuickTime movie from a Web page:

1. Click the button at the far right corner of the movie controller and drag to Save As QuickTime Movie (**Figure 2.16**).

2. In the Save dialog box that appears, choose a location and change the file name (if you wish).

Figure 2.16 To save a Web page movie to your hard disk, click the button on the far left of the controller and select Save As QuickTime Movie.

Figure 2.17 When an HTTP movie is being downloaded, the shaded portion of the slider represents the portion of the movie that has been downloaded. The Save options will be disabled until the entire movie has been downloaded.

The Difference Between Saving RTSP and HTTP Movies

HTTP movies are those that download completely to your hard drive—that is, if you save the movie as described on this page, the saved file contains all of the movie data. (You won't be able to save an HTTP movie until it has been completely downloaded. As the movie is being downloaded, the slider progressively becomes more shaded to represent the portion of the movie that has been downloaded, as shown in **Figure 2.17**. Only when the bar is completely gray will the Save As QuickTime Movie option be available.)

RTSP streaming movies are those in which movie data is sent but a file is never created. When you save one of these movies, a file is created on your hard drive, but that file doesn't contain all the movie data. Instead, it contains a pointer (or pointers) to the place (or places) on the Internet where the movie data is stored. When you open the file, the movie data is streamed over the Internet again. (You don't have to wait to save RTSP movies since no movie data is stored.)

✔ Tips

■ (Mac OS only) You can also drag the movie from the Web page to your desktop to save it.

■ The other option, Save As Source, may not save all the movie data. (This happens when the movie is not self-contained, a concept we'll explain in Chapter 6.)

■ In some cases, a Web page's HTML may make the button you would use to access the pop-up menu containing the Save choices unavailable. In other cases, the Save As QuickTime Movie and Save As Source menu items may be disabled—even after you've downloaded the entire movie. Nor will you be able to drag the movie to your desktop. This is because the movie has been set up to disallow saving. (We'll explain how you can set up your own movies this way in Chapter 17.)

■ To learn about the other options available through the button on the right side of the controller when a movie is on a Web page, see Appendix B, "Configuring QuickTime."

QuickTime Player Basics

Now that you know how to use the QuickTime standard controller, we'll introduce you to a very different interface—that of QuickTime Player.

Introduced with QuickTime 4, QuickTime Player provides much the same functionality as MoviePlayer, which was included in previous versions. Think of QuickTime Player as MoviePlayer with a face-lift.

QuickTime Player also includes some important additions, many of which are designed to enhance use of QuickTime over the Internet. These include a new bookmarking feature (called *Favorites*) as well as the ability to open a movie over the Internet.

In this chapter, we'll show you around the Player, pointing out the controls, drawers, and menu items that provide access to its many features. We'll also show you how to use QuickTime Player to open both local and remote files. You can open not only standard QuickTime movies but also video, animation, sound, and graphics files of various other formats. After that we'll cover how to use Favorites, how to change window sizes, and how to get copyright info. Finally, we'll introduce you to QuickTime Player's Info window, which you'll use throughout this book. In the next chapter we'll cover all the QuickTime Player features for playing movies.

About the QuickTime Player Window

When you initially open QuickTime Player, an empty Player window appears (**Figure 3.1**). This window is used for all movies except QuickTime VR movies, movies for which a different controller has been specified, or movies for which it has been specified that no controller should appear.

There are a number of components to the Player window; let's take a quick look around.

The controls that are always visible include those for playing and pausing the movie as well as for adjusting its volume. (We'll cover these in detail in the next chapter.) Also visible are the Controls button, the Info button, and the Favorites Drawer handle.

When you click the Controls button, the Controls Tray (**Figure 3.2**) slides down. You'll use the controls in this tray to step through a movie frame by frame; to fast-forward and fast-rewind; to jump to the beginning and end of the movie; and to adjust audio balance, bass, and treble. (We'll also cover these in the next chapter.) Click the Controls button to put this tray away, too.

When you click the Info button, the Info Tray (**Figure 3.3**) slides down, showing basic copyright information. Clicking the Info button again closes the tray.

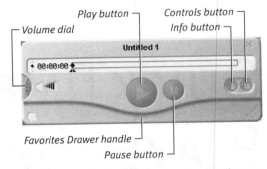

Figure 3.1 The Player window with no trays or drawers open.

Figure 3.2 The Player window with the Controls Tray open.

Figure 3.3 The Player window with the Info Tray open.

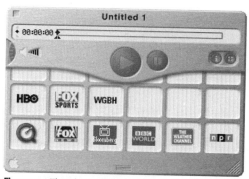

Figure 3.4 The Player window with the Favorites Drawer open.

When you drag down on the Favorites Drawer handle, the Favorites Drawer (**Figure 3.4**) opens. This drawer contains icons that allow you to quickly access and reorganize movies you've selected as Favorites. Close the Favorites Drawer by dragging up on the Favorites Drawer handle.

The box in the upper left of the Player window on the Mac is a close box. The X in the upper right of the Player window on Windows computers is a close button. Use either of these to close the Player window.

✔ Tips

- To open and close the Favorites Drawer, you can also double-click the Favorites Drawer handle or choose Open Favorites Drawer or Close Favorites Drawer from the Favorites menu.

- On a Windows computer, closing the last open Player window causes QuickTime Player to quit.

Locating QuickTime Player

In Windows, the QuickTime installer normally places QuickTime Player in the QuickTime folder, which is found inside the Program Files folder. (During installation, it's possible to specify a location different than this, however.) Windows users can also look for a shortcut on their desktop or use the Start menu (choose Programs, QuickTime, QuickTime Player) to access the Player. Windows 98 includes a QuickTime Player icon in the task bar.

On the Mac OS, the QuickTime installer places QuickTime Player in a folder called QuickTime Folder; it also puts an alias on the desktop. (If QuickTime 4 was included as part of your Macintosh operating system, it may be located in the QuickTime folder within the Applications folder.)

ABOUT THE QUICKTIME PLAYER WINDOW

Opening QuickTime Movies

The steps for opening a movie are the same as those for opening a document in most any other program.

To open a QuickTime movie from within QuickTime Player:

1. If QuickTime Player isn't already open, locate and double-click its icon to open it.

2. From the File menu, choose Open Movie (**Figure 3.5**).

3. In the Open dialog box, locate and select the movie file you wish to open and click the Open button (**Figure 3.6**).

   The selected movie appears in a window. (**Figure 3.7**). If another Player window was already open and the movie you opened was a linear, time-based movie, the new movie would replace the movie previously in the Player window. QuickTime VR movies won't replace what's in a Player window; they open in a new window, which uses the VR controller.

Figure 3.5 Choose Open Movie from QuickTime Player's File menu to open a QuickTime movie.

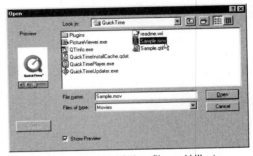

Figure 3.6 Select the QuickTime file you'd like to open, and click Open.

Figure 3.7 The movie appears in a window.

✔ Tips

- Instead of Open Movie, you may see Open Movie in New Player in the File menu. (Movies opened with this command won't replace whatever is currently open in a Player window.) Open Movie in New Player appears when QuickTime Player's preferences have been changed. (See "About Preferences" at the end of this chapter and "Having Multiple Windows Open in QuickTime Player" in Chapter 6.)

- If you haven't installed all of the QuickTime components (because you didn't follow our installation suggestions in Chapter 1) and you try to open a movie that requires one or more of the missing components, a dialog box will inform you that you're missing necessary QuickTime software. If you click the Do It Now button, QuickTime will retrieve the missing components and install them on your hard disk. If you're using a Macintosh, you may have to restart your computer before playing the movie. If you're using a Windows computer, you probably won't have to restart, although you may have to close and reopen the movie before you can play it.

Additional Methods of Opening Movie Files

You can also launch QuickTime Player automatically by dragging the movie file icon onto the QuickTime Player application icon. Or, if the movie was created with QuickTime Player, simply double-click the file's icon.

In addition, Windows users can double-click any file that has an .mov extension.

OPENING QUICKTIME MOVIES

Opening Non-QuickTime Files

QuickTime Player, like other QuickTime-savvy applications, can open movie, animation, and sound files in many other formats just as easily as it can open regular QuickTime movies. QuickTime can open the most common video, audio, and animation formats available on Mac and Windows as well as text files (see sidebar for a complete list).

Figure 3.8 Choose Open Movie from QuickTime Player's File menu to open many media files that aren't in the QuickTime format.

To open a non-QuickTime file in QuickTime Player:

1. From the File menu choose Open Movie (**Figure 3.8**).

2. In the Open dialog box, locate and select the movie file you wish to open.

   When you select a file in a non-QuickTime format, the Open button changes to a Convert button (**Figure 3.9**).

3. Click the Convert button.

   The file opens and appears in a standard QuickTime Player window (**Figure 3.10**).

Figure 3.9 When you select a file in another format that QuickTime Player can open, the Open button changes to a Convert button.

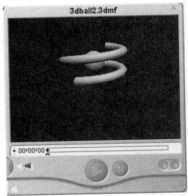

Figure 3.10 The file opens and appears just like any QuickTime movie.

✔ Tips

- If you are opening a karaoke or MIDI file, you'll see a Convert button in Step 2. If you want to open the file directly, you must hold down the Command key (Mac OS) or Ctrl key (Windows) before clicking this button. (When you do this, "Convert..." becomes "Convert.")

- To open text files directly, you must choose Import rather than Open Movie in Step 1. If you then hold down the Command key (Mac OS) or Ctrl key (Windows), the Convert... button becomes a Convert button, which you then click in Step 3.

- Even though you click a button called Convert, the original file is not being altered in any way. It is simply being opened in QuickTime Player. The only time the original file is changed is if you save from QuickTime Player using the same name as the original file.

- You can also drag files in any of the formats QuickTime supports to the QuickTime Player icon to open them in QuickTime Player.

- If, when you click a non-QuickTime file, the Convert button contains ellipses (Convert...) that you can't make disappear even if you hold down the Command or Ctrl key, you've selected a file type that QuickTime can't open directly. See "Converting Non-QuickTime Files" next in this chapter for more information.

File Formats That QuickTime Player Can Open Directly

◆ 3DMF	◆ MPEG-1 Layer 3 audio (MP3)
◆ AIFF	
◆ Animated GIF	◆ QuickDraw GX
◆ AU	◆ QuickTime Image File
◆ Audio CD	
◆ AVI	◆ QuickTime Movie
◆ BMP	
◆ DV	◆ Photoshop
◆ FlashPix	◆ PNG
◆ FLC/FLI	◆ SGI
◆ GIF	◆ Sound Designer II
◆ JPEG/JFIF	
◆ KAR (Karaoke)	◆ Targa Image File
◆ MacPaint	
◆ MIDI	◆ Text
◆ MPEG-1 (Mac OS only)	◆ TIFF
	◆ WAV
◆ MPEG-1 Layer 1 & 2 audio (Mac OS only)	

Converting Non-QuickTime Files

Compared to the number of file formats that QuickTime can open directly, there are a smaller number of formats that QuickTime will convert to QuickTime movies before opening. Once converted, these files act just like any other QuickTime file. Files that need to be converted include Macintosh System 7 sound files, PICT still image files, and PICS animation files. You can also convert text, MIDI, and karaoke music files, though you can also open these directly, as we described on the previous page.

Figure 3.11 Choose Import from QuickTime Player's File menu when you have a multimedia file that QuickTime won't open directly.

To convert a non-QuickTime file:

1. From the File menu, choose Import (**Figure 3.11**).

2. In the Open dialog box, locate and select the movie file you wish to open.

   The Open button changes to a Convert button (**Figure 3.12**). Note that the name of this button is followed by ellipses (...) to indicate that a further step is required.

3. Click the Convert button.

4. A Save dialog box appears (**Figure 3.13**) because you need to save the file as a movie so that the Player can open it.

5. Specify where you'd like to save the file, change the name of the file if you wish, and then click Save.

Figure 3.12 When you select a file that QuickTime can convert to a QuickTime file, the Open button changes to Convert.

✔ Tips

- For some files, an Options button will be active in the Save dialog box. If you click this button, you'll be able to change various settings particular to the type of media. We'll cover these options in later chapters.

- For System 7 sound files and PICS files, you can use the Open Movie command rather than the Import command in Step 1.

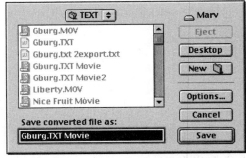

Figure 3.13 After you click the Convert button, a Save dialog box appears in which you specify the name and location of the new file that will be created by converting to QuickTime.

Figure 3.14 From the File menu, choose Open URL to open a movie on the Internet.

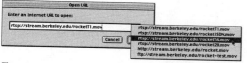

Figure 3.15 You can type a URL yourself...

Figure 3.16 ...or choose a URL from the pop-up menu.

Opening Files on the Internet

You can also use QuickTime Player to open QuickTime movie files (and other media files that QuickTime can open) over the Internet. There's no need to use for a Web browser or any other special software. All you need to know is the movie's URL.

To open a movie on the Internet:

1. From QuickTime Player's File menu, choose Open URL (**Figure 3.14**).

2. In the Open URL dialog box, type the URL that specifies the location of the movie or other media file (**Figure 3.15**), or choose a URL from the pop-up menu (**Figure 3.16**).

   The file opens as a movie in QuickTime Player.

✔ Tips

■ It won't work to try to type a Web page URL—even if that page contains a movie. You need to type in the URL of a movie or some other file of a format that QuickTime can open (see the next page for a list of file formats that QuickTime can open). QuickTime Player can open URLs starting with RTSP, HTTP, or FTP.

■ In the View menu of Netscape browsers, you can choose Page Info to get a listing of URLs for all the media on the page, including movies.

■ At this time, you can't open MIDI or karaoke files using the Open URL command.

■ See the following section, "Opening Favorites," for another method of opening movies on the Internet.

Opening Favorites

As we mentioned earlier, you can designate specific files as Favorites. These then appear as icons in the Favorites drawer and are also listed in the Favorites menu.

To open a Favorite:

◆ Open the Favorites drawer (by dragging down or double-clicking the Favorites drawer handle or double-clicking it), and click the icon for the movie you wish to open (**Figure 3.17**).

or

From the Favorites menu choose the name of the file you wish to open (**Figure 3.18**).

✔ Tip

■ When you first install QuickTime, QuickTime Player comes installed with some Favorites. One of these is the QuickTime Showcase, and is a movie that opens Apple's QuickTime Showcase Web page. There are a number of others, including HBO, Fox News, Fox Sports, Bloomberg TV, The Weather Channel, and NPR.

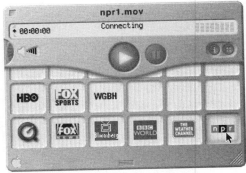

Figure 3.17 The Favorites drawer has includes graphical representations for Favorites; click any icon to open one of these Favorites.

Figure 3.18 The Favorites menu lists the names of your Favorites; choose one to open it.

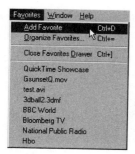

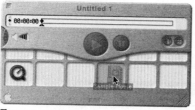

Figure 3.19 Open the movie you want to add to your Favorites drawer, and choose Add Favorite from the Favorites menu.

Figure 3.20 You can also drag a file to an open well in the Favorites drawer.

Icon for any URL-based movie that doesn't have another available image.

Icon for local audio-only movie.

Icon for local movie that doesn't have another available image.

Figure 3.21 QuickTime uses some special icons in the Favorites drawer.

Adding and Organizing Favorites

You control the contents and organization of the Favorites drawer.

To add a new Favorite:

◆ Open the movie you want to add, and from the Favorites menu choose Add Favorite (**Figure 3.19**).

or

Drag a file from the Macintosh Finder or Windows desktop to an open space (or *well*) in the Favorites drawer (**Figure 3.20**).

The movie's name appears in the Favorites menu, and an icon for the movie appears in the Favorites drawer. For movies that include a visual element, this icon is often a representative image from the movie. For audio-only movies (and in some other special cases), QuickTime Player uses special icons (these icons are shown in **Figure 3.21**).

✔ Tips

■ For movies with a visual track, the icon displayed in the Favorites drawer is usually a miniature version of the movie's poster. (We'll provide further detail about that in "Setting a Poster" in Chapter 6.)

■ The name used in the Favorites menu is the same as that which appears in the title bar and is determined by the Full Name annotation (if the movie's creator has added one; see "Adding Annotations" in Chapter 6). If there is no Full Name annotation, the movie's file name is used.

■ If you wish to add a movie viewed on a Web page to the Favorites drawer, you can first save it from the Web page, as described in "Saving Movies on the Web" in Chapter 2. You would then use one of the methods described above to designate it a Favorite. (For RTSP files, this saved file is nothing more than a pointer to the real movie data. For HTTP files, it is the full file.) To add an HTTP movie to your Favorites without storing it on your hard disk, you'll need to know its URL; open the movie in QuickTime Player using the Open URL command and then designate it a Favorite. (See "Opening Files on the Internet" earlier in this chapter.)

To change the order of Favorites:

◆ Simply drag icons around in the Favorites drawer (**Figure 3.22**).

or

1. From the Favorites menu choose Organize Favorites (**Figure 3.23**).

2. In the Organize Favorites dialog box (**Figure 3.24**) drag file names up or down.

3. Click Done.

Either method reorders Favorites in both the Favorites drawer and the Favorites menu.

To delete a Favorite:

1. From the Favorites menu choose Organize Favorites.

2. In the Organize Bookmarks window (**Figure 3.24**), select the movie file you wish to delete.

3. Click the Delete button.

Figure 3.22 You can drag icons around in the Favorites drawer to reorganize them.

Figure 3.23 To reorganize, delete, or rename Favorites, start by choosing Organize Favorites from the Favorites menu...

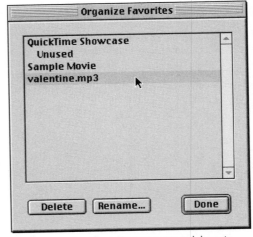

Figure 3.24 ...then drag file names up and down to reorganize them, or use the Delete or Rename Favorite buttons.

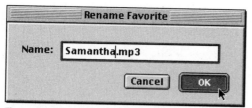

Figure 3.25 If you click the Rename button, you can then enter a new name.

To rename a Favorite:

1. From the Favorites menu choose Organize Favorites (**Figure 3.23**).

2. In the Organize Bookmarks window, select the movie file you wish to rename.

3. Click the Rename button, and in the Rename Favorite dialog box (**Figure 3.25**) enter a new name. Then click OK.

   Only the name listed in the Favorites menu is changed. The movie's file name remains the same.

✔ Tip

- On the Mac, you can drag icons from the Favorites Drawer to the Trash to remove them from the Favorites Drawer.

ADDING AND ORGANIZING FAVORITES

Changing Window Sizes

Typically, the first thing new QuickTime users want to do is resize the movie window. However, you generally get the best performance by *not* changing the window size. We know, though, that this knowledge is not going to stop you. And there are legitimate reasons for stretching out a window.

To change a window's size:

◆ From the Movie menu choose Half Size, Double Size, or Fill Screen (**Figure 3.26**).

or

Click in the notched area in the lower right corner of the window (called the *Resize Control*; see **Figure 3.27**), and drag in or out.

QuickTime is optimized to play movies at certain multiples or fractions of the movie's normal size. Thus, a movie will perform more smoothly at exactly double size than at some size slightly smaller than double.

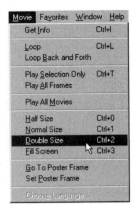

Figure 3.26 The Movie menu contains options for changing the window size.

Figure 3.27 You can also change the window size by dragging from the lower right corner of the window.

To drag a movie window to an optimal size:

◆ Hold down the Option key (Mac OS) or Ctrl and Alt keys (Windows) while you drag the lower right corner of the window.

Normally when you drag the window, the movie retains its original proportions. However, you can change the proportions, making the window wider or taller if you wish.

To change the proportions of a movie window:

◆ Hold down the Shift key as you drag the lower right corner of the window.

✔ Tip

■ (Windows only) To disproportionately change the size of VR movies, you can place your pointer over the window border until it changes to a double-headed arrow and then drag in or out.

CHANGING WINDOW SIZES

Showing Copyright Information

To find out more about the movie you're viewing—for example, who owns it, where it came from, who created it, and other copyright information—you can check the Info Tray.

To show copyright information:

◆ Click the Info button on the right side of the main Player window (**Figure 3.28**).

The Info Tray slides down, displaying either copyright information (**Figure 3.29**) or the statement "No copyright information available." The text shown here is a subset of the annotation information that is added to a movie. (We'll show how you can add annotations to your own movies in Chapter 6.)

Note that not everybody who creates a movie adds this information, so don't assume that the movie isn't copyrighted simply because no copyright information is available.

Figure 3.28 Press the Info button...

Figure 3.29 ...to open the Info Tray, where you can view copyright information.

Figure 3.30 To open the Info window for a movie, from the Movie menu choose Get Info.

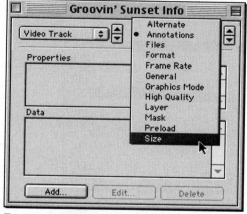

Figure 3.31 The choices in the right pop-up menu are dependent on what you've chosen in the left pop-up menu. Here you see what's available for a video track.

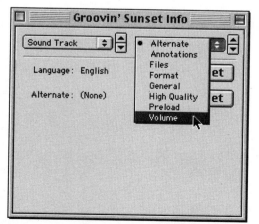

Figure 3.32 Here you see what's available for a sound track.

The Info Window

Now we'll introduce you to QuickTime Player's Info window. Although you won't need to use it to simply play movies, it's a vital piece of the Player interface. It enables you to get detailed information about both the structure of your movie and the individual tracks it contains. You also use this window to make various changes to tracks in your movie. We'll be returning to the Info window throughout the book.

To open the Info window for a movie:

◆ From the Movie menu choose Get Info (**Figure 3.30**).

The Info window for the movie appears. At the top of this window are two pop-up menus. In the left pop-up menu, you can choose the movie itself or any of its tracks. For each choice you make in the left pop-up menu, you'll find a different set of choices in the right pop-up menu (**Figures 3.31** and **3.32**). Altogether, more than 150 panels may appear (including more than 30 unique panels), which we'll cover throughout the book. Often we'll refer to what you see in the window by the choice made in the right pop-up menu—for example, "the Size panel."

✔ Tip

■ Don't confuse the Info Tray and the Info window. The Info Tray provides only a small amount of information about the movie. The Info window, in contrast, enables you to view and edit many characteristics of the movie.

Determining Which Tracks a Movie Contains

You don't have to do much to find out the number or type of tracks a movie contains.

To see which tracks a movie contains:

1. If the Info window isn't already open, from the Movie menu choose Get Info **Figure 3.33**).

2. In the Info window for the movie, pull down the left pop-up menu (**Figure 3.34**).

The items in the pop-up menu below the word *Movie* are the track names.

In most cases track names correspond to track types. For example, a video track will be listed as Video Track. However, because track names can be edited, you may occasionally have to dig a bit deeper to determine the type of track.

Figure 3.33 Choose Get Info from the Movie menu to access information about the movie and its tracks.

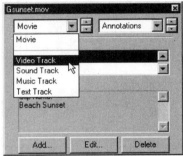

Figure 3.34 The left pop-up menu in the Info window lists the tracks in the movie.

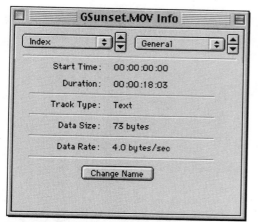

Figure 3.35 If you choose a track, and then choose General in the right pop-up menu, the track type is listed in the middle of the window. (This is useful when a track's name isn't the same as its type.)

To determine the track type if the track name doesn't correspond to a track type:

1. From the left pop-up menu in the Info window, choose the track you're interested in.

2. From the right pop-up menu, choose General.

   In the middle of the window you'll find a listing for track type (**Figure 3.35**).

✔ Tip

■ If you've opened an RTSP streaming movie, you'll probably see only a single track listed in the left pop-up menu in the Info window: Streaming Track. This track contains all the data from the original tracks that the movie was originally composed of before it was streamed to you. If Streaming Track is selected in the left pop-up menu, you can choose Format in the right pop-up menu to get a listing of the media types contained in the movie.

About Preferences

Using the General Preferences dialog box, you can specify defaults that determine how your QuickTime Player will behave. You access the dialog box by pulling down the Edit menu and choosing Preferences and then General (**Figure 3.36**).

In the General Preferences dialog box (**Figure 3.37**) you can specify preferences for:

◆ **Sound.** This specifies how audio plays when the movie isn't in front (see Chapter 12 for more information).

◆ **Auto-Play.** This determines whether movies will play automatically when opened in QuickTime Player.

◆ **Favorites Drawer.** This determines whether QuickTime Player asks if you really want to replace a Favorite when you drag a file to a well in the Favorites drawer that is already filled.

◆ **Open Movie.** This specifies whether movies should open in a new Player window or replace the movie that's already open in the window.

✔ Tip

■ When you choose Preferences in the Edit menu, you'll see that there are actually four choices for Preferences (**Figure 3.36**). However, choosing any of the last three (Connection Speed, Streaming Proxy, or Registration) merely opens panels in the QuickTime Settings dialog box. Because these potentially affect the behavior of all tools that use QuickTime, not just QuickTime Player, we'll cover them in Appendix B, "Configuring QuickTime."

The default preferences are fine in most cases: It makes sense to leave them alone unless they begin to annoy you.

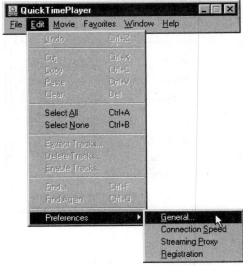

Figure 3.36 In the Edit menu, choose Preferences and then General Preferences.

Figure 3.37 The General Preferences dialog box lets you specify a number of default behaviors for QuickTime Player.

CONTROLLING MOVIES IN THE PLAYER

Now let's take a look at the kinds of things you can do to control movies from within QuickTime Player.

Although QuickTime Player looks quite different than the standard controller, you can use it to do many of the same things: play and pause movies, randomly access different points in a movie, and change audio level and playback rate. You can also use QuickTime Player to adjust additional audio characteristics, make a movie loop, show it full-screen, or search a text track—to name just a few of its capabilities. You can even control multiple movies simultaneously via QuickTime Player.

In this chapter we'll show you how to use the Player window buttons that affect playback (including those in the Player's trays). We'll also cover the menu commands for controlling movie playback.

Playing and Pausing Movies

Although QuickTime Player's Play and Pause buttons look different than their standard controller counterparts, they work in a similar fashion.

To play a movie:

◆ Click the Play button—the big round button marked with a triangle (**Figure 4.1**).

or

Press the Return key (Mac) or Enter key (Windows).

or

Press the spacebar.

or

Double-click the movie image.

or

Hold down the Command key (Mac) or the Ctrl key (Windows) and click the right Step button or press the right arrow key.

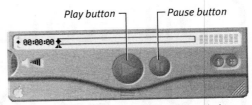

Play button *Pause button*

Figure 4.1 The largest buttons in the Player window are used to play and pause the movie.

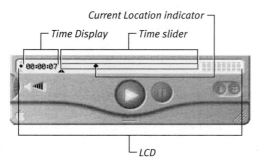

Current Location indicator

Time Display   **Time slider**

LCD

Figure 4.2 When a movie is playing, the triangle in the Play button glows. In the LCD, the Time Display updates and the Current Location indicator moves to the right in the Time slider.

When the movie is playing, the triangle in the Play button glows and the area with the white background above the Play button (called the LCD) changes as well (**Figure 4.2**). The Time Display (on the left side of the LCD) shows the elapsed time since the beginning of the movie (represented as hours:minutes:seconds). The Current Location indicator (the black diamond) moves to the right in the Time slider (the black-outlined rectangular bar).

To pause a movie:

◆ Click the Pause button (marked with two vertical bars to the right of the Play button) (**Figure 4.1**).

   or

   Click the Play button.

   or

   Press the Return key (Mac OS) or Enter key (Windows).

   or

   Press the spacebar.

   or

   Click the movie image.

PLAYING AND PAUSING MOVIES

Changing the Audio Level

You may want to adjust the volume of your movie's audio.

To change the audio level:

◆ Drag up or down on the Volume dial, which is located on the left side of the Player window (**Figure 4.3**).

As you slide the dial up or down, the number of lines in the Volume Feedback area changes: Dragging up increases the volume; dragging down decreases the volume.

When you play the movie, the audio volume will be correspondingly louder or softer.

or

Drag to the right or left in the Volume Feedback area.

Dragging right increases the number of visible lines (and thus the volume); dragging left decreases the visible lines (and thus the volume).

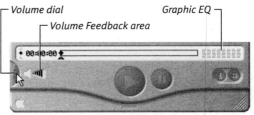

Volume dial *Graphic EQ*

Volume Feedback area

Figure 4.3 To adjust the volume, drag up or down on the Volume dial or right or left in the Volume Feedback area.

Figure 4.4 A movie must have a sound track for the Graphic EQ to be visible.

To quickly mute the audio:

◆ Click the speaker icon located to the right of the Volume dial.

✔ Tips

■ The meters to the right of the Time slider are called the Graphic EQ (**Figure 4.3**). (*EQ* stands for *equalizer.*) You'll only see the Graphic EQ if the movie you've opened has a QuickTime sound track. It won't appear for movies without audio, nor will it be visible for movies with music tracks, Flash tracks with audio, or MPEG tracks with audio. (Compare **Figure 4.3** with **Figure 4.4.**) You also won't see it if the movie has a Chapter List because the Chapter Control appears in the spot where the Graphic EQ would normally reside.

■ Using the Player, you can't overdrive audio in the same way you can with the standard controller. (See "Overdriving Audio" in Chapter 2.) You can, however, change the default volume of the audio. (See "Changing the Default Volume, Balance, Bass, and Treble of an Audio Track" in Chapter 12.) Also, you should know that when you move QuickTime Player's Volume dial as high up as possible, the audio plays at 150% of normal volume.

CHANGING THE AUDIO LEVEL

Randomly Accessing Points in a Movie

Figure 4.5 Drag the Current Location indicator in the Time slider to change your current location in the movie.

As with the standard controller, you can use QuickTime Player to quickly move to any point in a movie—without having to play the movie or step through it frame by frame.

To quickly move to any point in a movie:

◆ Drag the Current Location indicator in the Time slider to the right or left.

You'll see the movie image and Time Display change as you drag the indicator. When you release the mouse button, the movie remains at the point in time represented by Current Location indicator (**Figure 4.5**).

or

Click anywhere in the Time slider.

The Current Location indicator jumps to the point in the Time slider where you clicked. The Time Display is updated.

Figure 4.6 Click the Controls button to open the Controls Tray.

Step Back button ⌐ ⌐ Step Forward button

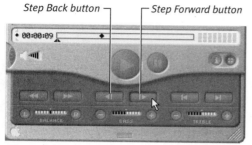

Figure 4.7 The Step Forward button moves you one frame forward; the Step Back button moves you one frame back.

Stepping Through a Movie Frame by Frame

You can also use Player to step through a QuickTime movie frame by frame.

To step through a movie frame by frame:

1. Unless the Controls Tray is already open, click the Controls button (**Figure 4.6**) to open it.

2. Click the Step Forward button to advance a frame and the Step Back button to move back a frame.

   Located in the middle of the top row of the Controller Tray, the Step buttons are represented by a triangle and vertical bar pointing right to advance and left to back up (**Figure 4.7**).

✔ Tips

- You can also press the right or left arrow keys to step forward or backward a frame.

- Some QuickTime movies—such as those containing only audio or 3D data—are not composed of frames, so the Step buttons do not work as described above. In 3D movies, the Step buttons advance the movie by a few fractions of a second. In audio-only movies, the Step buttons advance the movie in quarter-second increments.

Fast-Forwarding and Fast-Reversing a Movie

Using QuickTime Player buttons, you can play a QuickTime movie in fast motion: You can fast-forward or fast-reverse it. QuickTime player also includes buttons that jump you to the beginning or end of a movie.

To play a QuickTime movie in fast motion:

1. If the Controls Tray isn't already open, click the Controls button.

2. Hold down the Fast Forward or Fast Reverse button.

   Located on the left side of the top Controls Tray row, the Fast Forward button points to the right and the Fast Reverse button points to the left. (See **Figure 4.8.**)

   or

   Double-click the Fast Forward or Fast Reverse button.

✔ Tip

■ When you fast-forward or fast-reverse a movie, QuickTime Player will try to play it at twice its normal frame rate. If your computer isn't fast enough, the rate actually achieved may not be quite double the frame rate. For most computers and movies, fast-reversing rarely achieves double speed because compression algorithms are designed for forward play and so cannot decompress quickly enough during backward play.

Go to End button
Go to Start button
Fast Reverse button
Fast Forward button

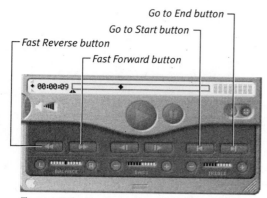

Figure 4.8 The Fast Forward and Fast Reverse buttons let you play a movie forward or backward in fast motion. The Go to Start and Go to End buttons jump you to the beginning or end of a movie.

To jump to the beginning or end of a movie:

1. If the Controls Tray isn't already open, click the Controls button.

2. In the Controls Tray, click the Go to Start button to jump to the beginning of the movie or the Go to End button to jump to the end of the movie.

   This pair of buttons is located on the right side of the top Controls Tray row. (See **Figure 4.8.**)

Changing Balance, Bass, and Treble

The Controls Tray also provides buttons for changing various audio track qualities. These buttons are located along the bottom row of the Controls Tray (**Figure 4.9**), which you open by clicking the Controls button. For stereo audio tracks, you can change balance, increasing the volume on the left or right. For some types of audio tracks, you can increase the low frequencies (bass) or high frequencies (treble).

To change balance:

◆ Click in the bar above the word BALANCE. The further to the right you click, the louder the right channel will be; the further to the left you click, the louder the left channel will be.

or

Click the L button in the balance area to make the left-channel audio slightly louder; click the R button to make the right-channel audio slightly louder. Hold down either to continue altering the balance.

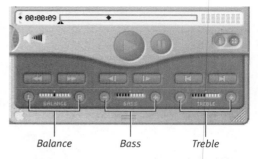

Balance   Bass   Treble

Figure 4.9 Audio control buttons in the Controls Tray

To increase the bass:

◆ Click in the bar above the word BASS.

or

Click the "+" button in the bass area to increase the low frequencies; click the "-" button to decrease the low frequencies. Hold down either to continue altering the bass.

To increase the treble:

◆ Click in the bar above the word TREBLE.

or

Click the "+" button in the treble area to increase the high frequencies; click the "-" button to decrease the high frequencies. Hold down either to continue altering the treble.

✔ Tip

■ The changes you make using these controls remain in effect only as long as the movie is open. The next time you open the movie, settings will be in the same positions they were before you altered them.

PRESENTING A MOVIE FRAME BY FRAME

Presenting a Movie

A QuickTime Player option will display your movie against a black screen. The Player window is not visible, and the movie plays all the way to the end. This is called *presenting* a movie, and it's an effective way to show your movie on your monitor—particularly when you want a dramatic effect.

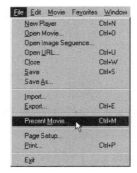

Figure 4.10 To present a movie so that it plays from the current frame to the end, choose Present Movie from the File menu.

To present a movie so that it plays automatically:

1. Position the Current Location indicator at the point in the movie where you'd like playback to begin.

2. From the File menu choose Present Movie (**Figure 4.10**).

   The Present Movie dialog box appears.

3. Use the Movie Size pop-up menu to choose your desired movie window size (**Figure 4.11**).

4. For Mode, make sure the Normal radio button is selected (**Figure 4.12**).

5. Click the Play button at the bottom of the Present Movie dialog box.

   The movie appears against a black background with no controller (**Figure 4.13**), and it plays from its current location to the end.

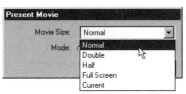

Figure 4.11 Choose a window size in the Present Movie dialog box.

Figure 4.12 Select the Normal radio button; then click Play.

Figure 4.13 The movie appears against a black background and plays from the current image to the end. To stop the movie before its end, click anywhere.

PRESENTING A MOVIE

To stop a movie presentation before the movie reaches its end:

◆ Press the Esc key.

   or

   Click anywhere on the screen.

   or

   Press Command-period (Mac OS only).

✔ Tip

■ Present Movie is not available for audio-only movies.

Choosing Movie Size When Presenting Movies

If you choose Normal, Double, or Half from the Movie Size pop-up menu and your monitor and system software allow you to switch resolutions, QuickTime will automatically switch your screen resolution to that closest to the movie's size (without being smaller; thus, the movie may appear larger than you expect). If you choose Current, the movie will always appear the same size that it is currently.

Presenting a Movie Frame by Frame (in Slide-Show Mode)

There may be times that you'd like to present a movie a frame at a time—for example, if your movie comprises a sequence of still images that make little sense when shown in rapid succession, or if you want to closely analyze a clip.

To present a movie a frame at a time:

1. Position the Current Location indicator at the frame you'd like to show first.

2. From the File menu (**Figure 4.14**) choose Present Movie.

3. In the Present Movie dialog box, use the Movie Size pop-up menu to choose your movie window size (**Figure 4.15**).

4. Click the Slide Show radio button to select it as the mode (**Figure 4.16**).

5. Click Play.

   The current frame appears against a black background (**Figure 4.17**).

6. Press your mouse button to show each subsequent frame. (You can also use the right and left arrow keys to move forward and backward a frame at a time.)

To exit Slide Show mode:

◆ Press the Esc key.

   or

   Press Command-period (Mac OS only).

✔ Tip

■ If you try to play a movie that's not composed of frames (for example, one with only a 3D track) in Slide Show mode, just the current image shows. The movie won't advance, even when you click.

Figure 4.14 To present a movie frame by frame, first choose Present Movie from the File menu.

Figure 4.15 Choose a window size in the Present Movie dialog box.

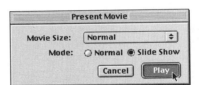

Figure 4.16 Select the Slide Show radio button; then click Play.

Figure 4.17 The current frame appears against a black background. Click anywhere to show the next frame, or use the right and left arrow keys to move forward and backward a frame at a time. To exit the slide show, press the Esc key.

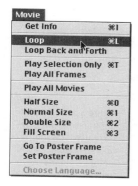

Figure 4.18 To make a movie loop, choose Loop from the Movie menu and then play the movie.

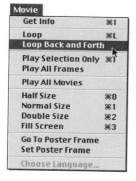

Figure 4.19 To make a movie play continuously forward then backward, choose Loop Back and Forth from the Movie menu and then play the movie.

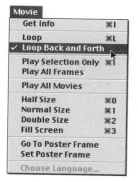

Figure 4.20 To return a movie to normal (nonlooping) play, select whichever option (Loop or Loop Back and Forth) is checked.

Looping a Movie or Playing It Backward

Normally, when you play a movie, it stops when it reaches the end. There may be times, however, when you want a movie to play continuously, not halting until you choose to pause it. You may also want to play it in reverse.

To make a movie play over and over again:

1. From the Movie menu choose Loop (**Figure 4.18**).

2. Play the movie.

To make a movie play continuously forward then backward:

1. From the Movie menu choose Loop Back and Forth (**Figure 4.19**).

2. Play the movie.

   The movie plays forward from beginning to end, then backward from end to beginning, then forward again, and so on.

To set a movie to play normally:

1. Pull down the Movie menu.

   If you previously chose Loop or Loop Back and Forth, that command is checked (**Figure 4.20**).

2. Choose the command that is checked.

   The next time you play the movie it will stop when it reaches the end.

To play a movie backward:

◆ Hold down the Command key (Mac) or the Ctrl key (Windows) and press the left arrow key.

   or

   Hold down the Shift key and double-click the movie image.

Playing Every Frame

If you're playing movies on a computer that's not quite as powerful as you'd like, you should know that QuickTime normally skips (or *drops*) frames if the computer doesn't have sufficient power to show the frames as quickly as they are supposed to be shown. You can, however, tell QuickTime Player to show each and every frame—no matter how long it takes.

To play all of a movie's frames:

1. From the Movie menu choose Play All Frames (**Figure 4.21**).

2. Play the movie.

   Because QuickTime won't necessarily be able to keep the audio synchronized with the video, no audio plays. Movies designed for very fast machines take longer than normal to show all the frames on slow machines.

✔ Tip

■ To determine whether the computer on which you're playing a movie is capable of playing all frames in real time, see "Checking the Frame Rate" later in this chapter.

Figure 4.21 To play all the frames in a movie— no matter how long it takes—choose Play All Frames from the Movie menu.

PLAYING EVERY FRAME

Figure 4.22 To play all open movies simultaneously, choose Play All Movies from the Movie menu.

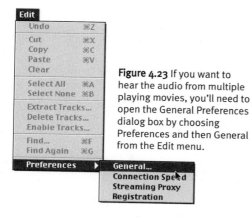

Figure 4.23 If you want to hear the audio from multiple playing movies, you'll need to open the General Preferences dialog box by choosing Preferences and then General from the Edit menu.

Figure 4.24 In the General Preferences dialog box, make sure that "Only front movie plays sound" is not checked.

Playing and Pausing All Open Movies

With QuickTime Player, you can have many movies open simultaneously—all of which you can start and stop simultaneously as well.

To play all open movies:

◆ From the Movie menu, choose Play All Movies (**Figure 4.22**).

To play sound from all playing movies:

1. From the Edit menu, choose Preferences and then from the submenu General (**Figure 4.23**).

   This opens the General Preferences dialog box.

2. Make sure that the option labeled "Only front movie plays sound" is not checked (**Figure 4.24**).

To pause all open and playing movies:

◆ From the Movie menu, choose Stop All Movies (**Figure 4.25**).

✔ Tip

■ If the first checkbox in the General Preferences dialog box—"Play sound in background"—is checked, you'll be able to hear the audio from any playing movie, even when QuickTime Player is in the background and you're using a different application.

Figure 4.25 To halt all open movies, choose Stop All Movies from the Movie menu.

Figure 4.26 To check the frame rate, choose Get Info from the Movie menu to open the Info window.

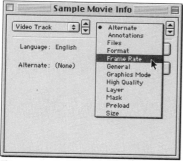

Figure 4.27 In the Info window, choose Video Track from the left pop-up menu and Frame Rate from the right pop-up menu.

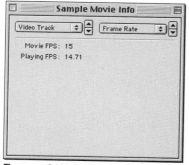

Figure 4.28 Movie FPS shows the average number of frames per second contained in the movie; Playing FPS shows the number of frames per second that are actually being played.

Checking the Frame Rate

As long as your movie has a video track, you can always check to see how many frames per second are playing and how many frames per second are contained in the movie—regardless of whether you're playing a movie at normal speed, fast-forwarding or fast-reversing it, or playing all frames.

To check the frame rate:

1. From the Movie menu choose Get Info (**Figure 4.26**).

2. From the left pop-up menu choose Video Track.

   If you have more than one video track, you'll need to check them one at a time.

3. From the right pop-up menu choose Frame Rate (**Figure 4.27**).

4. Play the movie.

   The top line shows the average number of frames per second (FPS) contained in the track. The second line—Playing FPS—shows the actual number of frames per second being played (**Figure 4.28**).

   Note that the Playing FPS is an estimate: If a movie has a changing frame rate, it sometimes takes a while for the display to catch up with the action.

✔ Tip

- You can also check the frame rate of a streaming (RTSP) track that originally contained a video track. Follow the steps above but choose Streaming Track from the left pop-up menu in Step 2.

Using Chapter Lists

When you open some movies, you'll find that the movie LCD contains an extra element in the position where audio meters usually appear: a text area with up-arrow and down-arrow icons to the right of the Time slider (**Figure 4.29**). This is the Chapter Control, which provides a way to jump quickly to designated points—or *chapters*—in a movie.

Figure 4.29 The Chapter Control only appears for some movies.

To jump to the next chapter:

◆ Click the down or up arrow to go to the movie's next or previous chapter (**Figure 4.30**).

   or

   Click and drag up or down on the text to flip quickly through the list of chapters.

Figure 4.30 To jump to the next or previous chapter, click the down or up arrow.

With either method, the Current Location indicator jumps to the beginning of the portion of the movie represented by the chapter you selected.

✔ Tips

■ To learn how to create chapter lists for your movies, see Chapter 10.

■ The Chapter List interface in QuickTime Player is currently not very useful, since you can't see a list of all the chapters at one time. (Compare it to the way Chapter Lists are implemented in the standard controller, as discussed in Chapter 2.) We hope future versions of QuickTime Player will address this issue.

Figure 4.31 Select Choose Language from the Movie menu.

Figure 4.32 Select the language of your choice in the Choose Movie Language dialog box.

Choosing a Language for Playback

Some movies contain tracks (usually sound or text) in multiple languages. If you have such a movie, you can switch from one language to another. (We'll cover how to create such movies in Chapter 7.)

To choose a language for playback:

1. From the Movie menu select Choose Language (**Figure 4.31**).

2. In the Choose Movie Language dialog box, select the language of your choice, and click OK (**Figure 4.32**).

   When you play the movie, the tracks in the selected language are enabled (that is, you can see and hear them). Tracks designated as alternates to those tracks are automatically disabled.

Running a Non-English Version of Your Operating System

When a movie is initially opened, it will automatically enable tracks that match the current system language and disable those tracks' alternates. For example, if you're running the Japanese version of your operating system, the tracks designated as Japanese will be enabled when the movie is opened.

CHOOSING A LANGUAGE FOR PLAYBACK

Searching a Text Track

You can navigate movies with text tracks by searching for specific text strings. This is particularly useful for long movies that don't include significant visual changes—for example, lecture videos or audio-only movies.

To search for text in a text track:

1. From the Edit menu choose Find (**Figure 4.33**).

2. Type the text string you want to locate and click Find (**Figure 4.34**).

   The movie jumps to the first point in time after the current location where the text is located. The string you typed is highlighted if the text track is visible (**Figure 4.35**). If the specified text is not found in the text track, you'll hear an alert sound, regardless of whether the text track is visible.

To search for a repeat occurrence of the text:

◆ From the Edit menu choose Find Again (**Figure 4.36**).

To find a previous instance of the text:

1. From the Edit menu choose Find.

2. In the Find dialog box, click the Backward button before clicking Find.

Figure 4.33 Choose Find from the Edit menu.

Figure 4.34 Type a text string.

Figure 4.35 The movie jumps to the point where the text is located; the string you typed is highlighted.

Figure 4.36 Find Again lets you locate a repeat occurrence of the text.

INTERACTING WITH QUICKTIME VR

QuickTime VR is one of the newer additions to the QuickTime architecture. Although *VR* stands for virtual reality, this isn't virtual reality with special gloves and headsets. Instead, it's what's often called *desktop virtual reality*. Computer users can experience QuickTime VR using just a keyboard and a mouse.

QuickTime VR files share the same format as standard QuickTime files, which means that QuickTime VR movies can be played in QuickTime Player as well as in most other applications that can handle QuickTime. (With a few exceptions, however, the Player can't be used to create or edit VR movies.)

There are two fundamental types of VR movies—*panoramas and objects*. Panoramas give you the experience of being in the center of a space and looking around (usually a full 360 degrees), whereas object movies give you the experience of looking at and rotating an object. Individual VR movies of either type are sometimes combined into one large file to provide the experience of exploring an extensive space.

In this chapter we'll look at how you interact with all types of QuickTime VR movies. You'll do this by dragging in the image area as well as with the help of a controller. (This controller is used in the Player as well as on the Web and in other applications.)

Looking Around in Panorama Movies

Panorama movies place you at the center of a space, where you can then look around.

To look around in a panorama movie:

1. Press the mouse button and drag across the image in the direction you want to look.

   The pointer changes to an arrow pointing in the direction you are dragging (**Figure 5.1**). The view changes in the same way it would had you moved your head in that direction.

2. Keep holding the mouse button down to continue changing the view in the direction the arrow is pointing.

   The further you drag from your initial location, the faster the view changes. (You can drag beyond the window borders to make the image spin very rapidly. Be fore-warned, however: People have become nauseous spinning around a room at high speeds!)

   When you have altered the view the maximum amount allowed in any direction, the pointer changes to include a bar indicating that you've gone as far as you can go (**Figure 5.2**). Usually you'll only run up against this limit when looking up or down because most QuickTime VR panorama movies provide a 360-degree view: You just continuously loop around. (Some movies may provide a less-than-360-degree view, however, in which case you will bump up against a right or left edge.)

Figure 5.1 Drag in a QuickTime VR panorama in the direction you want to look. The pointer shows the direction in which you're dragging.

Figure 5.2 The pointer changes to show a bar when you've dragged as far as possible in a certain direction.

Figure 5.3 The normal object movie pointer.

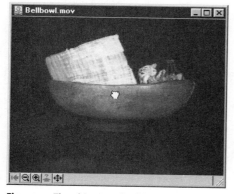

Figure 5.4 The object movie pointer as it appears when you click.

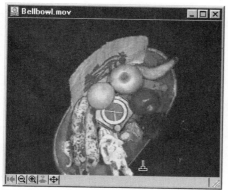

Figure 5.5 When an object has been rotated as far as it can go in a particular direction, the pointer changes to an arrow with a bar.

Manipulating Objects in Object Movies

Object movies comprise a sequence of views—usually of a single object in different rotational positions.

To manipulate an object in an object movie:

1. Click in the movie window.

   Your pointer changes from an open hand (**Figure 5.3**) to a clenched fist (**Figure 5.4**) to indicate that you've grabbed the object.

2. Continuing to hold down the mouse button, drag in the direction you wish to rotate the object.

   You can drag beyond the movie window's border to continue rotating the object. However, it's often easier to repeatedly release the mouse, and click and drag again in the movie window.

   If you've already rotated the object as far as it can go in a particular direction, the pointer, when near the window border, changes to an arrow with a bar (**Figure 5.5**).

   Some object movies provide views of an object only in a single vertical position, so your view doesn't change if you drag up or down.

Finding and Using Hot Spots

Hot spots are predefined areas in QuickTime VR movies that trigger an action when clicked. You click hot spots to move from one panorama or object to another when they're combined in a single file. (Each individual panorama or object is referred to as a *node*; a file with multiple nodes is referred to as a *multinode movie*.) You can also click hot spots to send a predefined URL to a Web browser, causing the browser to open (if it's not already) and the page to load. (When used in certain multimedia applications that support QuickTime VR or on Web pages, hot spots can be assigned additional tasks. This is accomplished via a program or script that's external to the VR movie but which references the hot spot by number.)

To locate hot spots:

◆ In the controller click the Show Hot Spots button—the one with the question mark and squished arrow pointing upwards (**Figure 5.6**).

As long as you continue holding the mouse button, hot spots will be highlighted with translucent blue shapes.

If you double-click the Show Hot Spots button, it will remain depressed. This way, you can drag in the movie window while the hot spots remain highlighted.

or

Move your pointer in the movie window: You will see that it changes when dragged over a hot spot.

Typically, a squished upward-pointing arrow (**Figure 5.7**) indicates a hot spot that opens another node. A pointing finger over a globe (**Figure 5.8**) usually means that the hot spot opens a Web page. The pointer appears as a hand over

Hot spot

Show Hot Spots button

Figure 5.6 When you click the Show Hot Spots button, hot spots in a movie are highlighted with translucent blue shapes.

Figure 5.7 This is how the pointer appears when over a hot spot that takes you to another panorama or object contained in the movie file.

Figure 5.8 The pointer looks like this when it's located over a hot spot that opens a Web page.

Figure 5.9 Here the pointer is over a hot spot that doesn't necessarily do anything in QuickTime Player, though it may serve some function in another environment.

Back button

Office Multinode Pano Movie

Figure 5.10 Click the Back button to open the node you were in before you clicked the hot spot to get to the current node. This button is not active unless the open movie is a multinode movie; it becomes active once you have used a hot spot to jump from one node to another.

a bulls-eye (**Figure 5.9**) when a hot spot has been defined but no action has been assigned to it; such hot spots can be assigned an action on a Web page or in a multimedia authoring tool, but not currently in QuickTime Player.

To use a hot spot:

◆ Click in the translucent blue rectangle or where the cursor has changed.

To return to a node after using a hot spot to jump to another node:

◆ Click the Back button. (This is the button with the left-pointing arrow; see **Figure 5.10.**)

✔ Tip

■ As you move your pointer over the buttons in the QuickTime VR controller, their names appear in the area to the right of the buttons. Text may also appear in that same area when you move your cursor over some hot spots.

QuickTime VR Pointers

While the pointers we describe here are the default pointers for QuickTime VR, developers can specify alternative pointers for their QuickTime VR movies. So, you may encounter pointers different than those shown here.

Zooming In and Out

Zooming in on a QuickTime VR movie is like using a zoom lens on a camera: It allows you to get a closer look at the image. Zooming out is just the opposite: It allows you a wider perspective.

To zoom in:

◆ Click the Zoom In button. (This is the button with the plus sign in the middle of the magnifying glass; see **Figure 5.11**.)

or

With the pointer in the movie window, press the Shift key.

If you keep holding down your mouse button or pressing the Shift key, you continue to zoom in until the image has been magnified as much as possible, or as much as the movie's creator has specified (**Figure 5.12**).

To zoom out:

◆ Click the Zoom Out button. (This is the button with the minus sign in the middle of the magnifying glass; see **Figure 5.11**.)

or

With the pointer in the movie window, press the Control key or the Ctrl key.

If you keep holding down your mouse button or pressing the Control or Ctrl key, you continue to zoom out until the image has been zoomed out as much as possible (**Figure 5.13**).

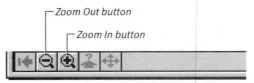

— Zoom Out button
— Zoom In button

Figure 5.11 Use the Zoom buttons to change the magnification of the image in the movie window.

Figure 5.12 This shows a movie that has been zoomed in as much as possible.

Figure 5.13 This shows a movie that has been zoomed out as much as possible.

ZOOMING IN AND OUT

─ *Drag Zoomed Object button*

Figure 5.14 Use the Drag Zoomed Object button or hold down the Option key (Mac OS) or the Ctrl and Alt keys (Windows) when you want to move a zoomed-in object.

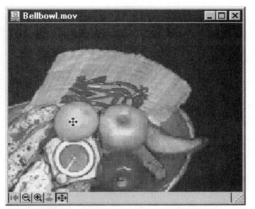

Figure 5.15 The cursor changes to show that you are in object-moving rather than object-rotating mode.

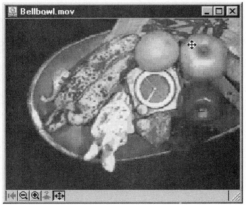

Figure 5.16 Notice that the object has not changed its rotational position.

Moving Zoomed-In Objects

Normally, when you drag in an object movie, you change the rotational position of the object. However, when an object movie is zoomed in, you sometimes want to view a portion of the image that is offscreen. You can do so by adjusting the object so that the portion you want to view becomes visible onscreen.

To move zoomed-in objects:

1. Click the Drag Zoomed Object button (the one with the arrows pointing in four directions; see **Figure 5.14**) or hold down the Option key (Mac OS) or the Ctrl and Alt keys (Windows).

   The pointer changes to look like the icon on the Drag Zoomed Object button (**Figure 5.15**).

2. Click and drag in the direction you want to move the object.

   The object retains its rotational position as you drag it (**Figure 5.16**).

Presenting QuickTime VR Movies

You can show a QuickTime VR movie on a black background just as you can a linear QuickTime movie. This is how we recommend showing VR movies to large groups of people.

To present a QuickTime VR movie:

1. Drag your movie into the rotational position you'd like it to appear in when the presentation begins.

2. From the File menu choose Present Movie (**Figure 5.17**).

   The Present Movie dialog box appears.

3. Use the Movie Size pop-up menu to choose your desired movie window size.

4. Click Play (**Figure 5.18**).

   Your screen goes black and the movie appears in the center of the screen with a QuickTime VR controller below it (**Figure 5.19**). You can control the movie as you would normally.

To stop a QuickTime VR presentation:

◆ Press the Esc key.

   or

   Type Command-period (Mac OS only).

Figure 5.17 Choose Present Movie from the File menu.

Figure 5.18 Change the movie size (if you want); then click Play.

Figure 5.19 The VR movie is shown on a black background and can be controlled in the usual fashion. Press Esc to get out of Presentation mode.

BASIC MOVIE EDITING

We call this chapter "Basic Movie Editing," but you'll still be impressed with some of the things you'll be able to do when we're done. Windows users who have played around with Windows Media Player will be blown away by QuickTime Player's editing features. And even many Mac users may not be aware of all of QuickTime Player's long-standing editing features. (Remember, QuickTime Player is essentially the same tool as the old MoviePlayer.)

While the Player doesn't include all of the fancy features of an editing program such as Adobe Premiere, it remains the best tool for certain tasks. In fact, even though we use Premiere for many functions, we've found that QuickTime Player is more efficient for simple cut, copy, and paste editing.

We start this chapter by covering one of the first skills you need if you plan to edit QuickTime movies in QuickTime Player: selecting portions of a movie. Once you've selected data, you can copy it and paste it elsewhere, remove it, or use it in various other ways.

We'll also discuss techniques for editing parts of a movie that you *don't* see or hear—posters, previews, and annotations. And finally, we'll take a look at what you need to know when it comes time to save your edited movie.

Selecting and Deselecting Movie Data

To select data in a word processor, you drag across the text you wish to select, and it becomes highlighted. Because you can't view all of the data in a QuickTime movie at once, you specify the beginning and end of your selection as points on the Time slider. You can select movie data in two basic ways: The first makes use of new Selection indicators in QuickTime Player; the second involves the Shift key—a method familiar to previous MoviePlayer users.

To select a portion of a movie using selection indicators:

1. Click the Selection End indicator—the rightmost triangular indicator below the Time slider—to activate it (**Figure 6.1**).

   When the Selection End indicator is active, the bottom triangle in the area to the left of the Time Display (the Timecode Mode Selector) becomes black. The Time Display shows the time represented by the Selection End indicator.

2. Drag the Selection End indicator to the point where you want the selection to end.

   As you drag the indicator, the Time Display continues to show the time represented by the Selection End indicator, and the movie display area shows the movie image for that time. A portion of the Time slider becomes gray (**Figure 6.2**). (Or if it was already gray, that portion extends to your new out point.) When you release the mouse button, the movie image switches back to that indicated by the Current Location indicator.

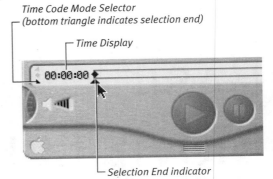

Time Code Mode Selector
(bottom triangle indicates selection end)

Time Display

Selection End indicator

Figure 6.1 When you click the Selection End indicator, it becomes active, as shown in the Timecode Mode Selector. The Time Display also changes to match the location of the Selection End indicator.

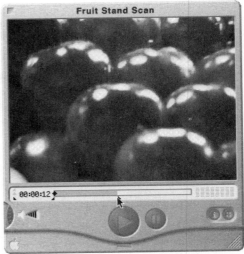

Figure 6.2 The gray area in the Time Slider represents the selected portion of the movie.

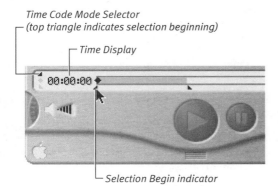

Time Code Mode Selector
(top triangle indicates selection beginning)

Time Display

Selection Begin indicator

Figure 6.3 When you click the Selection Begin indicator, it becomes active, as shown in the Timecode Mode Selector. The Time Display also changes to match the location of the Selection End indicator.

Figure 6.4 Choose Select All to select all of a movie's data.

3. Click the Selection Begin indicator—the leftmost triangular indicator below the Time slider—to activate it (**Figure 6.3**).

When the Selection Begin indicator is active, the top triangle in the Timecode Mode Selector becomes black. (Now the Time Display shows the time represented by the Selection Begin indicator.)

4. Drag the Selection Begin indicator to the point where you want the selection to begin.

Again, as you drag, the Time Display and the movie image are updated to match the location of the Selection Begin indicator, and the length of the gray portion of the Time slider changes accordingly.

To select a portion of a movie using the Shift key:

1. Move the Current Location indicator to the point in the movie where you want to begin selecting data.

2. Hold down the Shift key and move the slider to the point in the movie where you want the selection to end.

The play bar turns gray to represent your selection. QuickTime's Selection Begin and End indicators move to the beginning and end of the selected area.

To select all of the data in a movie:

◆ From the Edit menu choose Select All (**Figure 6.4**).

The entire play bar turns gray.

To cancel a selection:

◆ From the Edit menu choose Select None (**Figure 6.5**).

or

Hold down the Shift key and click the Delete key, Clear key (Mac OS), or Backspace key (Windows).

✔ Tips

■ You can also click the triangles in the Timecode Mode Selector to activate the Selection indicators.

■ The image you see when you are done selecting is actually not part of your selection—unless you are at the very end of the movie. Instead, you see the image immediately following your selection.

■ If you use the Shift key method of making a selection, you'll want to start with no movie data selected. Use one of the methods described above for canceling a selection.

■ If you use the Shift key method to make your selection, remember that you can move the Current Location indicator in any number of ways: You can drag it directly, move it a frame at a time (using the Step buttons or arrow keys), or even play the movie and then pause it when it reaches the point where you'd like the selection to end. (Just remember to hold down the Shift key while performing any of these actions.)

Figure 6.5 Choose Select None to *deselect* any data in the movie.

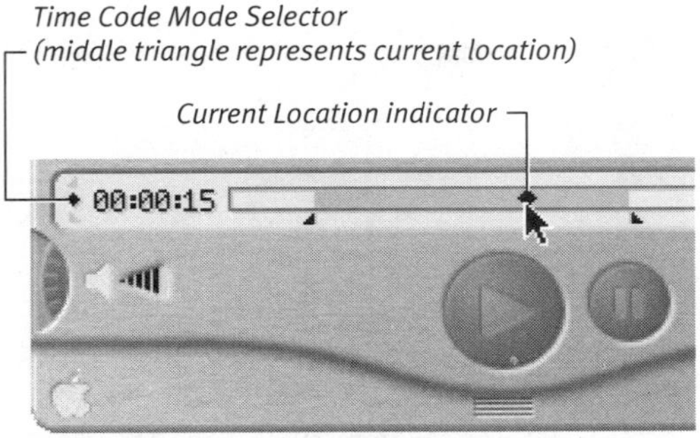

Time Code Mode Selector
(middle triangle represents current location)

Current Location indicator

Figure 6.6 Activate the Current Location indicator by clicking either it or the diamond in the middle of the Time Code Mode Selector.

Fruit Stand Scan

Figure 6.7 If the Current Location indicator starts to the left of the selection...

Jumping to the Beginning or End of a Selection

When you're trying to determine if you've selected the right data, it's helpful to be able to jump to the beginning or end of the selection.

To jump to the beginning or end of the selection:

1. Activate the Current Location indicator by clicking either it or the diamond in the middle of the Timecode Mode Selector (**Figure 6.6**).

2. If the Current Location indicator is situated to the left of the selection, hold down the Option key (Mac OS) or Ctrl and Alt keys (Windows) and click the right arrow key. (**Figure 6.7**).

continues on next page

This will jump you to the beginning of the selection (**Figure 6.8**). If you repeat the action, it will jump you to the end of the selection (**Figure 6.9**).

3. If the Current Location indicator is situated to the right of the selection, hold down the Option key (Mac OS) or Ctrl and Alt keys (Windows) and click the left arrow key.

   This will jump you to the end of the selection. If you repeat the action, it will jump you to the beginning of the selection.

✔ Tip

■ After you've jumped to the beginning or end of the selection, it may help to step forward or backward a frame or two using the Step buttons or arrow keys to verify that you've selected the desired portion of the movie.

Figure 6.8 ...holding down the Option key (Mac OS) or Ctrl and Alt keys (Windows) while clicking the right arrow key jumps you to the beginning of the selection.

Figure 6.9 Clicking again (with the modifier key or keys down) jumps you to the end.

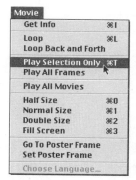

Figure 6.10 Choose Play Selection Only from the Movie menu.

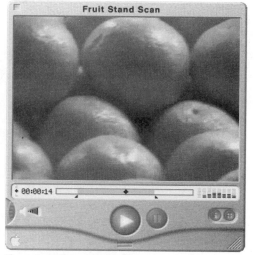

Figure 6.11 When you play the movie, the slider moves only in the area that has been selected.

Playing Only What's Selected

If you want to verify your selection, you can play just the data you've selected.

To play selected data only:

1. From the Movie menu choose Play Selection Only (**Figure 6.10**).

2. Play the movie.

   Only the portion of the movie that you've selected plays (**Figure 6.11**).

   You can return the movie to normal playback by again choosing Play Selection Only (which is now checked) from the Movie menu.

✔ Tip

■ If you going to play only your selection, you may find it helpful to also turn looping on so that the selected portion repeats several times. (Choose Loop from the Movie menu.) We've found that oftentimes we can only be sure that we have the right selection if we see it several times in a row.

Fine-Tuning a Selection

Once you've made a selection, you may want to alter it a frame (or a small portion) at a time. There are several ways to do this.

To alter the selection a frame at a time when the Selection Begin or Selection End indicator is already active:

◆ Press the right or left arrow keys to move the active indicator a frame at a time.

To alter the selection a frame at a time when the Current Location indicator is active:

1. Use the technique described in "Jumping to the Beginning or End of the Selection" to set the Current Location indicator to match whichever Selection indicator you want to change.

2. Hold down the Shift key and click the right or left arrow keys to move the Selection indicator and the Current Location indicator a frame at a time (**Figure 6.12**).

Figure 6.12 Once you've jumped to the beginning or end of the selection, your arrow keys will move the current time and the selection together.

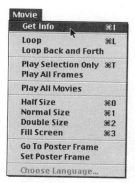

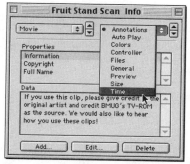

Figure 6.13 Choose Get Info from the Movie menu to open the Info window.

Figure 6.14 Choose Time from the right pop-up menu.

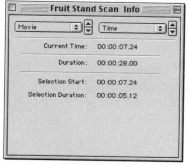

Figure 6.15 The Time panel provides time-related information.

Getting Time Information about the Movie and Selection

When editing it's sometimes useful to know the precise duration of your movie and selection.

To get time information:

1. From the Movie menu choose Get Info to open the movie's Info window (**Figure 6.13**).

2. In the movie's Info window, make sure Movie is chosen in the left pop-up menu; from the right pop-up menu choose Time (**Figure 6.14**).

   The Time panel provides four pieces of information concerning time (**Figure 6.15**): The first line (Current Time) shows the point in time relative to the start of the movie at which the Current Location indicator is positioned. The second line shows the duration of the movie. And the bottom two lines show the point in time relative to the start of the movie at which the selection begins as well as how long the selection lasts. Time values in the Time panel are represented as hours: minutes:seconds:thirtieths of a second. Thus, 00:12:45:15 represents zero hours, 12 minutes, 45 seconds, and fifteen-thirtieths (or one-half) of a second.

Copying and Cutting Movie Data

QuickTime Player provides the standard Copy and Cut commands that you find in just about all Mac OS and Windows applications. However, because you can't see all the data you're working with, these commands work a bit differently here than they do in most programs.

To copy movie data:

1. Select the movie data you wish to copy (**Figure 6.16**), as described at the beginning of this chapter.

2. From the Edit menu choose Copy (**Figure 6.17**).

   As with most programs, nothing appears to happen when you copy your data; nonetheless, it has been copied and is ready to be pasted elsewhere.

Figure 6.16 Before copying or cutting, make a selection in the Time slider.

Figure 6.17 Choose Copy from the File menu when you want to copy the data without removing it.

Figure 6.18 Choose Cut from the File menu when you want to copy and remove the data at the same time.

To cut movie data:

1. Select the movie data you wish to cut.

2. From the Edit menu choose Cut (**Figure 6.18**).

   The gray area representing the selection disappears from the Time slider, and both Selection indicators move to the beginning of the Time slider (**Figure 6.19**). Unless you had moved the Current Location indicator into the area you've selected, the movie image appears unchanged. If you play the movie, however, you'll see that the portion of the movie that was selected isn't played at all. That portion is ready to be pasted elsewhere.

✔ Tips

- Use the Undo command in the Edit menu to return the movie to its previous state (that is, before you performed your last action).

- If you have not selected any data (that is, the Selection Begin and Selection End indicators are as close together as possible), QuickTime treats the current frame as your selection when you copy or cut.

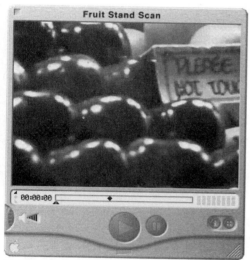

Figure 6.19 Once you've cut data, the selection disappears.

Having Multiple Windows Open in QuickTime Player

By default, when you open a new linear movie in QuickTime Player, that movie will replace whatever movie appears in your already-open window—somewhat inconvenient for many editing tasks. Far more convenient would be to have multiple windows open simultaneously.

To open a movie in its own window:

1. From the File menu choose New Player (**Figure 6.20**).

   An empty Player window opens.

2. From the File menu, choose Open Movie.

   An Open dialog box appears in which you can locate and select the movie you wish to open.

   or

1. Hold down the Option key (Mac OS) or Ctrl and Alt keys (Windows) while pulling down the File menu.

2. Open Movie in New Player replaces Open Movie in the File menu.

3. Choose Open Movie in New Player.

   An Open dialog box appears in which you can locate and select the movie you wish to open.

Figure 6.20 If you want a movie to appear in its own window, choose New Player before choosing Open Movie.

Figure 6.21 You can change your general preferences...

Figure 6.22 ...to specify that you always want movies opened in a new player window.

Figure 6.23 The menu item changes to Open Movie in New Player (rather than just Open Movie).

To always have movies open in their own windows:

1. From the Edit menu, select Preferences and then General (**Figure 6.21**).

2. In the General Preferences dialog box, check "Open movie in new player" and click OK (**Figure 6.22**).

   Once you've altered your preferences in this fashion, the File menu will display an Open Movie in New Player command rather than Open Movie, so you won't have to hold down the Option or Ctrl and Alt keys, or choose New Player before opening a movie (**Figure 6.23**).

✔ Tips

■ Once you've changed QuickTime Player's preferences as described above, you'll find that holding down the Option key (Mac OS) or Ctrl and Alt keys (Windows) while pulling down the File menu causes Open Movie to replace Open Movie in New Player.

■ Always opening movies in their own window may sometimes result in having lots of windows open. On a Mac OS computer, if you want to quickly close all those windows, hold down the Option key and click the close box of any movie window. All the windows will close. (On Windows computers you can hold down the Ctrl and Alt keys and click the close button, but since closing the last open Player window causes QuickTime Player to quit, it doesn't make much sense to do this.)

Pasting Movie Data into a Movie

Pasting is not a terribly complicated operation; however, it does have some idiosyncrasies. One of the slightly confusing aspects of pasting is that things happen one way if you place the new data at the end of the movie and another if you place it anywhere else. We'll explain both here.

To paste previously copied or cut data at the end of a movie:

1. Move the Current Location indicator as far to the right as possible in the Time slider (**Figure 6.24**).

2. From the Edit menu choose Paste (**Figure 6.25**).

   The Current Location indicator remains at the end of the Time slider. The last frame of the data you previously copied or cut appears in the movie window. A portion of the Time slider, which represents the pasted data, is selected.

   The data has been pasted after the original data.

Figure 6.24 When you want to paste data at the end of the movie, move the Current Location indicator as far to the right as possible.

Figure 6.25 Choose Paste from the Edit menu to paste previously copied or cut movie data.

Pasting Data into Other Applications

Data that you've copied or cut from a movie can often be pasted into other applications that are able to handle that type of data. For example, you can paste video-track data into a graphics program such as Adobe Photoshop, and you can paste text-track data into some text or word processors. Typically, only the first frame of the selection is pasted.

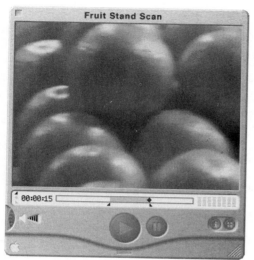

Figure 6.26 When you want to paste data anywhere except the end of a movie, move the Current Location indicator to the frame before which you want the data pasted. The current image will be the one immediately following the pasted data.

To paste previously copied or cut data anywhere except the end of a movie:

1. Move your Current Location indicator to the point in the movie just past where you want the data pasted.

2. From the Edit menu choose Paste.

   A selection appears in the Time slider to the left of the Current Location indicator, representing your pasted data (**Figure 6.26**). If you play or step through the movie, you'll see that the data has been inserted just before the point where the Current Location indicator was positioned when you pasted.

✔ Tip

- In QuickTime Player, when you paste into a movie with a selection the pasted data does not replace the selected data, as is the case with many other applications. QuickTime Player does, however, have a Replace command that works this way; see "Replacing Part of a Movie with a Portion of Another" later in this chapter.

Transitional Edits

When you combine movies by copying and pasting as described in this section, you are performing what's called a *straight-cut edit*, where one clip ends and another begins. A *transitional edit*, on the other hand, is one in which one clip begins before the other ends, with some kind of visual effect—for example, a dissolve—occurring during the overlap. QuickTime has built-in effects that editing software can use to provide transitional editing capabilities; unfortunately, QuickTime Player can't make use of these effects. However, Apple does have a free utility, called MakeEffectMovie, that will allow you to experiment with these effects; you can get it at http://www.apple.com/quicktime/developers/tools.html#effects.

Pasting Text and Graphics into a Movie

As long as you're not pasting into an empty movie, you can paste data from applications that handle text or images: You simply follow the same steps you use to paste movie data. The rules for where the data gets pasted are also the same: Unless the Current Location indicator is situated at the end of the movie, the data is pasted immediately *before* the current image.

Pasting images from a graphics application

If the movie into which you are pasting already includes a visual component, pasted images are resized and reproportioned to fit the movie window's current dimensions (**Figure 6.27**). So, it's best to make sure that the graphic is the same size as the existing window before pasting. If the movie is an audio-only movie, the image retains its original dimensions.

A new frame is added to the movie when you paste graphics. If there was a video track in the movie before the paste, the new frame becomes part of the existing video track. If the movie didn't include a video track before the paste, a video track is added.

In addition, if the movie contained a video track before the paste, the new frame is usually the same duration as the frame that was visible when you pasted. If the movie didn't contain a video track prior to pasting, the new frame has a duration of 2 seconds.

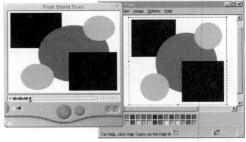

Figure 6.27 When you paste an image copied from a graphic application into a movie, the image is resized and reproportioned to fit the existing movie window. It's given a duration of 2 seconds.

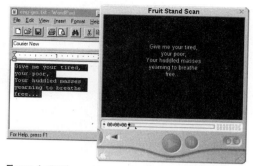

Figure 6.28 When you copy text from a word processor and paste it into a movie, the text is white on a black background and centered. It may retain other formatting characteristics.

Pasting text from a word processor

Pasted text appears centered in a new frame and is white on a black background (**Figure 6.28**). Depending on what word processor you've copied the data from, the text may retain other formatting, such as font, size, and style. (Some word processors don't copy styled text in a way that other applications, such as QuickTime Player, can understand.)

The width of the window does not change. If you paste an extremely large block of text, the movie window's height is extended to fit the text and white is added to the bottom of the window in the rest of the movie. (The height is only extended as much as your current screen will allow; only the text that will fit in that height appears.)

The duration of the frame containing the text is 2 seconds.

✔ Tips

- A technique that will allow you to change these default durations is discussed in Chapter 7 in the section "Scaling a Track to a Specific Duration."

- If you have a lot of graphics or text to paste, you may be better off importing the data and creating a new movie with a video or text track. See Chapters 9 and 10 for more on this. In these chapters we also discuss techniques for performing such tasks as adding a graphic that can be used as a logo or changing the look of text.

- In some situations, QuickTime Player may not interpret data copied from other applications as you might expect. For example, when you copy multiple cells from an Excel spreadsheet, QuickTime Player treats it as a graphic.

PASTING TEXT AND GRAPHICS INTO A MOVIE

Creating a New Movie and Pasting Movie Data into It

There's nothing terribly complicated about creating a new movie and placing copied movie data into it. We'll assume that you have already copied data from another movie. (Note that you can only paste data copied from a QuickTime movie into an empty movie; you cannot paste text or graphics copied from another application.)

To create a new movie and paste something into it:

1. From the File menu choose New Player (**Figure 6.29**).

   An empty Player window appears (**Figure 6.30**).

2. From the Edit menu choose Paste (**Figure 6.31**).

   Assuming the pasted data has a visual component, the movie window will expand to fit the data's dimensions. The entire play bar is selected (**Figure 6.32**).

   When you play the movie you'll see that it now contains the pasted data.

Figure 6.29 Choose New Player from the File menu.

Figure 6.30 A new empty Player window appears.

Figure 6.31 Choose Paste to paste previously copied movie data.

Figure 6.32 The movie window expands to the dimensions of the pasted data.

Figure 6.33 Choose Select All from the Edit menu in one movie.

Figure 6.34 Choose Copy from the Edit menu.

Figure 6.35 Click in the other movie, move the Current Location indicator, and choose Paste form the Edit menu.

Combining Two Movies

Once you know how to copy and paste movie data, you also understand how to combine movies so that one plays after the other. However, we'll review the steps here anyway.

To combine two movies:

1. In the movie window that contains the data you want to play second, choose Select All from the Edit menu (**Figure 6.33**).

2. From the Edit menu choose Copy (**Figure 6.34**).

3. Click in the other movie window.

4. Move the Current Location indicator to the far right of the Time slider.

5. From the Edit menu choose Paste (**Figure 6.35**).

   You can, of course, select less than the whole movie in Step 1. In addition, in Step 4 you can position the Current Location indicator somewhere other than to the far right of the Time slider if you wish to paste data in a location other than at the end of the movie.

✔ Tip

■ You can use the Tab key to or the Windows menu switch between QuickTime Player windows.

COMBINING TWO MOVIES

Deleting Parts of a Movie

When you want to get rid of movie data, you have two choices: You can delete the selected data, or you can delete everything but the selection.

To delete a section of a movie:

1. Select the portion of the movie you wish to delete.

2. From the Edit menu choose Clear (**Figure 6.36**), or press the Delete key.

To retain a portion of a movie while deleting everything around it:

1. Select the portion of the movie you wish to retain.

2. Hold down the Option key (Mac OS) or Ctrl and Alt keys (Windows), and from the Edit menu choose Trim (**Figure 6.37**). (Holding down the modifier keys causes Trim to replace Clear in the Edit menu.)

✔ Tip

- If you haven't selected any data when you clear or trim in a movie with a track composed of frames (such as video, sprite, and text tracks), QuickTime Player treats the current frame as the selection. So, clearing removes the current frame, and trimming gets rid of everything *but* the current frame. With 3D movies when no data is selected, all but one-thirtieth of a second of the movie is deleted when you choose Trim; a few fractions of a second of the movie are removed when you choose Clear. You can't clear or trim in audio-only movies without selecting some portion of data.

Figure 6.36 Choose Clear from the Edit menu to delete the selection.

Figure 6.37 Trim appears in the Edit menu when you hold down the Option key (Mac OS) or Ctrl and Alt keys (Windows). Use this command to delete everything but the selection.

Figure 6.38 Hold down the Shift key while pulling down the Edit menu to choose Replace.

Replacing Part of a Movie with a Portion of Another

You can easily replace part of one movie with a portion copied from another.

To replace a section of a movie with data from another movie:

1. Select the data you want to use as replacement data.

2. From the Edit menu choose Copy.

3. Click in the movie window that includes the data you want replaced.

4. Select the data you want replaced.

5. While holding down the Shift key, from the Edit menu choose Replace (**Figure 6.38**).

   (When you hold down the Shift key, Replace appears instead of Paste in the Edit menu.)

   The movie may be longer or shorter than it was originally, depending on the length of the replacement data.

Drag-and-Drop Editing

Drag-and-drop editing allows you to easily drag data from one window to another within and between applications (such as QuickTime Player) that support that type of editing. It provides the same functionality as copying and pasting but is usually faster.

To perform a simple drag-and-drop edit in QuickTime Player:

1. Arrange your desktop so that at least portions of two movie windows are visible. Select part of one of the movies. (If you don't select any data, QuickTime Player assumes that the current frame is the selection.)

2. Click in the image and, continuing to hold down the mouse button, drag toward the other window. You'll see a ghosted frame the size of the movie image containing a small translucent image of the movie (**Figure 6.39**). As you drag over the other movie window, a moving border (which looks something like a barber pole) appears in that window, indicating that it can receive the data (**Figure 6.40**).

3. Release the mouse button when the data is positioned over the other movie window. (In other words, "drop" the data.) The data is pasted into the movie prior to the location of the Current Location indicator (or at the end of the movie if that's where the Current Location indicator is).

Figure 6.39 When you click in the movie window and drag, a ghosted image appears.

Figure 6.40 When you drag over another movie window, an animated border appears to show that you can drop the data there.

✔ Tips

- You can drag movie data in this way to many applications that support drag-and-drop editing—as long as the application can handle the type of data contained in the movie window where you've made the selection. (For example, you can drag an image from the movie window into some graphics applications, and you can drag text into some word processors.) You can even drag movie data to the Mac OS Finder: The first time you do this a movie file called Movie Clipping 1 is created; the second time a Movie Clipping 2 file is created; and so on. (These clipping files are dependent on the movie from which you dragged; see Saving Movies at the end of this chapter.) If you drag movie data to the Windows desktop, a still-image file (in BMP format) is created.

- You can also drag from drag-and-drop–aware applications to a movie window. You can even drag files of formats that QuickTime understands from the Mac OS Finder and the Windows desktop to a movie window; data will be pasted as if you had selected and copied all the data in the file.

Adding and Editing Annotations

QuickTime movies can contain textual information about various important properties pertaining to the movie's creation and ownership. Collectively referred to as *annotations*, more than 20 such properties exist (see sidebar on page 106 for a complete list).

When you're working on a movie (or at least before you hand it over it to anyone else), it's a good idea to add some of this information so viewers can find out more about the movie's background if they wish.

To add annotation data:

1. From the Movie menu choose Get Info (**Figure 6.41**).

2. If the Annotations panel isn't already visible, from the left pop-up menu choose Movie and from the right pop-up menu choose Annotations.

3. In the Annotations panel click the Add button (**Figure 6.42**).

4. In the Add Annotation dialog box, select the property you'd like to add (**Figure 6.43**).

5. In the field at the bottom of the window, type the appropriate text for the property (or paste it if you previously copied it from elsewhere).

6. At the bottom of the Add Annotation dialog box click the Add button.

   When you click the name of the property you chose in Step 4 in the movie's Info window, you'll see the text you typed in Step 5 in the bottom field labeled Data.

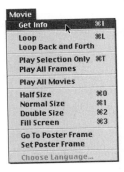

Figure 6.41 Choose Get Info to open the movie's Info window.

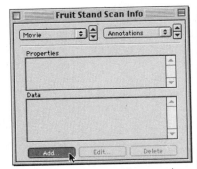

Figure 6.42 In the Annotations panel, click Add.

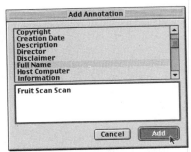

Figure 6.43 Select the property you want to add, type the text for that property, and then click Add.

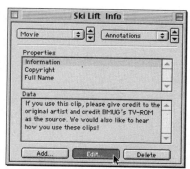

Figure 6.44 To alter existing annotation data, select the property you want to change and click Edit.

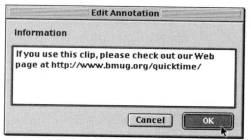

Figure 6.45 Make changes to the text, and click OK.

Figure 6.46 To delete annotation data, select the property you want to delete and click Delete.

To change annotation data:

1. In the Annotations panel, select the property for which you wish to change data and click Edit (**Figure 6.44**). (You can also double-click the property.)

2. In the Edit Annotation dialog box, edit the text and click OK (**Figure 6.45**).

To delete annotation data:

1. In the Annotations panel, select the property for which you want to delete data and click Delete (**Figure 6.46**).

   An alert dialog box appears asking if you really want to delete the property.

2. Click Delete.

✔ Tips

- Annotation names represent the properties that the QuickTime team anticipated would be most useful to multimedia developers. While it makes sense to provide data appropriate to any particular annotation name, there's nothing preventing you from adding whatever alphanumeric information you want for any annotation. Also, feel free to use as few or as many of these annotations as you wish.

- As many as three of your annotations can appear in the Info Tray, which you access by clicking the Info button in the Player window. (See next page for details.) One of these, the Full Name property, appears as the Movie Title (**Figure 6.47**); it's also how your movie appears in the Favorites menu if users choose to add it to their Favorites.

Figure 6.47 Whatever you enter for the Full Name property appears as the Movie Title. (If you don't enter anything for Full Name, the movie's file name is used as the title.)

Annotations a Movie Can Contain	
◆ Album	◆ Producer
◆ Artist	◆ Product
◆ Author	◆ Software
◆ Comment	◆ Special Playback Requirements
◆ Copyright	
◆ Creation Date	◆ Warning
◆ Description	◆ Writer
◆ Director	◆ Edit Date 1
◆ Disclaimer	◆ Edit Date 2
◆ Full Name	◆ Edit Date 3
◆ Host Computer	◆ Edit Date 4
◆ Information	◆ Edit Date 5
◆ Make	◆ Edit Date 6
◆ Model	◆ Edit Date 7
◆ Original Format	◆ Edit Date 8
◆ Original Source	◆ Edit Date 9
◆ Performers	

Figure 6.48 The annotations you enter (up to three of those chosen from those in the sidebar on this page) will determine what text is displayed in the Info Tray.

Changing What's Shown in the Info Tray

When a viewer clicks the Info button, the Info Tray opens (**Figure 6.48**). For your own movies, you can enter certain annotations to control what gets shown here. As many as three annotations will appear in the Info Tray, and these three must belong to a certain subset (see sidebar).

To add the text that will appear in the Info Tray:

◆ Add annotations chosen from those listed in the sidebar on this page. (To learn how to add annotations, see the previous section of this chapter, "Adding and Editing Annotations.")

QuickTime Player will use the order listed in this page's sidebar to determine which annotations will appear and in what order. The first listed annotation that includes data will appear on the first line of the Info Tray; the second one with data will appear on the second line; and the third one with data will appear on the third line.

For example, if Copyright, Full Name, Creation Date, and Album are provided with data, Full Name, Copyright, and Album will appear in the Info Tray. They'll appear in that order because that's the order in which they're listed in the sidebar. Creation Date is ignored because it is not one of the properties that can be displayed in the Info Tray.

Annotations That Appear in the Info Tray

◆ Full Name	◆ Performers
◆ Copyright	◆ Album
◆ Information	◆ Director
◆ Artist	◆ Producer
◆ Author	◆ Description
◆ Writer	◆ Comment

To change the text that appears in the Info Tray:

◆ Change the displayed annotations.

If you're not sure which these are, you can open the Annotations panel and click the items in the properties field until you locate the ones being used. (To learn how to change annotations, see "Adding and Editing Annotations" earlier in this chapter.)

✔ Tips

■ If you type too much text, part of it will be replaced by ellipses. When your movie is opened on a Mac OS computer, the end of the line will be missing (**Figure 6.49**); when your movie is opened on a Windows machine, the middle of the line will be missing (**Figure 6.50**).

■ Returns in your text will be ignored when shown in the Info Tray on a Mac OS computer; on a Windows computer they'll be replaced by other characters. If you care how the text looks in the Info Tray, avoid using returns when you type text in the Add Annotation dialog box.

Figure 6.49 If there's too much text to fit, the end is replaced by ellipses when the annotation is shown on a Mac OS computer.

Figure 6.50 If there's too much text to fit, the middle is replaced by ellipses when shown on a Windows computer.

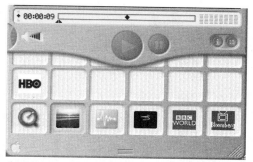

Figure 6.51 The Poster is the image used in the Favorites Drawer.

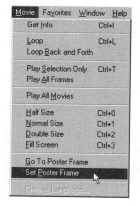

Figure 6.52 Choose Set Poster Frame from the Movie menu to use the current image as the poster.

Figure 6.53 Choose Go To Poster Frame to jump to the poster image.

Setting a Poster

A *poster* is the image that represents a movie in the Favorites Drawer (**Figure 6.51**). It is also sometimes shown in the Open dialog box, and it can be printed when you print a movie.

The poster is a single image from the movie. By default, the poster is the first frame or image of the movie—that is, even movies that aren't composed of frames, like 3D movies, can have a poster.

To set a poster:

1. Move the Current Location indicator to the position where the image that you want for the poster is located.

2. From the Movie menu choose Set Poster Frame (**Figure 6.52**).

To ensure that the correct image is used for the poster:

1. Move the Current Location indicator to a random point on the play bar.

2. From the Movie menu choose Go To Poster Frame (**Figure 6.53**).

   The Current Location indicator moves to the location that you set as the poster.

Setting a Preview

The Open dialog box for QuickTime applications usually includes a preview area on the left (**Figure 6.54**). This can be a static image, or it can be a portion of the movie that can be played. (On Mac OS computers, it's usually the poster. On Windows computers, it's usually the first ten seconds of the movie.) However, for either platform, you can specify exactly what you want to appear here by setting a preview.

To set a preview:

1. Select the portion of the movie you want to use for a preview (**Figure 6.55**).

2. From the Movie menu choose Get Info.

3. In the Info window, from the left pop-up menu choose Movie (if not already chosen) and from the right pop-up menu choose Preview.

4. In the Preview panel, click the button labeled Set Preview to Selection (**Figure 6.56**).

To view the current preview:

1. In the Preview panel click Set Selection to Preview.

2. From the Movie menu choose Play Selection Only (**Figure 6.57**).

3. Play the movie.

To remove a preview:

◆ In the Preview panel click Clear Preview.

Figure 6.54 A dynamic preview often appears on the left side of the Open dialog box for applications that can open QuickTime movies.

Figure 6.55 To set the preview for your movie, select the portion of the movie you want.

Figure 6.56 Then, in the Preview panel of the Info window, click Set Preview to Selection.

Figure 6.57 If you want to check the current preview while the movie is still open, click Set Selection to Preview, and then choose Play Selection Only from the Movie menu.

SETTING A PREVIEW

Figure 6.58 You can select data in a different movie to be used as a preview. Simply drag from the other movie window and drop in the Preview panel of the movie for which you're setting a preview.

Setting a Preview Using Data from Other Movies

Just as "coming attractions" for a film aren't always composed of exact scenes from the film, you may want your QuickTime movie preview to show segments from some other movie (perhaps one composed of highlights edited together expressly for this purpose).

To set a preview that's composed of data from another movie:

1. Open the other movie and make a selection in that movie.

2. Click on the image and drag to the Preview panel of the Info window for the movie for which you're setting a preview.

3. Release the mouse button when a frame appears around the words *Drop Preview Movie Here* (**Figure 6.58**).

Saving Movies

Once you're done editing, you'll want to save your work. When saving it's important to understand the concept of *file dependencies*. After you've pasted data into a movie, the movie actually contains *references* (pointers) to the file or files from which you copied the data. The file is said to have *dependencies*. You can leave it this way (which saves disk space), but the movie won't play unless the other files are available. Or, you can specify when you save that all the data be moved into the file, making it larger but *self-contained*.

To save a movie file, allowing dependencies:

1. From the File menu choose Save As (**Figure 6.59**).

   QuickTime Player displays a standard Save dialog box with a pair of radio buttons at the bottom of the window.

2. Make sure the "Save normally (allowing dependencies)" radio button is selected (**Figure 6.60**).

3. Name the file, navigate to the location where you want to save it, and click the Save button.

To save a movie file so that it is self-contained:

1. From the File menu choose Save As.

2. In the Save dialog box, provide a new name and navigate to a new location for the file, if you wish. (If you have edited an existing file on a Windows computer, you must do one of these—change the name or location— to go on to the next step.)

Figure 6.59 Choose Save As from the File menu when you want to save a file.

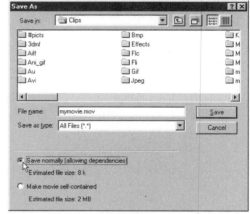

Figure 6.60 If you want the file to be saved with dependencies, choose the "Save normally (allowing dependencies)" radio button.

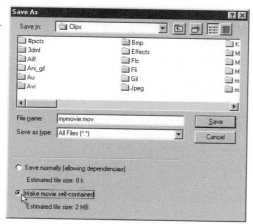

Figure 6.61 If you want to make sure that the file doesn't depend on other files to play, choose the "Make movie self-contained" radio button.

3. Select the "Make movie self-contained" radio button (**Figure 6.61**).

4. Name the file, navigate to the desired location, and click Save.

✔ Tips

■ If you choose Save rather than Save As for a movie that's had new data pasted into it but has previously been saved, it will automatically be saved with dependencies.

■ If you've resized the window or selected Loop, Loop Back and Forth, Play All Frames, or Play Selection Only, these settings will remain when the movie is saved.

■ You can open an RTSP streaming movie over the network (using the Open URL command) and copy data from it and paste into another movie. When you save the movie (that you've pasted into), it will not actually contain the data, even if you save as a self-contained movie. It will only contain a pointer to the movie stored over the network.

Checking File Dependencies

QuickTime Player's Info window provides a way for you to see which files a movie is dependent on, if any.

To check file dependencies:

1. From the File menu choose Get Info (**Figure 6.62**).

2. Make sure Movie is selected in the left pop-up menu, and then from the right pop-up menu select Files.

   The Files panel lists the files upon which this movie depends.

   If only one file is listed, it is usually the file currently open and active. This means that the movie is dependent only on itself (**Figure 6.63**).

   If the listed file doesn't match the name of the open file, or if more than one file is listed, the movie depends on other files to play (**Figure 6.64**).

   You can also determine which tracks are dependent on other files by looking at the Files panel for each track. This lists the files upon which the track depends.

   You can double-click the file name to open any of these reference files.

✔ Tip

■ When checking the Files panel to see if anything other than the currently open file is listed, recall that the open file's filename may not be what appears as the Movie Title. (The Movie Title may instead be what's entered for the Full Name annotation; see "Adding and Editing Annotations" earlier in this chapter.)

Figure 6.62 Choose Get Info from the File menu to open the Info window.

Figure 6.63 If the Files panel shows only the current file, the movie has no dependencies other than itself—that is, it's self-contained.

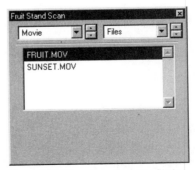

Figure 6.64 When more than one file is listed, the movie needs all the files listed to be present in order to play.

WORKING WITH TRACKS

In the previous chapter you learned editing techniques that treat a movie as if it were a single entity, ignoring that a movie is often actually composed of separate tracks.

In this chapter we'll show you how you can decompose a movie into its component media tracks, combine tracks to make a new movie, delete tracks, hide tracks, and scale individual tracks to a specific duration

We'll also explain the process of assigning alternate languages to tracks.

Finally, we'll demonstrate how you can get slightly better performance by specifying how certain tracks can be loaded into memory.

Combining Tracks with the Add and Add Scaled Commands

When you use the Paste command, as covered in the previous chapter, pasted data gets placed before or after existing data. Sometimes, however, you may want to add data that plays at the same time as the existing data—for example, to add a new audio track to a movie, to add text for subtitles, or to add new graphics to enhance an existing image.

You can add the data so it runs as long as it did originally—a good idea for audio, unless you want to speed up or slow down the audio. You can also add data so its duration is scaled to a certain length—as you'll often want to do when adding text or graphics.

To add data so it lasts for its original duration:

1. Select and copy the data you wish to add.

2. In the movie you want to add the data to, move the Current Location indicator to the point where you want the new data to begin playing.

3. Hold down the Option key (Mac OS) or Ctrl and Alt keys (Windows), and from the Edit menu choose Add (**Figure 7.1**).

   (Add replaces Paste in the Edit menu when you hold down the Option or Ctrl and Alt keys.)

   When you play the movie and reach the point where you've added the data, you'll find that it begins playing along with whatever data was already there.

Figure 7.1 To add data so it plays concurrently with existing data, hold down the Option key (Mac OS) or Ctrl and Alt keys (Windows) while pulling down the Edit menu and choosing Add.

Track Names

If you already have a track of the type you are adding, QuickTime automatically changes the track names to include sequential numbers (for example, Video Track 1 and Video Track 2). To simplify later editing, you can rename tracks with more meaningful labels. In the Info window, select the track you want to rename in the left pop-up menu and choose General in the right pop-up menu. Then click the Change Name button, type a new name, and click OK.

Figure 7.2 When you want added data to last for a certain length of time, make a selection of that length in the movie you're adding the data to...

Figure 7.3 ...and then hold down the Option and Shift keys (Mac OS) or the Ctrl, Alt, and Shift keys (Windows), and from the Edit menu choose Add Scaled.

To add data so it lasts for a duration of your choosing:

1. Select and copy the data you wish to add.

2. In the movie you want to add the data to, select the portion of the movie where you want the added data to play (**Figure 7.2**).

3. Hold down the Option and Shift keys (Mac OS) or the Ctrl, Alt, and Shift keys (Windows), and from the Edit menu choose Add Scaled (**Figure 7.3**).

   (Add Scaled replaces Paste in the Edit menu when you hold down the Option and Shift keys or the Ctrl, Alt, and Shift keys.)

   When you play the movie, you'll see or hear that the added data lasts for the duration of the selection. For data that originally had a time component (in other words, that changed over time), this gives you a fast- or slow-motion effect, depending on whether the selection was shorter or longer than the original duration of the added data.

✔ Tips

■ Don't be confused by the term *scaled*. You're scaling the data in time, not space.

■ When you use the Add Scaled command to add data to a movie with no selection, the new data is actually scaled to the entire movie, as if you had selected it all in Step 2.

Annotating Tracks

You can add and edit annotations for individual tracks, just as you can for the whole movie. Simply follow the steps in "Adding and Editing Annotations" in Chapter 6; however, instead of choosing Movie in the left pop-up menu, select the track for which you'd like to add or edit an annotation.

COMBINING TRACKS

Extracting Tracks

Just as you can create single-track movies by importing various media files, you can also pull a single track out of an existing movie.

To extract a track from a movie:

1. With the movie open, from the Edit menu choose Extract Tracks (**Figure 7.4**).

2. In the Extract Tracks dialog box, select the track you want to extract and click the Extract button (**Figure 7.5**).

   A new movie window appears. When you play this new movie, you'll see or hear that it contains only the data from the track you extracted.

   If you save this movie (or another movie that you paste data from this movie into), make sure to save it as a self-contained file. Otherwise, the movie will depend on the original file you extracted the track from.

✔ Tip

■ You can select more than one track in the Extract Tracks dialog box. If you hold down the Shift key, you can make a contiguous selection. If you hold down the Command key (Mac OS) or Ctrl key (Windows), you can make a noncontiguous selection.

Figure 7.4 From the Edit menu, choose Extract Tracks.

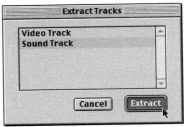

Figure 7.5 Select the track or tracks you wish to extract, and click Extract.

Figure 7.6 From the Edit menu, choose Delete Tracks.

Figure 7.7 Select the track or tracks you wish to remove, and click Delete.

Deleting Tracks

At times you may want to get rid of a single track in a movie while retaining the remaining tracks.

To delete a track:

1. With the movie open, from the Edit menu choose Delete Tracks (**Figure 7.6**).

2. In the Delete Tracks dialog box, select the track you want to delete, and click the Delete button (**Figure 7.7**).

   If the track you selected was a visual track that appeared in the movie window, you will notice that it has now disappeared. If the track was the sole audio track in the movie, the Graphic EQ in the LCD will have disappeared. (This assumes that the Graphic EQ was previously visible; if a movie has a chapter list, no Graphic EQ would have been previously visible.)

   When you play the movie, you'll see or hear that the deleted track no longer plays.

✔ Tips

- Deleted data remains in the movie until you save it as a self-contained file—even though you can't access that data and there's no way to get it back.

- You can select more than one track in the Delete Tracks dialog box. By holding down the Shift key, you can make a contiguous selection; by holding down the Command key (Mac OS) or Ctrl key (Windows), you can make a noncontiguous selection.

DELETING TRACKS

119

Disabling and Enabling Tracks

You can selectively disable and enable tracks in a movie. For visual tracks, this gives you a way to hide or reveal tracks. You may find this capability useful during editing, when you want to focus on individual tracks without being distracted by others. You may also want to do this for a final movie (for example, you can make a text track invisible yet still searchable). Unlike a deleted track, a disabled track can always be enabled—even after the movie is saved.

To disable a track:

1. From the Edit menu, choose Enable Tracks (**Figure 7.8**).

2. In the Enable Tracks dialog box (**Figure 7.9**), click the line in the list that contains the name of the track you want to disable.

   The text in the box to the left of the track name changes from a green ON to a red OFF.

3. Click OK.

To enable a disabled track:

1. From the Edit menu, choose Enable Tracks.

2. In the Enable Tracks dialog box, click the line containing the name of the disabled track (one with a red OFF to the left of the track name) you wish to turn back on.

   The text in the box to the left of the track name changes from a red OFF to a green ON.

3. Click OK.

Figure 7.8 If you want to enable or disable a track, from the Edit menu, choose Enable Tracks.

Figure 7.7 Select the track or tracks you wish to remove, and click Delete.

Figure 7.10 Use the Extract Tracks command to extract the track you want to scale.

Figure 7.11 From another movie, select a portion that is equal to your desired duration.

Scaling a Track to a Specific Duration

Using the QuickTime Player features covered in this and the preceding chapter, you can change the duration of an existing QuickTime track to whatever length you wish. The technique, however, isn't quite as simple as you might like.

To change the duration of a track:

1. If the track in question is combined with other tracks, go to the Edit menu and use the Extract Tracks command to create a movie containing only that track (**Figure 7.10**).

2. Click in the window that contains the track with the duration you wish to change, and then from the Edit menu choose Select All. Finally, from the Edit menu choose Copy.

3. Locate and open another movie whose duration is equal to or greater than that what you desire for your track. (It doesn't matter what's in this movie; you're only interested in its duration.)

4. If the movie's duration is greater than what you desire, select a portion that's equal to what you want (**Figure 7.11**). (Use the Time panel in the Info window to help do this; see "Getting Time Information About the Movie and the Selection" in the previous chapter.)

continues on next page

5. Hold down the Shift and Option keys (Mac OS) or the Shift, Ctrl, and Alt keys (Windows), and in the Edit menu choose Add Scaled (**Figure 7.12**).

   The added track is now your desired duration.

6. From the Edit menu use the Extract Tracks command to separate the track you just added from the rest of the tracks (**Figure 7.13**).

Figure 7.12 When you use the Add Scaled command—which you access by holding down the Shift and Option keys (Mac OS) or Shift, Ctrl, and Alt keys (Windows)—the added track scales to the duration of the selection.

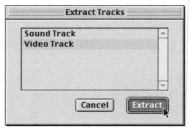

Figure 7.13 Extract the scaled track from the movie you just added it to.

Setting Up Tracks with Alternate Languages

In Chapter 4, you saw how viewers switch between languages in movies containing alternate versions of certain tracks. In addition, when a movie contains alternate tracks in different languages, the matching track will automatically play when the user is running an operating system version that matches one of the languages.

In the next few pages we'll show you how to create these alternate-language tracks.

You can use any set of tracks as alternate-language tracks, although this is typically done for sound and text tracks.

To set up alternate-language tracks:

1. Specify the language for each track (see "Specifying a Language for a Track," on the next page).

2. Designate the tracks as alternates for each other (see "Designating a Set of Alternate Tracks," later in this chapter).

   After you've taken these steps, you'll see that the Choose Language command is available in the Movie menu.

Alternate Languages on the Web

If you're preparing movies for the Web, and want to deliver different media depending on the user's preferred language, you'll use *alternate movies* rather than alternate tracks. See "Creating Alternate Movies" in Chapter 17.

Specifying a Language for a Track

You generally want to designate specific languages for tracks when you are setting up alternate-language tracks (as described on the previous page). However, you may also want to designate specific languages for tracks in multimedia projects for which you are using an authoring tool that can refer to tracks by language.

To specify the language of a track:

1. From the Movie menu, choose Get Info (**Figure 7.14**).

   The Info window for the movie appears.

2. In the left pop-up menu, select the track you'd like to assign a language to, and in the right pop-up menu, choose Alternate.

3. In the Alternate panel (**Figure 7.15**), click the upper Set button.

4. In the Set Track Language dialog box, select the appropriate language for your track, and click OK (**Figure 7.16**).

   The selected language appears in the Info window (**Figure 7.17**).

Figure 7.14 From the Movie menu, choose Get Info to open the Info window.

Click this button to designate a language.

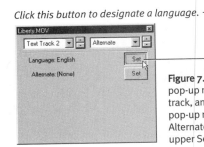

Figure 7.15 In the left pop-up menu select a track, and in the right pop-up menu select Alternate. Click the upper Set button.

Figure 7.16 Pick a language from the list, and click OK.

Figure 7.17 The selected language is listed as the language for the track.

Click this button to designate an alternate.

Figure 7.18 In the Info window's Alternate window, click the lower Set button.

Figure 7.19 Select the track you wish to designate as an alternate.

Figure 7.20 The track you selected is listed as an alternate...

Figure 7.21 ...and if you switch to the track listed as alternate, you will see that it has automatically been assigned the first track as its alternate.

Designating a Set of Alternate Tracks

When you have a set of tracks, only one of which you want to play at a time, you can specify the set as an *alternate track group*. For movies being played back in QuickTime Player, this is only useful if the tracks in the group are also assigned languages (as described on the previous page). However, other tools can use alternate tracks for other purposes.

To designate tracks as alternates for each other:

1. In the Info window, open the Alternate panel for one of the tracks you wish to designate as belonging to a group of tracks that will be alternates for each other.

2. Click the lower Set button (**Figure 7.18**).

3. In the Set Track Alternate dialog box, select the track you want to designate as an alternate for the track selected in the Info window and click OK (**Figure 7.19**). The track you selected is listed as the alternate in the Info window (**Figure 7.20**).

   If you use the left pop-up menu in the Info window to switch to the track you selected, you'll see that the other track is already designated as its alternate (**Figure 7.21**).The two tracks are now an alternate track group.

4. If you wish to include more than two tracks in the alternate track group, select an additional track in the left pop-up menu and repeat Step 3, assigning any of the tracks already in the alternate track group as an alternate for the new track. Note that in the Alternate panel of the Info window, only one of the alternates is listed, even though a track may have multiple alternates. You can continue adding additional tracks to the group in this manner.

Loading Tracks into Memory

Normally, when QuickTime movies play, only small amounts of data are loaded into memory (RAM) at a time. For very small tracks you can achieve slightly better performance by specifying that all of a track's data be put into or kept in memory

To specify that a track be loaded into memory:

1. From the Movie menu, choose Get Info to open the movie's Info window. (**Figure 7.22**).

2. From the left pop-up menu, choose the track you want loaded into memory, and from the right pop-up menu choose Preload (**Figure 7.23**).

   The Preload panel has two checkboxes (**Figure 7.24**).

3. Select Preload if you want the track loaded into memory before it is played.

   This option is ideal for tracks containing small amounts of data, such as text and music tracks. It allows the movie to play smoothly while the system is doing other things (for example, loading another movie from a CD-ROM).

4. Select Cache hint if you want the track to stay in memory for as long as possible after it has been played.

   This option is useful for small files you wish to loop. However, if the track is too large to remain in memory, it will perform poorly.

✔ Tip

■ Use these preloading options only for tracks that contain small amounts of data. Crashes or other unpredictable behavior may occur if QuickTime tries to load large amounts of data into memory.

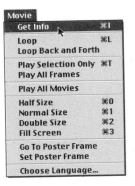

Figure 7.22 Choose Get Info to open the Info window.

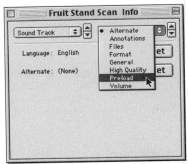

Figure 7.23 From the left pop-up menu, select a track; from the right pop-up menu, choose Preload.

Causes the track data to stay in memory after being played the first time

Causes the track to be fully loaded before playing

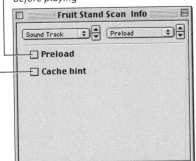

Figure 7.24 Choose either the Preload or Cache hint options to load track data into memory.

WORKING WITH VISUAL TRACKS

Several QuickTime track types—video, sprite, 3D, text, and Flash—have visual components. Streaming tracks also often contain visual data. In addition, Mac OS users have the MPEG track.

In this chapter we'll show you how to use QuickTime Player functions that apply to all of these visual tracks: to change their size, shape, and location in the window; to make portions transparent or translucent so you can see other tracks layered below; and to alter the colors used to display them. You'll find many of these techniques to be most useful when you've combined tracks (using the Add or Add Scaled commands covered in Chapter 7); however, you may discover that some are helpful even if your movie only contains one visual track.

We'll also go over what you need to know if you want to add visual data to a QuickTime VR movie or a custom color table to any movie. And finally, we'll cover the process of exporting QuickTime visual tracks as still image or animation files of other formats.

To find out more about what you can do with visual tracks, make sure to read the following chapters, which cover individual track types. In addition, Chapter 15, "Delivery Basics," explains how you can add visual effects to movies when you perform your final export.

Flipping, Rotating, Resizing, and Skewing

Flipping, rotating, resizing, and skewing tracks are all functions typically performed in still-image processing software. With QuickTime Player, you perform these operations on entire visual tracks at one time. Because all of these tasks are accessed from the same panel of the Info window—the Size panel (**Figure 8.1**)—we cover all of them together here.

To open the Size panel:

1. From the Movie menu, choose Get Info to open the movie's Info window.

2. From the left pop-up menu, choose the visual track; from the right pop-up menu, choose Size.

To rotate a track's image 90 degrees:

◆ Click the button with the looping arrow pointing clockwise to rotate the image 90 degrees clockwise (**Figure 8.2**).

   Click the button with the looping arrow pointing counterclockwise to rotate the image 90 degrees counterclockwise.

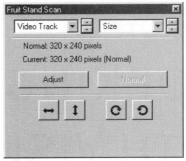

Figure 8.1 The Size panel is accessible via the Info window for all visual tracks.

Figure 8.2 A track can be rotated 90 degrees.

Figure 8.3 If you start with a track that looks like this...

Figure 8.4 ...you can flip it horizontally to look like this...

Figure 8.5 ...or vertically to look like this.

To flip a track's image:

◆ Click the horizontal arrow to flip the track horizontally. The result is a mirror image of the original (**Figure 8.3** and **Figure 8.4**).

Click the vertical arrow to flip the track upside down (**Figure 8.5**).

FLIPPING, ROTATING, RESIZING, AND SKEWING

To change the dimensions of a track, reposition it, skew it, or rotate it other than 90 degrees:

You can also change the dimensions of a track, skew it, rotate it more or less than 90 degrees, and reposition it.

1. In the Size panel, click the Adjust button (**Figure 8.6**).

   In the movie window, red marks appear on the selected track, and the name of the button you clicked changes from Adjust to Done.

2. Click in the movie window.

3. Make your changes.

   To resize: Click any of the red corners and drag to stretch or shrink the image (**Figure 8.7**). (If you hold down the Option key on a Mac OS or the Ctrl and Alt keys on a Windows computer, the image will be halved when you drag in and doubled when you drag out.)

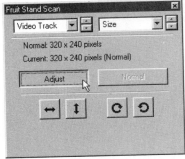

Figure 8.6 Click the Adjust button.

Figure 8.7 By grabbing one of the red corner marks, you can drag toward the center of the image to shrink it or away from the center to stretch it.

Figure 8.8 Use the red marks on the image's edges for skewing.

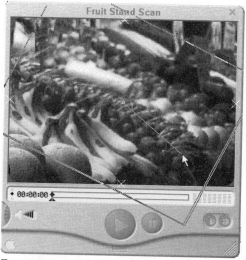

Figure 8.9 Drag from the red circle in the center to rotate the image.

To skew: Click one of the semicircular marks at the middle of the image's edges (**Figure 8.8**) and drag. (Drag right or left if using the marks on the bottom or top to slant the vertical edges; drag up or down if using the marks on the left or right to slant the horizontal edges.)

To rotate: Click the circle in the center of the image and drag (**Figure 8.9**).

To reposition: Click anywhere in the image except on a red mark and drag the image to the desired location.

4. Click back in the Info window.

5. Click Done.

To return a track to normal:

◆ Click the Normal button.

Masking a Visual Track

QuickTime Player allows you to mask a visual track so that it can play within a nonrectangular shape. This is useful for layered tracks as well as for instances when you'd like to make a movie play within a nonrectangular shape on a Web page.

To mask a visual track:

1. Using a graphics program, create on a white background a black image of the shape you'd like to use as the mask (**Figure 8.10**). Ideally, make the black image go to the edge of the background.

2. From the Movie menu in QuickTime Player, choose Get Info.

3. From the left pop-up menu within the movie's Info window, choose the track you'd like to mask; from the right pop-up menu, choose Mask.

4. In the Mask panel, click the Set button (**Figure 8.11**).

5. In the Open dialog box, locate and select the file you created in Step 1 and click Open.

   The image appears in the Info window, and the movie window displays the visual track only in the black area of the shape (**Figure 8.12**).

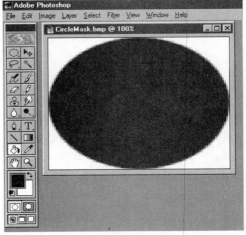

Figure 8.10 First, use your favorite graphics program to create a black-and-white graphic of the mask.

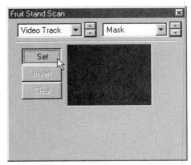

Figure 8.11 In the Mask panel, click the Set button and locate the file containing the mask graphic.

Figure 8.12 The track you are masking appears only in the black area of the graphic...

MASKING A VISUAL TRACK

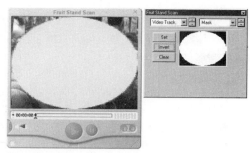

Figure 8.13 ...or in the white area if you click the Invert button in the Mask panel.

6. If you'd prefer to have the visual track show in the area defined by the white region of the image, click the Invert button (**Figure 8.13**).

✔ Tips

■ If proportions of the masking graphic and its background don't match those of the track you're masking, QuickTime will adjust the mask to fit those proportions. For example, if your graphic is a circle and you apply it to a 320 by 240 movie, the mask will be an oval.

■ If the black graphic doesn't go to the edges of its background, you'll get unpredictable results.

MASKING A VISUAL TRACK

Placing Visual Tracks Side by Side

You may want to display two visual tracks side by side, particularly when analyzing visual data. To do this, you simply place the two tracks in the same movie (as covered in the previous chapter) and then position them (as described earlier in this chapter). Here's a review of those steps:

To place visual tracks side by side:

1. Open two movies.

2. Select data from one (see "Selecting and Deselecting Data," in Chapter 6), and from the Edit menu choose Copy.

3. Click in the other movie, move the Current Location indicator to the far left of the Time slider, hold down the Option key (Mac OS) or Ctrl and Alt keys (Windows), and from the Edit menu choose Add (**Figure 8.14**).

   The added visual data is layered on top of the existing visual data.

4. From the Movie menu, choose Get Info to open the movie's Info window.

5. From the left pop-up menu, choose the added visual track—the one lower in the list—and from the right pop-up menu, choose Size.

6. Click the Adjust button (**Figure 8.15**), and then click in the movie window to make it active.

7. Click in any part of the added image (except one of the red marks) and drag right or left to position the image correctly (**Figure 8.16**).

   The movie window expands to fit both images.

8. Click in the Info window, and then click Done.

Figure 8.14 Use the Add command to place two visual tracks in the same movie.

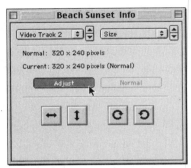

Figure 8.15 In the Size panel of the Info window, click Adjust.

Figure 8.16 Drag the track on top to the right or left to position it next to the original track.

Figure 8.17 After changing the image's size, drag it to the position you want.

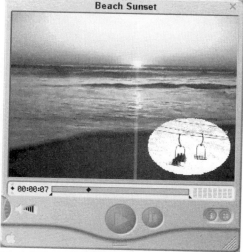

Figure 8.18 A picture in a picture can be non-rectangular if a mask is applied to the track.

Creating a Picture-in-a-Picture Effect

Another interesting effect, this one adapted from television, is the picture in a picture. This, too, can be accomplished using techniques already covered.

To create a picture-in-a-picture effect:

1. As we just did in "Placing Visual Tracks Side by Side," open two movies, select data from one, copy that data, and add it to the other.

2. Click the Adjust button, and then click in the movie window to make it active.

3. Click one of the red marks in the image's corners and drag toward the center of the image to shrink it.

4. If you want to move the image, click anywhere other than on a red mark and drag the image to your desired location (**Figure 8.17**).

✔ Tip

■ By applying what you've already learned about using masks (see "Masking a Visual Track" earlier in this chapter), you can make the inner image nonrectangular (**Figure 8.18**).

Relayering Tracks

When adding visual tracks to a movie you may do so in the wrong order, so that one track is layered on top of another when you really want it to be in back. (Added tracks are placed on top of existing tracks.) QuickTime Player lets you reorder the track layers so that you can fix this problem.

To change the layer of a track:

1. From the Movie menu, choose Get Info.

2. From the left pop-up menu select the track you want to reorder, and from the right pop-up menu choose Layer.

3. In the Layer panel (**Figure 8.19**), click the downward-pointing arrow to decrease the layer number or the upward-pointing arrow to increase the layer number.

✔ Tips

- When a new track is added to a movie, it is assigned a number that is one less than the lowest existing number, and it is placed in front of any existing tracks. Think of the Layer panel as the place to change the default layer numbers.

- The thing to remember here is precisely what it says in the Info window: "Smaller layer numbers are further forward." This means that if you want a track to go behind all of the other tracks, its layer number must be greater than that of any other track. If you want a track to be at the front, its layer number should be smaller than that of any other track—it can even be a negative number. If you are working with many visual tracks, you may need to click one of the arrow buttons multiple times to correctly position your track.

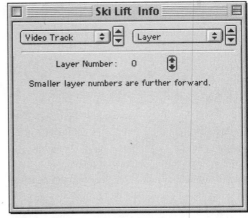

Figure 8.19 Through the Layer panel, you can reorder your movie's visual tracks.

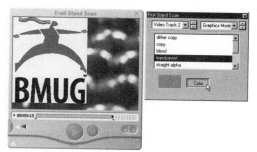

Figure 8.20 After choosing transparent from the scrolling list, click the Color button to bring up a Color Picker dialog box.

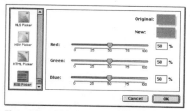

Figure 8.21 This is a Mac OS Color Picker dialog box.

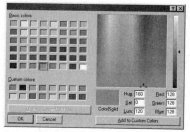

Figure 8.22 This is a Windows Color Picker dialog box.

Figure 8.23 The color you chose in the Color Picker dialog box becomes transparent in the track you selected in the Info window.

Making a Color Transparent in a Track

When you have layered one track on top of another, you can define a particular color in the image to be transparent. This works best in images with solid areas of color—computer-generated images or animations rather than photographic images.

To make a color in the track transparent:

1. From the Movie menu, choose Get Info.

2. In the Info window, from the left pop-up menu select a visual track, and from the right pop-up menu choose Graphics Mode.

3. From the scrolling list, choose transparent.

4. Click the Color button (**Figure 8.20**).

   A Color Picker dialog box appears (**Figure 8.21** and **Figure 8.22**).

5. Pick the color that you want to make transparent, and click OK.

   Any portions of the image that are in the color you selected become transparent (**Figure 8.23**).

✔ Tip

- To identify which color should be transparent, users of Mac OS 8 or later can hold down the Option key to get an eyedropper pointer; using it, you can then click anywhere on the screen; the color under the cursor will automatically be selected in the Color Picker dialog box. Other users may need to open the image in a program such as Adobe Photoshop to obtain the numeric values that identify a particular color.

MAKING A COLOR TRANSPARENT IN A TRACK

Blending Tracks

When one track is layered on top of another, you can make the top track translucent. This way, it looks like the tracks are blended together.

To make a track translucent:

1. From the Movie menu, choose Get Info.

2. In the Info window, from the left pop-up menu choose your top track, and from the right pop-up menu choose Graphics Mode.

3. In the scrolling list, choose blend (**Figure 8.24**).

   You'll be able to see through the selected track to the tracks below (**Figure 8.25**).

✔ Tip

■ If you're not satisfied with the degree of translucency or you want a tinted effect, click the Color button in the Graphics Mode panel. In the Color Picker dialog box, choose a light tone to make the track less translucent and a dark tone to make the track more translucent. Gray tones remove all colors from the image equally; if you pick a color, you'll find that the image is colorized.

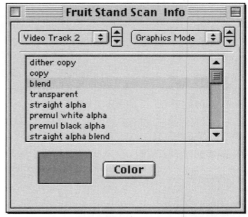

Figure 8.24 Choose blend for a track you want to be translucent.

Figure 8.25 You can see through the track to the others behind it.

Figure 8.26 Here's an image we'll use to make an alpha channel.

Figure 8.27 Here's the image's alpha channel created with an image processing tool such as Photoshop.

Using Alpha Channels

Alpha channels are used by graphic artists to achieve sophisticated transparency effects. Although an alpha channel is a type of mask, it can include partly transparent pixels so that when the image containing the alpha channel is layered on top of another image, the transition between the two is less abrupt and looks more seamless. (See **Figure 8.26** and **Figure 8.27** for an example of an image and its alpha channel.)

To use alpha channels:

1. Create an image with an alpha channel, using a program such as Adobe Photoshop.

2. In QuickTime Player, open or import the image with the alpha channel and add it to another track.

The Copy Modes

The Graphics Mode panel offers three *copy* modes: dither copy, copy, and composition (dither copy). Choose one of these modes if you don't want any part of the image to be transparent. Dither copy is the default mode for most tracks and is usually the best copy choice. The difference between dither copy and copy is only apparent when your system is in 256-color mode; dithering adjusts adjacent pixels of different colors to give the illusion of a color that's not in the set of available 256 colors. Dithered images look better, but copy mode may provide better performance.

Composition (dither copy) is more appropriate for certain files (usually animated GIF files); these are automatically assigned composition mode when opened in QuickTime Player.

3. In the Graphics Mode panel, choose one of the alpha channel modes in the scrolling list—straight alpha, premul white alpha, or premul black alpha—depending on how the file was created. (See Tip below.)

The image below shows completely through the black area of the alpha channel (**Figure 8.28**).

✔ Tip

■ Choose one of the premul modes only if the graphic was created with a premultiplied alpha channel. The premul white alpha choice is for images created on a white background, and the premul black alpha choice is for those created on a black background. If you don't know if the image has a premultiplied alpha channel, try each of the modes and pick the one that looks best. The fourth alpha choice, straight alpha blend, is a combination of straight alpha and blend, so the masked areas will be transparent and the unmasked areas will be translucent. As with blending, you can use the Color Picker to alter the degree of translucency.

Figure 8.28 Here's the image after being imported into QuickTime Player and combined with another track using one of the alpha channel modes.

Creating Tracks with Alpha Channels

Only certain programs create alpha channels. When you save in such a program, be sure to save the file appropriately: as a 32-bit image. With many file formats that QuickTime Player can open, the alpha channel remains a 32-bit image. However, if you import a PICT file, QuickTime applies compression, so make sure you choose a video compressor that supports 32-bit color, such as Animation, PNG, TIFF, TGA (Targa) None, or Planar RGB. See Chapter 9 for more on compressing and importing still images.

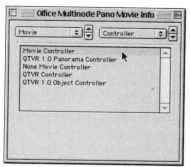

Figure 8.29 The trick to adding data to a QuickTime VR movie is to switch to the movie controller.

Figure 8.30 A VR panorama or object can have a graphic (such as this logo) that is always visible.

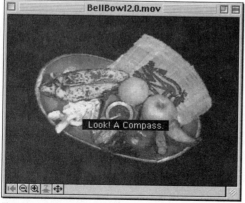

Figure 8.31 A VR object movie can have different graphics or text on different frames.

Adding Visual Data to QuickTime VR Movies

There's not a lot you can do to alter QuickTime VR movies using QuickTime Player, but you can bring in extra visual data by adding a visual track to your QuickTime VR movie. See the sidebar "Why Add Data to a VR Movie?" to learn why you might want to do this. First, though, we'll cover the general technique for adding data to a QuickTime VR movie.

To add tracks to a QuickTime VR movie:

1. From the Movie menu, choose Get Info to open the movie's Info window.

2. In the Info window, from the left pop-up menu choose Movie, and from the right pop-up menu choose Controller.

   A list of controller names appears. The default VR controller is determined by the QuickTime VR version used to create the movie as well as whether the movie is a panorama or object. You should remember which controller is selected.

3. From the list of controller names, select Movie Controller (**Figure 8.29**).

   Switching to the Movie Controller gives you access to QuickTime Player's editing features.

4. From another movie or file, select and copy the visual data you want to add, and use the Add or Add Scaled commands to add it to the VR movie. (Refer back to Chapter 7 for a refresher on how to do this.)

5. Manipulate the added data, using what you learned earlier in this chapter about resizing, repositioning, applying a mask, and using transparencies in a movie.

6. In the Info window, choose the VR controller that was selected prior to switching to the Movie Controller in Step 3.

✔ Tip

■ You can use the masking technique described in "Masking a Visual Track" to add a black-and-white copyright mark to a QuickTime VR movie.

Why Add Data to a VR Movie?

◆ You can give your VR movie a logo, frame, or caption that always appears in the movie window by using the Add Scaled command (**Figure 8.30**).

◆ You can designate that graphics or text appear only when the object is in a certain position by adding data to selected frames in an object movie (**Figure 8.31**). If you add text to selected frames in an object movie, viewers can search for a text string to locate a certain viewing angle.

◆ You can make data *play* as you move an object if you add data that changes over time to multiple frames of an object movie.

◆ Some object movies have multiple frames per rotational position, providing an animated effect even when the user isn't moving the object. If you add data (including audio) that changes over time to one of these files, the data plays even when the user isn't moving the object.

◆ If you add data that changes over time to a panorama, users can double-click the area of the window where this data is visible to make it play. This added data needs to include at least one visual track (for the user to double-click), but added audio will also play when the user double-clicks the visual track.

◆ If you add data that changes over time to a multinode movie, a different image from the added data appears in each node. If there's a one-to-one correspondence between frames in the added data and the nodes, you get one frame to a node. This is a good way to title nodes or provide a "you are here" map that appears in each node.

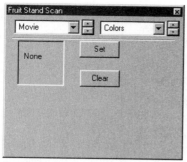

Figure 8.32 In the movie's Colors panel, click the Set button and navigate to the file that has the color table you wish to use.

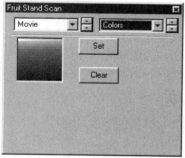

Figure 8.33 The color table is displayed in the window. (Sorry, you can't see the colors in this gray-scale image.)

Where to Get a Custom Color Table

If you have an existing file with a custom color table, you can attach that table to your movie. Files that may already include a custom color table include graphics files (such as GIFs).

To define a custom color table for your own movie, you need software that can analyze your movie and figure out which 256 colors to use. DeBabelizer and Media Cleaner Pro are examples of commercial products that can create custom color tables for QuickTime movies.

Adding a Custom Color Table to a Movie

When a movie whose visual data consists of thousands or millions of colors plays on a computer system that can show only 256 colors, the viewing experience is often less than ideal. This isn't simply because there aren't enough colors but also because the system's standard 256 colors aren't usually the *best* colors for that particular movie. Standard system colors on both platforms, for example, don't have many flesh tones or earth tones.

Fortunately, you can designate a custom set of 256 colors that are better suited to your movie. This way, when the movie plays on a system that can show only 256 colors, the computer uses the colors you've specified. A movie with a custom color table playing on a 256-color computer still doesn't look as good as it would on a system that can show more colors, but it looks better than it would using the standard system colors.

To add a custom color table to your movie:

1. From the Movie menu, choose Get Info.

2. From the left pop-up menu choose Movie, and from the right pop-up menu choose Colors to open the Colors panel.

3. Click the Set button (**Figure 8.32**), and locate a file with a custom color table you want. (See "Where to Get a Custom Color Table.")

   The colors of the selected color table will appear to the left of the Set button (**Figure 8.33**).

   When the movie is played on a computer that shows only 256 colors, it will use the colors in the color table. When played on a computer that can show more than 256 colors, it will not use the color table but instead be shown in full-color.

Creating a Still-Image File from a Movie Image

Whenever you have a movie window with a visual element, you can create a still-image file in BMP or PICT formats of what appears in that window.

To export an image as a PICT or BMP:

1. Move QuickTime Player's Current Location indicator until the image you want appears in the window.

2. From the File menu choose Export (**Figure 8.34**).

3. From the Export pop-up menu near the bottom of the window, choose Movie to Picture, for a PICT file, or Movie to BMP (**Figure 8.35**).

4. Click Save.

   The exported image contains everything visible in QuickTime Player's window—even if the image is composed of data from multiple tracks.

Figure 8.34 To create a still image from an image in the movie window, choose Export from the File menu.

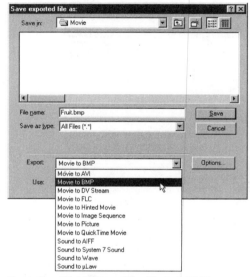

Figure 8.35 Then choose either Movie to BMP or Movie to Picture, depending on whether you want a BMP or PICT file.

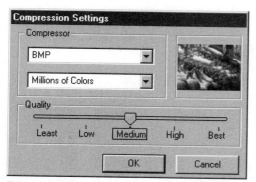

Figure 8.36 You can click the Options button to make a dialog box appear that lets you choose compression settings. (We'll look at compression settings in the next chapter.)

✔ Tips

■ Recall from Chapter 6 that you can always copy data from the QuickTime Player window and paste it into a graphics application; use this technique if you need a still image in a format other than BMP or PICT. By exporting an image, however, you get a file without having to use another application.

■ You can click the Options button before clicking Save to open a Compression Settings dialog box. There, you can choose compression settings for the image (**Figure 8.36**). (See Chapter 9 for more on compression settings.) However, the default settings are usually fine. Whether or not you switch compression settings, the image is compressed when you save it. In general, any system you want to open the image on must have QuickTime installed to decompress the image. BMP files, however, will open on any Windows machine—even without QuickTime installed—and several Mac OS applications will read BMPs without QuickTime.

Creating a Set of Still Images from a Movie

You can export your entire movie as a series of still images—a handy capability when you need to use your movie content in an application that can't import a QuickTime or AVI movie but can import a series of still images.

In most cases, the application you plan to use will require that these images be in a certain format. QuickTime Player provides a choice of BMP, JPEG, MacPaint, Photoshop, PICT, PNG, QuickTime Image, SGI, TGA (Targa), or TIFF. You can also specify how many frames per second you want exported as well as a few other options for certain formats.

To export a series of still images:

1. With your movie open, from the File menu choose Export.

2. From the Export pop-up menu near the bottom of the window, choose Movie to Image Sequence (**Figure 8.37**).

3. Click the Options button, and in the Export Image Sequence Settings dialog box (**Figure 8.38**), choose a format and frame rate.

   If you want to export all of the frames in the movie, leave the "Frames per second field" empty.

   For some formats, an Options button may be available in the Export Image Sequence Settings dialog box, allowing you to further specify such things as compression settings.

4. Click OK to return to the Export dialog box.

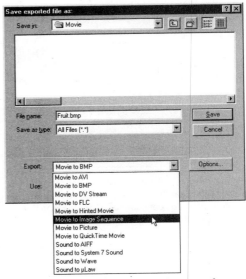

Figure 8.37 Choose Movie to Image Sequence from the Export pop-up menu.

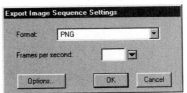

Figure 8.38 By clicking the Options button in the Export dialog box, you open the Export Image Sequence Settings dialog box, where you choose a format and frame rate for your exported files.

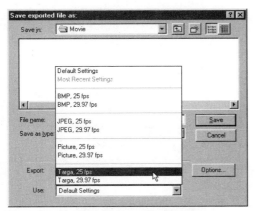

Figure 8.39 The Use pop-up menu offers some preconfigured choices that can save time if they match your requirements.

5. Specify a location, change the file's name (if desired), and click Save.

   Image files are saved using the name you provide, with sequential numbers immediately preceding the file extension (for example, mymovie 1.bmp, mymovie 2.bmp, mymovie 3.bmp).

✔ Tips

■ After Step 2 and before you click the Options button, you may want to look at the Use pop-up menu (**Figure 8.39**) to see if your desired format and frame rate is listed. If so, simply choose it and skip Steps 3 and 4. Note that if you pick Default Settings, all the frames in your movie will be exported in the PNG format.

■ If you do click the Options button and use the Export Image Sequence Settings dialog box to pick settings, you'll see that the Use pop-up menu is set to Most Recent Settings when you return to the Export dialog box. QuickTime Player remembers these settings, so the next time you want to export a movie as a sequence of images you can choose Most Recent Settings to get the same results.

■ Be aware of how many still images you'll export, and be sure you want that many. As an example, a one-minute clip exported at 29.97 frames per second will create almost 1800 images. If you will have hundreds or thousands of images, do yourself a favor and save all of the images in a new folder so you can easily find and work on them.

CREATING A SET OF STILL IMAGES FROM A MOVIE

Creating a FLC Animation from a Movie

You can export a QuickTime movie in the FLC format, which is commonly used for animations on Windows systems. This format doesn't include sound, so only the visual data in your movie will be exported. FLC files also contain only 256 colors, so you will need to specify which set of 256 colors you want to use. You can choose the 256 colors that the Mac employs or the 256 colors that Windows uses. (On a Mac, you can also have QuickTime pick the set of 256 colors that most closely matches the original image.)

To export a movie in FLC format:

1. From the File menu choose Export.

2. From the Export pop-up menu, choose Movie to FLC (**Figure 8.40**).

3. Choose your set of colors and frame rate.

   If you know which set of colors and frame rate you want, choose them from the Use pop-up menu if they are listed (**Figure 8.41**).

Figure 8.40 From the Export pop-up menu, choose Movie to FLC.

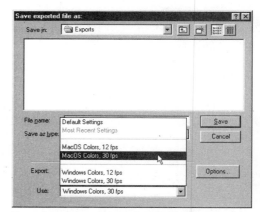

Figure 8.41 If your choice is listed in the Use pop-up menu, select it and click Save.

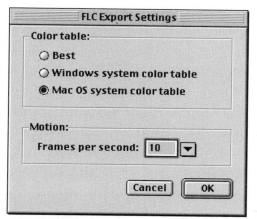

Figure 8.42 If you need to specify your own settings, click the Options button in the Export dialog box to bring up the FLC Export Settings dialog box. (Windows users won't have the Best choice for Color table.) Pick your settings, and click OK to return to the Export dialog box, where you can save the file.

If your choice is not listed in the Use pop-up menu, click the Options button, and in the FLC Export Settings dialog box (**Figure 8.42**), choose your desired color table and frame rate. Click OK to return to the Export dialog box.

If you don't know what file format you want, from the Use pop-up menu choose Default Settings. This will give you a 10-frame-per-second FLC animation file. If you are using a Mac, the file will use the best set of colors; on a Windows computer it will use the Windows set of colors.

4. Specify a location for the file, change its name (if desired), and click Save.

✔ Tip

- If you click the Options button and use the FLC Export Settings dialog box to pick settings, you'll see that the Use pop-up menu is set to Most Recent Settings when you return to the Export dialog box. QuickTime Player remembers these settings, so the next time you want to export a movie as a FLC file you can choose Most Recent Settings to get the same results.

CREATING A FLC ANIMATION FROM A MOVIE

VIDEO AND MPEG TRACKS

Video tracks are the most commonly found tracks in QuickTime movies and are, in fact, what most people associate with QuickTime.

Because video tracks are almost always compressed, we'll provide some background information about video compression and then take a look at the Compression Settings dialog box, which comes up in this chapter as well as in later chapters where movie delivery is discussed.

Although people often create video tracks by capturing video from a camcorder or VCR into a QuickTime file, QuickTime Player doesn't have capture functions, so we won't cover that topic here. You can, however, use the Player to create video tracks when you have existing still-image, video, or animation files, so we will explain those techniques.

For Mac users, we'll also go over how you can create a QuickTime file from an MPEG movie file, which results in an MPEG track rather than a video track.

Note that in this chapter we'll cover only those aspects of QuickTime and QuickTime Player that apply to video and MPEG tracks and not to any other track types. To learn about additional techniques for manipulating video and MPEG tracks, be sure to read Chapter 8, "Working with Visual Tracks."

About Video Compression

What is compression? Essentially, it's a method of cheating: Although viewers may see what appears to be many megabytes of information per second, the stored data they're viewing is actually much smaller, thanks to the various techniques used to reduce the data required to display images and efficiently represent that information.

Compression is crucial to the video track, particularly for movies with a high frame rate. An individual full-screen image is about 1 MB in size, which means that full-screen video at 30 frames per second—what you're accustomed to seeing on television—would contain close to 30 MB of information per second of video. (We could also say that it has a *data rate* of 30 MB per second.) You wouldn't want to store even a few minutes of data at that size. Nor could your computer move that quantity of data to your screen quickly enough (unless you had special hardware). Plus, that's way too much data to move over modems, which have speeds of far less than 1 MB per second. Even if you use only a portion of the screen and lower the frame rate—as is done with many QuickTime movies—without compression, it's still too much information.

Thus, just about all QuickTime video tracks are compressed in some way. QuickTime gives you access to a wide variety of compressors, each of which works slightly differently and is appropriate for different types of media. (Many compressors come with QuickTime; see **Table 9.1** for a list. You can also obtain additional compressors, some of which we'll discuss in Chapters 16 and 18.)

Table 9.1

Video Compressors Included with QuickTime 4	
COMPRESSOR NAME	**COMMENTS**
Animation	Works best on computer-generated animations with broad areas of flat color. Doesn't work well for scenes with lots of color changes.
BMP	Used for still images when exporting in the BMP format. Does minimal compression. Inappropriate for video-based movie playback.
Cinepak	Commonly used for video movies that require CD-ROM playback. Compresses very slowly.
Component Video	A high-quality compressor. Good for capture on Macs with built-in video capture capabilities and as an intermediate storage format. Low compression ratios (larger files).
DV-NTSC, DV-PAL	Used with Digital Video cameras.
Graphics	Good for 8-bit graphics files. Usually better than the Animation compressor in 8 bits. Slower to decompress than Animation.
H.261 and H.263	Designed originally for videoconferencing. Very high compression ratios.
Intel Indeo Video 4.4	High image quality. Requires a Pentium for compression and decompression. Mac OS version is not built into QuickTime but can be downloaded from http://www.apple.com/quicktime/technologies/indeo/.
Motion JPEG A, Motion JPEG B	Used to decompress files made with certain Motion-JPEG cards when the card isn't available, or to compress in a format that can be played by certain hardware Motion-JPEG cards.
None	Good for capture only. Does almost no compression.

table continues on next page

Table 9.1 *continued*

Video Compressors Included with QuickTime 4

COMPRESSOR NAME	COMMENTS
Photo JPEG	Ideal for high-quality compressed still images. Also useful as an intermediate storage format for movies and QuickTime VR panoramas. Decompresses too slowly for video-based playback.
Planar RGB	For images with an alpha channel.
PNG	Typically used for still-image compression. Can get high compression ratios.
Sorenson Video	Very high compression ratios and high quality. Excellent for Web and CD-ROM. On Mac OS computers, requires a PowerPC processor for compression.
Targa	Typically used for still-image compression. Does minimal compression.
TIFF	Typically used for still-image compression. Does minimal compression.
Video	Very fast video compression and decompression. Decent compression ratios. Good for real-time capture of video, particularly when hard disk space is at a premium. Good for testing clips. OK for hard disk playback. Image quality is poor when compressing enough for CD-ROM playback.

Note: *The Minimum Install of QuickTime (which many end-users will choose) doesn't install all of these compressors. However, if the computer being used to play a movie requiring one of these compressors has an Internet connection, QuickTime will download the necessary compressor when needed for decompression.*

Compressors perform their jobs in two basic ways: through *spatial compression* and *temporal compression.*

With spatial compression, the compressor essentially throws out redundant data from individual frames. With temporal compression, the compressor discards information that is repeated from one frame to the next. It saves a single frame in its entirety, but in subsequent frames it saves only those parts of the picture that have changed. The first frame is called a *key frame,* and the subsequent frames are referred to as *difference frames.*

Since you generally won't use QuickTime Player to compress your movies until it's time to distribute them, we won't explain the process in detail until Chapter 15, "Delivery Basics." There will be a few places in this chapter, however, where you'll have to make some compression choices, so it's a good idea to have a sense of what compression is.

✔ Tip

- Compressors are also called *codecs,* for *co*mpressors-*dec*ompressors; if a file has been compressed, a decompressor is necessary during playback.

About the Compression Settings Dialog Box

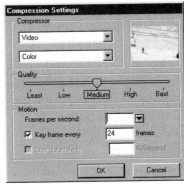

When working with video tracks in QuickTime Player, there are a number of places where you may come across an important dialog box—the Compression Settings dialog box (**Figure 9.1**). Let's preview it now.

The top right area of the dialog box displays a sample frame from the movie. As you make changes in the dialog box, the sample frame reflects the effects of those changes. You can zoom in on the image by holding down the Option key (Mac OS) or the Ctrl and Alt keys (Windows) and clicking. You can zoom out by adding the Shift key to the key or keys you're holding down to zoom in. After you've zoomed in, you can click and drag in the image to move it around.

Figure 9.1 The Compression Settings dialog box is used frequently in QuickTime Player and other QuickTime applications to choose compression settings for video tracks.

You can use the upper pop-up menu in the Compression Settings dialog box (**Figure 9.2**) to choose a particular compressor; all built-in compressors as well as any added compressors appear in this list.

Depending on the compressor selected, you can use the lower pop-up menu to choose how many colors should be used to represent the image (for some compressors you aren't given a choice).

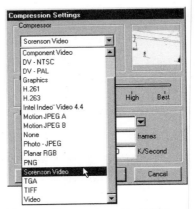

Figure 9.2 You can choose any of the compressors available to QuickTime.

You can use the slider in the middle of the dialog box (labeled Quality) to indicate your desired image quality. Although you might instinctively choose the highest quality, you should be aware that higher quality also means less compression—and therefore larger files and higher data rates. (We'll explain the significance of these in Chapter 15, "Delivery Basics.")

The bottom area of the window (labeled Motion) lets you choose settings that affect how smoothly the movie plays. You can specify frame rate, key-frame rate, and for some

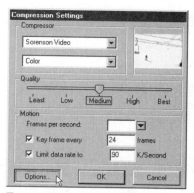

Figure 9.3 For some compressors, you'll see an Options button at the bottom of the window that provides access to additional settings and information.

compressors, data rate. We'll suggest settings for each of these in specific situations we'll cover later.

In some cases, depending on the compressor you've chosen, you may see an Options button in the bottom left of the window (**Figure 9.3**). Click this button to view information or set additional options specific to the compressor.

✔ Tip

■ The Compression Settings dialog is part of QuickTime itself, so many other applications use it as well. Thus, what we've covered here will apply to other tools and situations.

Determining How a Video Track Was Compressed

Now that you know video tracks can be compressed with different compressors, you may be interested in finding out how a particular video track was compressed.

To determine how a video track was compressed:

1. From the Movie menu, choose Get Info to open the movie's Info window (**Figure 9.4**).

2. From the left pop-up menu, choose the video track, and from the right pop-up menu, choose Format to open the Format Panel (**Figure 9.5**).

   The third line in the Format panel shows the number of colors in the image.

   The fourth line, labeled Data Format, generally tells you how the track was compressed.

   In some cases—such as when a track was created by importing a still image and wasn't compressed using a QuickTime codec—the Data Format instead lists the file format, such as GIF or FlashPix.

✔ Tip

- In rare cases, when a video track has been compressed with a codec not included with QuickTime, the movie will open but show no image. An error message appears stating that "the required compressor can not be found." You can check to see the name of the compressor used, although QuickTime won't necessarily tell you where to find the appropriate codec.

Figure 9.4 From the Movie menu choose Get Info to open the Info window for the movie.

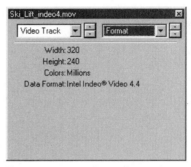

Figure 9.5 Colors tells you the number of colors used in the image. Data Format indicates how the movie was compressed (if it was compressed).

Compression on a Streaming Track

If you open an RTSP streaming movie in QuickTime Player, you won't find a video track. However, you can get information about how the streaming video was originally compressed. Once the movie starts playing, open the Info window. From the left pop-up menu choose the streaming track (probably named "Streaming Track"), and from the right pop-up menu choose Format. You'll see the media types contained in the stream. Look for Video as a media type, and below it you'll see compression information.

Figure 9.6 When you have a numbered sequence of images that you want to turn into a QuickTime movie, choose Open Image Sequence from the File menu.

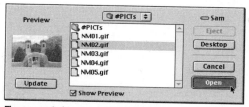

Figure 9.7 Select any of the files in the sequence, and click Open.

Creating Video Tracks from a Sequence of Still Images

Since video tracks are normally composed of a sequence of images, it makes sense that you can create a video track by putting together a bunch of still images. You might want to do this if you have a collection of images you want in a slide show. Or you could have an animation program that does not support QuickTime but will export an animation as a sequence of still images.

To create a video track from a sequence of still images:

1. Give each still-image file a common name with a sequential number appended to it (for example, picture1, picture2, picture3). Then place all of the files in the same folder.

2. From the File menu, choose Open Image Sequence (**Figure 9.6**).

3. In the Open dialog box, locate and select any one of the sequentially named files and click Open (**Figure 9.7**).

continues on next page

4. In the Image Sequence Settings dialog box that appears, specify a frame rate for the movie (**Figure 9.8**).

5. Click OK.

A new movie window appears. The movie contains the images you numbered sequentially and plays at the frame rate you specified.

6. From the File menu, choose Save As, and save the file as a self-contained movie. (If you don't do this, the movie will require the presence of the original still images for playback.)

✔ Tip

■ As shown in **Figure 9.8**, you have many choices of frame rates. In general, a frame rate of less than two seconds per frame is best if you want a slide-show effect; a frame rate of at least six frames per second is usually necessary to convey a sense of motion.

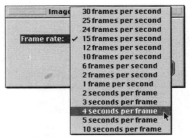

Figure 9.8 In the Image Sequence Settings dialog box, pick a frame rate: The choices at the bottom of the list are best for slide shows; the choices at the top are best for conveying a sense of motion.

Still-image Formats that QuickTime Can Open	
◆ BMP	◆ PICT
◆ DV	◆ PNG
◆ FlashPix	◆ QuickTime Image File
◆ GIF	
◆ JPEG/JFIF	◆ SGI
◆ MacPaint	◆ Targa
◆ Photoshop	◆ TIFF

Figure 9.9 You open most still-image files as you would any QuickTime movie.

Figure 9.10 The only difference is that there's a Convert button rather than an Open button.

Figure 9.11 The image opens in a movie window.

Creating a Video Track from a Single Still Image

You can also create a single-frame video track from a single still image—something you might do if you wanted to merge the still image with other QuickTime tracks. This capability is also useful for creating a poster movie to be used on the Web, as we'll discuss in Chapter 17.

The procedure you follow to create a video track from a still image varies depending on whether the file is a PICT file. (Most still-image formats can be opened directly, whereas the PICT file format must be imported, as described in Chapter 3.)

To create a video track from a single still image in any format other than PICT:

1. From the File menu, choose Open Movie (**Figure 9.9**).

2. In the Open dialog box, locate the still-image file and click the Convert button (**Figure 9.10**).

   The image that you selected appears in a new movie window (**Figure 9.11**), which has the same name as the file you opened.

   continues on next page

continues on next page

CREATING A VIDEO TRACK FROM A STILL IMAGE

If you click the Play button, the slider will move to the end of the play bar but the image won't change; the movie is a single frame with a duration of 2/30 of a second (indicated as 00:00:00.02 in the Time panel of the Info window; see **Figure 9.12**).

The data in this movie can be copied and pasted or added to other QuickTime movies. However, you have not actually created a QuickTime movie *file* until you save. If you quit QuickTime Player without saving, the file remains in its original still-image format.

To create a video track from a single PICT file:

1. From the File menu, choose Import (**Figure 9.13**).

2. In the Open dialog box, locate the PICT file and click the Convert button (**Figure 9.14**).

   A Save dialog box appears (**Figure 9.15**) because you need to create a new file.

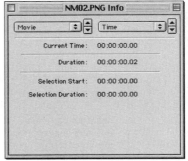

Figure 9.12 You get a very short movie— 2/30 of a second.

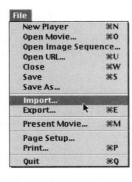

Figure 9.13 For PICT files, choose Import rather than Open Movie.

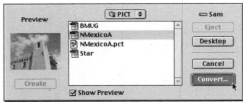

Figure 9.14 When you select a PICT file, the Open button changes to a Convert button. (The ellipses indicate that there will be another step.)

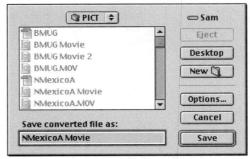

Figure 9.15 The next step is to save the file.

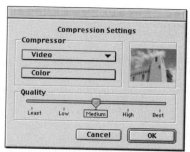

Figure 9.16 If you click the Options button in the Save dialog box before saving, you can alter the compression settings of the single-frame movie that will be created.

3. If you want to apply specific compression settings to this image, click the Options button. This will bring up a Compression Settings dialog box without the motion settings area (see **Figure 9.16**). However, since the default settings generally work fine, we recommend not changing them.

4. If desired, change the name and location for the file to be created.

5. Click Save.

A new window opens containing a movie that consists of a single frame with a duration of 2/30 of a second.

Because a new file has been created, you don't need to save this movie unless you alter it.

Creating Video Tracks from Non-QuickTime Animation and Video Files

As with still-image files, the file format of a time-based file dictates the process you use to create a video track from the file. You can directly open Animated GIF files (a standard animation format on the Web) and FLI/FLC files (the standard Windows animation format). In addition, you can directly open AVI files (the format for Microsoft's Video for Windows and DV files (the new digital video standard). However, you must import PICS animations (the standard Mac format), converting and saving the file before it can be viewed.

Figure 9.17 You open Animated GIF, FLI/FLC, AVI, and DV files just like any QuickTime file.

To create a video track from an Animated GIF, FLI/FLC, AVI, or DV file:

1. From the File menu, choose Open Movie (**Figure 9.17**).

2. In the Open dialog box, locate the animation or video file, and click the Convert button (**Figure 9.18**).

   A new movie window appears with the same name as the file you selected.

   When played, the animation or video should behave as it did in its original format.

   You can copy and paste or add the data in this movie to other QuickTime movies. However, you have not actually created a QuickTime movie *file* until you save. If you quit QuickTime Player without saving, the file remains in its original format.

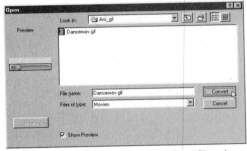

Figure 9.18 When you click on one of these files, the Open button changes to a Convert button.

Figure 9.19 Choose Import when you have a PICS animation file that you want to turn into a QuickTime movie.

To create a video track from a PICS animation file:

1. From the File menu, choose Import (**Figure 9.19**).

2. In the Open dialog box, locate the PICS file and click Convert (**Figure 9.20**).

Figure 9.20 When you click on a PICS file, the Open button changes to a Convert button. (The ellipses indicate that there will another step.)

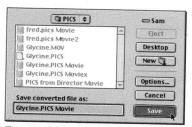

Figure 9.21 The next step is to save the file.

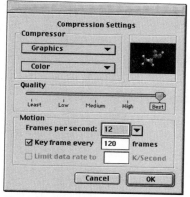

Figure 9.22 If you click the Options button before saving the file, you'll get a standard Compression Settings dialog, where you can specify compression settings.

Problems with AVI Files

AVI files can be compressed with a variety of compressors. Sometimes when you open an .avi file you'll get an error message saying, "You may experience problems playing a video track in 'yourmovie.avi' because the required compressor could not be found." This is because the file was compressed using a codec that's not currently available in QuickTime. You can see what the compressor is by opening the Format panel for the video track in the Info window. Often the compressor is a version of Intel's Indeo Video (listed as "IV32" for Indeo 3, "IV41" for Indeo 4, "IV50" for Indeo 5.) You can get Indeo compressors from Apple (See Appendix C).

3. A Save dialog box appears; here you can click Save to create a new QuickTime file (**Figure 9.21**).

If you wish to specify compression settings, click the Options button to open the Compression Settings dialog box (**Figure 9.22**) before clicking the Save button.

✔ Tips

■ If you are having problems creating QuickTime movies from PICS files on a Windows computer, we recommend trying it on a Mac OS computer and then copying the QuickTime movies to a Windows machine.

■ If you open a DV movie file, you may not see the sharp, clear image you'd expect. This is because QuickTime's default setting is to show the movie at low resolution so it will play more smoothly. You can view the file in high resolution by opening the movie's Info window, choosing the video track in the left pop-up menu and High Quality in the right pop-up menu, and then checking the High Quality Enabled checkbox.

■ You can't create a video track from a Flash animation file. Instead, when you open a Flash file in QuickTime Player, you create a Flash track. See Chapter 11 for more information.

Adding Images to an Existing Movie

Just as you can use the Paste command to insert a graphic from another application into a movie (as described in Chapter 6), you also can use the Add or Add Scaled commands (as described in Chapter 7) to layer a graphic over other visual tracks.

A common reason to do this would be to add a visual element, such as a logo, to a corner of the movie window (as you see on many TV programs).

Adding a graphic also provides a way to create a new video track. (Contrast this with pasting, in which the graphic is *appended* to the existing video track, and no new video track is created.)

To add a small graphic from another application to a movie:

1. Select and copy an image created in a graphics application.

2. In QuickTime Player, open the movie you want to add the graphic to.

3. From the Edit menu, choose Select All, or select the portion of the movie you want to add the graphic to.

4. Hold down the Shift and Option keys (Mac OS) or the Shift, Ctrl, and Alt keys (Windows), and from the Edit menu choose Add Scaled (**Figure 9.23**).

   When you play the movie, the graphic will appear during the portion of the movie you selected in Step 3.

   The movie now contains an additional video track; you can verify this in the Info window (**Figure 9.24**).

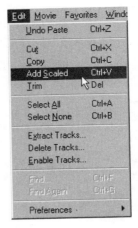

Figure 9.23 Choose Add Scaled to add a graphic that appears for the duration of the selection. You'll need to hold down the Shift and Option keys (Mac OS) or Shift, Ctrl, and Alt keys (Windows) to get this choice.

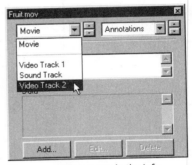

Figure 9.24 You can see in the Info window that you've added a video track.

✔ Tip (Mac only)

- If you hold down the Control key while adding data, a Compression Settings dialog appears, which allows you to specify the compressor, number of colors, and quality for the new track. Otherwise, QuickTime chooses the default settings based on the image's format.

Graphic Too Large or in the Wrong Place?

Use the Size panel in the Info window, as described in Chapter 8, to move the graphic to the correct location or to resize it.

ADDING IMAGES TO AN EXISTING MOVIE

Figure 9.25 You can open an MPEG file in QuickTime Player using the Open Movie command.

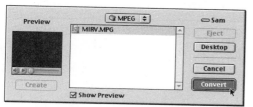

Figure 9.26 When you select an MPEG file, the Open button changes to a Convert button. Click it to open the file.

Creating MPEG Tracks from MPEG Files (Mac Only)

MPEG (which stands for Motion Picture Experts Group) is a commonly used video and audio standard. Apple's QuickTime MPEG extension lets you import MPEG-1 data into a QuickTime movie. However, rather than going into a standard video track, the data goes into a special MPEG track that contains both audio and video.

Once it's in a QuickTime track, you can play back and edit MPEG data like any other QuickTime data type. You can also combine it with other track types.

Unlike other QuickTime track types, however, the data from the entire track comes along when you copy and paste selected portions of an MPEG track; the data you didn't explicitly copy doesn't play, but it remains in the file. In the same way, when you delete data from an MPEG track, it doesn't really go away—it's just not played. Therefore, files with edited MPEG tracks can be much larger than you might think from simply viewing the movie.

Currently, QuickTime's MPEG extension works only on Mac OS computers with PowerPC microprocessors. However, Apple plans to release a Windows version. It is also likely that the company will release a new version that works with other formats of MPEG.

To create an MPEG track from an MPEG file:

1. From the File menu, choose Open Movie (**Figure 9.25**).

2. Locate the MPEG file you want to open, and click Convert (**Figure 9.26**).

continues on next page

The file is opened like any other QuickTime movie. When you check the movie composition in the Info window, however, you'll see that there is a single MPEG track (**Figure 9.27**).

✔ Tips

■ MPEG audio tracks (including MP3) are a different matter. We'll cover these in Chapter 13.

■ Tracks on a Video CD (a format—which never gained wide acceptance—designed to play on CD-i players) are actually MPEG-1 tracks and can be opened by QuickTime Player. On the Video CD, the files have a table of contents that can be used to jump to specific predesignated points in the video. When opened in QuickTime Player, the entries in the table of contents appear as a chapter list (see "Using Chapter Lists" in Chapters 2 and 4.)

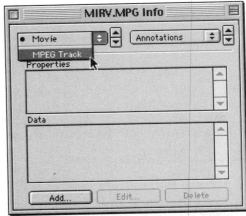

Figure 9.27 When you open an MPEG file in QuickTime Player, you create a single MPEG track, even if the file also contains audio.

Seeing Black Lines?

Normally, when you double the window size for an MPEG movie, the pixels are doubled horizontally but not vertically. Instead, black lines are added for every other row of pixels. Because the computer doesn't have to display every other horizontal line, it performs better, allowing the movie to play back more smoothly. QuickTime Player allows you to avoid this black-lining technique and choose to double the pixels both horizontally and vertically. To do this, use the Info window to select the MPEG track in the left pop-up menu and High Quality in the right pop-up menu. Then select the High Quality Enabled checkbox.

10

TEXT TRACKS

Of all the QuickTime track types, text tracks are perhaps the least used. However, they have tremendous potential. Not only do they allow you to caption a movie, but because they are searchable (as described in Chapter 4) they add a level of interactivity to movies.

Text tracks are easy to create from scratch, requiring no special tools other than a simple text processor or word processor (in conjunction with QuickTime Player).

In this chapter, we'll show you how to create text tracks as well as how to alter their appearance and behavior. Once you have a text track, you can combine it with other tracks as described in Chapter 7; you can also change its position and appearance as described in Chapter 8.

At the end of his chapter, we'll also cover turning text tracks into chapter lists.

Creating a Text Track by Importing a Text File

It's simple to create a text track, as long as you have a text or word processor.

To create a text track from a text file:

1. In a text or word processor, type the text you'd like your text track to contain; use Return characters to separate material that you want to see in different frames (**Figure 10.1**). Save this file as text only.

2. In QuickTime Player, from the File menu choose Import (**Figure 10.2**).

3. Locate and select the text file you created, and click the Convert button.

4. In the Save dialog box that appears, provide a name for the file, navigate to the location where you'd like it saved, and click Save.

   A new window appears, containing a text track with your text in it (**Figure 10.3**). The resulting track has centered, white text on a black background; each line of text in the file is a frame with a duration of 2 seconds. (On subsequent pages we'll show you how to change these defaults.)

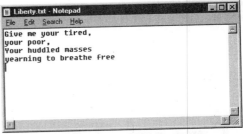

Figure 10.1 Type your text in a word or text processor, pressing Return after each line.

Figure 10.2 Use QuickTime Player's Import command to import the text file.

Figure 10.3 The resulting track is centered white text on a black background. Each line of text is a different frame.

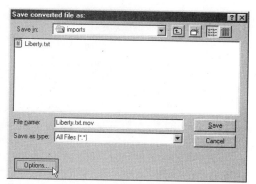

Figure 10.4 In the Save dialog box, click the Options button to change text settings.

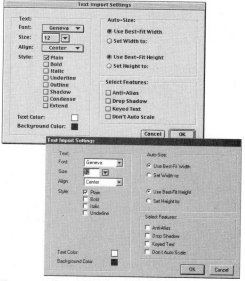

Figure 10.5 The Text Import Settings dialog box—which is slightly different for the Mac OS (top) and Windows—lets you change text properties.

Specifying Text Track Appearance when You Import

When you import your text, you can specify such characteristics as font, size, and color as well as the track's width and height.

To change text features:

1. Import the text as described on the previous page, but before clicking the Save button, click the Options button (**Figure 10.4**).

   The Text Import Settings dialog box appears (**Figure 10.5**).

2. Make your changes.

   Use the Font, Size, and Align pop-up menus and the Style options to change basic text properties.

   To select a text or background color for the text track, click the square next to Text Color or Background Color, and use the Color Picker dialog box that appears. (Click OK to return to the Text Import Settings dialog box.)

   Select Use Best-Fit Width and Use Best-Fit Height, or enter your own values for width and height. When you use Best-fit width and height, QuickTime creates a movie that is 160 pixels wide and tall enough to fit the longest line of text being imported.

   Select Anti-Alias to fuzz the edges of the characters. (This makes them look smoother when they're displayed in a large font size.)

   Select Drop Shadow to place a drop shadow behind the text.

   Select Keyed Text to specify a transparent background.

   continues on next page

Select Don't Auto Scale if you want the text to remain the size you defined even if the movie window is resized.

3. Click OK to close the Text Import Settings dialog box and return to the Save dialog box, where you can click Save to create your new text-track movie (**Figure 10.6**).

✔ Tip

■ Antialiased, drop-shadowed, and keyed text can look quite nice when the text is placed over a video track. However, these features require a lot of computing power and will bog down all but the fastest machines.

Figure 10.6 The resulting text track can be quite different than the default.

Antialiasing Text in an Existing Text Track

Normally, text in a text track is not antialiased unless the person creating the text track chooses this option when importing text. However, the Info window has a panel that allows you to switch to antialiased text. To do this, go to the Info window, and in the left pop-up menu choose the text track and in the right pop-up menu choose High Quality. Then select the High Quality Enabled checkbox.

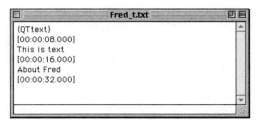

Figure 10.7 Here's a file that can be imported into QuickTime Player.

Specifying the Duration and Appearance of Individual Frames of Text

By adding some commands to a text file *before* you import, you can control how long the text appears and how it looks in each frame. **Figure 10.7** shows an example text file containing such commands.

To create a text track that specifies the duration and appearance of individual frames:

1. In a text or word processor file, type {QTtext} on the first line.

   This shows QuickTime that the file contains special commands (rather than just straight text), which it must process when imported.

2. On the following lines, type your text, using the time stamps and text descriptors listed below.

3. Save and import the file into QuickTime Player as described in the section "Creating a Text Track by Importing a Text File" earlier in this chapter.

To use time stamps to specify a duration for individual frames of text:

1. Before each line of text, enter a time-stamp value in square brackets—for example, [00:00:08.000]—indicating when the frame containing that line of text should appear. (You can have the time stamp immediately precede the text, but for readability we suggest you put it on a separate line.)

   Time stamps are specified as hours:minutes:seconds.1/600 of a second.

   continues on next page

Alternative Ways to Specify Time Stamps

If it works better for you, after each line of text you can enter time stamps that indicate how long the frame should appear on the screen rather than when the frame should end. You'll need to type {timestamps:relative} once before any time stamps and [00:00:00.000] before the first line of text, too.

Also, you don't have to specify time stamps as 1/600 of a second. Using a special "timescale" tag, you can also specify time stamps with a final number that is a fraction of a second. For example, if you type {timescale: 30} at the top of the file, the final number will be read as 1/30 of a second.

2. After the last line of text, type a final time stamp followed by a return. (This last time stamp designates when the last frame ends and the duration of the text-track movie that will be created when you import this file.)

To use text descriptors to specify the appearance of the text in individual frames:

◆ Before a line of text, add text tags such as font and size (see **Figure 10.8**).

A tag like this is called a *text descriptor* and can be on a line of its own or share the same line as the text.

You can also place text descriptors at the top of the file, in the same line as the {QTtext} tag. Text descriptors affect all subsequent text in the file to the point where you put in the same text descriptor with a different value. See **Table 10.1** for some other tags you can use.

✔ Tips

■ You'll probably find it easier to create a file like this if you follow the steps in the next task.

■ Be sure to use valid and logical time stamps and descriptors in your file; otherwise, QuickTime Player won't be able to import it. (For example, a time stamp is bad if it's formatted incorrectly or specifies a time earlier than a previous time stamp; a text descriptor is bad if it is misspelled or has an inappropriate value.)

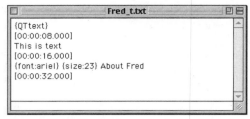

Figure 10.8 This file will change the font and size of the last line.

Table 10.1

Some Text Descriptors That Can Be Used for Individual Lines of Text		
DESCRIPTOR	POSSIBLE VALUES	EXAMPLES
{font: fontname}	Any font name	{font: Courier}, {font: Ariel}
{fontstyle}	Plain, bold, italic, underline	{italic}
{size: pointsize}	Numbers representing font size	{size: 14}
{justify: alignment}	Left, right, center	{justify: right}
{textColor: redvalue, greenvalue, bluevalue}	Numbers from 0 to 65535, representing how much of each color should be used.	{textColor: 0,65535,0} (this value represents pure green)
{backColor: redvalue, greenvalue, bluevalue}	Numbers from 0 to 65535, representing how much of each color should be used.	{backColor: 65535,0, 65535} (this value represents magenta)
{scrollIn:onOrOff}	On, off	{scrollIn:on}
{scrollOut:onOrOff}	On, off	{scrollOut:on}

These and additional text descriptors are documented more completely at http://www.apple.com/quicktime/authoring/textdescriptors.html.

Note that capitalization doesn't matter for the descriptors or the values. They are specified this way to improve legibility.

Figure 10.9 From the File menu, choose Export.

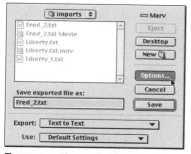

Figure 10.10 Choose Text to Text, and click the Options button.

Exporting a Text Track with Text Descriptors and Time Stamps

Now that you know how to create by hand a text track with all the extra codes, we'll show you an easier way to create a text file containing text descriptors and time stamps—that is, exporting a text track that already includes the codes. This way, you can simply edit the text rather than type it all yourself.

To create a text file with text descriptors and time stamps:

1. Pick a QuickTime file with a text track, or create one following the steps in "Creating a Text Track by Importing a Text File" earlier in this chapter. Don't worry about timing or styling issues at this point.

2. Open the movie containing the text track, and from the File menu choose Export (**Figure 10.9**).

3. From the pop-up menu at the bottom of the dialog box, choose Text to Text and click the Options button (**Figure 10.10**).

continues on next page

Hyperlinks in a Text Track

New to QuickTime 4 are text descriptors that you can use to turn text in your track into a *hyperlink*. (By this we mean text that when clicked causes a Web page to load.) See "Creating Hyperlinks in a Text Track" in Chapter 17 for a description of these.

EXPORTING TEXT DESCRIPTORS & TIME STAMPS

4. In the Text Export Settings dialog box (**Figure 10.11**), click the Show Text, Descriptors, and Time button.

More options appear (**Figure 10.12**).

5. In general, you can leave the options as they are and click OK.

To match your personal editing preferences, however, you may want to change the time stamps so they are shown relative to the start of the sample. In other words, each time stamp indicates how long the preceding line of text will appear. If you want to change the default setting for fractions of a second from 1/600, enter a number in the field at the bottom.

6. In the Save dialog box, specify a location for the file, change its name (if desired), and click Save.

You can open the new file in a text or word processor, edit it as described on the previous pages, and then reimport it. This method saves you time and decreases the likelihood of errors, since you only have to edit specific items rather than type everything from scratch.

✔ Tips

■ If you know you don't want to change any of the additional options in the Text Export Settings dialog box (**Figure 10.12**), after choosing Text to Text in Step 3 simply choose Text with Descriptors in the Use pop-up menu, and skip to Step 6.

■ You can also export a text track without the text descriptors or time stamps if you need to have a text file with only the words from your text track. Choose Text Only in the Use pop-up menu in the Export dialog box, or select the Show Text Only radio button in the Text Export Settings dialog box.

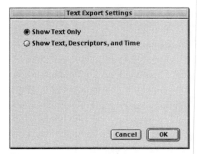

Figure 10.11 A simple Text Export Settings dialog box appears.

Figure 10.12 Click the Show Text, Descriptors, and Time button. Additional options appear. Once you've specified changes to any of these options, click OK. The file can then be edited and reimported.

Why 1/600?

The default is 1/600 because 600 is the smallest number that 30, 25, and 24 evenly divide into. These are the frame rates of the different video and film formats used today.

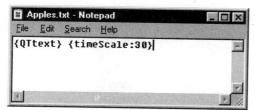

Figure 10.13 Start your file by entering this line of text.

Creating a Text Track That's Synced to Other Tracks

If you have a lot of text to add to a movie and it needs to appear at precise times, the following technique may help you efficiently create a properly timed text track. When added to the movie, it should display the correct text at the correct time.

To create a text track that's synced to other tracks:

1. Open the movie you want to add text to, and from the Movie menu, choose Get Info to open the movie's Info window.

2. In the right pop-up menu, choose Time. (The left pop-up should have Movie chosen.)

3. Open your word processor and arrange the open windows so you can see the movie, Info window, and word-processing window.

4. In the first line of the word-processing file, type {QTtext}{timeScale:30} (**Figure 10.13**).

   The descriptor {timeScale:30} indicates that your values are entered as thirtieths of a second. You'll want to enter values this way because this is how the Info window shows time, and you'll be copying values from there.

5. Click in the movie you're indexing, and move the Current Location indicator to the first location where you'd like text to appear.

continues on next page

6. Click in the word-processing window, and on the next line type (in brackets) the current time as it appears in the Info window, press Return, and then type the text you want to appear at this point in time (**Figure 10.14**).

7. Repeat the two previous steps at each point you want to add text. After the last word, press Return and enter (in brackets) the value that's listed for Duration in the Info window.

8. Save the text file (as text only), and import it into QuickTime Player.

9. In the text movie, from the Edit menu choose Select All and then choose Copy.

10. In the movie you want to add the text to, move the Current Location indicator to the beginning of the movie. Hold down the Option key (Mac OS) or Ctrl and Alt keys (Windows) and from the Edit menu choose Add to add the text.

✔ Tip

■ If you create a text track this way and then disable it (as described in Chapter 7), the movie can still be searched. This is a good way to create an index to a movie.

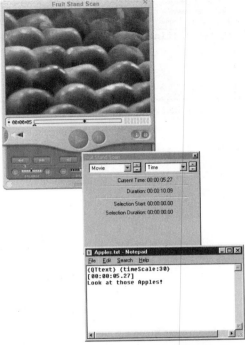

Figure 10.14 Then type the current time (listed in the Info window), and on the next line type the text that you want to appear at that time. Repeat for each line of text.

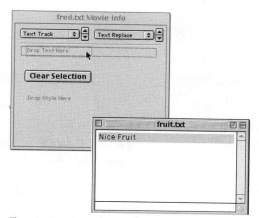

Figure 10.15 To replace words in a text track, drag to the area labeled Drop Text Here.

Changing Text That's Already in a Text Track

You can replace selected text that's already in a movie using drag-and-drop editing. You can also change the style of the text.

To replace existing text:

1. Select the portion of the movie that has the text you want to replace.

2. In a text editor or word processor, type your replacement text. (You must be able to drag and drop text from the text editor or word processor. On a Mac, Apple's SimpleText works; on a Windows computer, WordPad works.)

3. From the Movie menu, choose Get Info.

4. From the left pop-up menu choose the text track, and from the right pop-up menu choose Text Replace.

5. Select and drag the replacement text from the text processor to where the words *Drop Text Here* appear in the Info window, as shown in **Figure 10.15**. (A border appears around the words when your pointer is in the right location to drop the text.)

   The selected text in the movie changes to the text you dropped.

To change the font, size, and style of the text in a text track:

1. Select the portion of the movie displaying the text you want to apply a new font, size, or style to.

2. In a text editor or word processor that lets you style individual elements of text, type any text and set its font, size, and style.

continues on next page

3. From QuickTime's Movie menu, choose Get Info to open the Info window.

4. From the right pop-up menu choose Text Replace.

5. From the text processor, select the styled text and drag it to QuickTime's Info window where the instructions Drop Style Here appear (**Figure 10.16**).

The selected text in the movie changes to match the style of the text you dropped. (The content of the text is unaffected.)

To delete portions of text from a text track:

1. Select the portion of the movie that contains the text you want to clear.

2. From the Info window's right pop-up menu, choose Text Replace, and in the panel click Clear Selection.

✔ Tips

■ You cannot use the Undo command to undo changes made in the Text Replace panel.

■ With the current version of QuickTime, Windows users can't change the font, size, and style of text in a text track as described above. We expect this feature to be implemented in a future version of QuickTime, however.

Figure 10.16 To change the font, size, or style of text in a text track, drag any styled text to the area labeled Drop Style Here.

Figure 10.17 If you've copied text from a word processor, you can use the Add command to add it to a movie. (You can also use the Add Scaled command.)

Adding Small Amounts of Text

By far the simplest method of getting small amounts of text into a movie is to add the text directly to the movie where you'd like it to appear. You don't need to first create a separate text track and then add it to the other tracks.

To add small amounts of text to a movie:

1. In a text or word processor, type the text you want to add, select it, and copy it.

2. In the movie you want to add the text to, move the slider to the point where you want the text to first appear.

3. You have several choices for setting the length of time the text appears.

   If you want the text to last 2 seconds, hold down the Option key (Mac OS) or the Ctrl and Alt keys (Windows) and choose Add from the Edit menu (**Figure 10.17**).

   If you want the text to last for a duration other than 2 seconds, select the duration you'd like in the Time slider. Then hold down the Option and Shift keys (Mac OS) or the Ctrl, Alt, and Shift keys (Windows), and from the Edit menu choose Add Scaled.

continues on next page

A text track is added below the visual data that's already visible in the window; the image area is stretched vertically to accommodate it (**Figure 10.18**). However, portions of the movie that don't include text are gray in the text track area (**Figure 10.19**). The only way to make that area black is to add empty text for those portions. In general, we recommend adding text this way only if you plan to add text for the duration of the movie or if the text track will be disabled. Note also that each time you add text like this, a new text track is created; therefore, this is not a good technique to use when you need to add a lot of text.

✔ Tips

■ In the current version of QuickTime, when you add text copied from a word processor, the text track does not appear directly below the existing visual tracks; it is shifted to the left and up. This is a bug that will likely be fixed in an update. In the meantime you will want to adjust the position of the text track using the Size panel (as covered at the beginning of Chapter 8), unless you intend to disable the text track.

■ (Mac OS only) If you want to change the text's properties, hold down the Control key while you add the text. The Text Settings dialog box (described in "Specifying Text Track Appearance when You Import," earlier in this chapter) appears so you can specify your choices.

Figure 10.18 The text track is added below the other tracks.

Figure 10.19 During portions of the movie where no text was added, gray shows at the bottom of the window.

Figure 10.20 In the Set as Chapter panel of the Info window, click the Set Chapter Owner Track button.

Figure 10.21 In the Select Chapter Owner Track dialog box, choose any track from your movie.

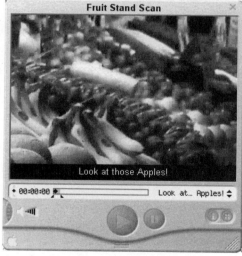

Figure 10.22 You get a chapter list composed of the frames from your text track. (You'll probably want to disable the text track to make it invisible.)

Creating Chapter Lists

Chapter lists give users a quick way to move to designated spots—called *chapters*—in a movie.

To create a chapter list:

1. Create a text track containing the text you want to use as chapter names.

    The text, of course, needs to appear at the times you wish the chapters defined. (The technique we described earlier in this chapter, in "Creating a Text Track That's Synced to Other Tracks," will probably be useful.) Add the text track to the movie you want chapters in. (Use the Add command, covered in Chapter 7.)

2. From the Movie menu, choose Get Info.

3. In the left pop-up menu choose the text track you just added, and in the right pop-up menu choose Set as Chapter Track.

4. Click Set Chapter Owner Track (**Figure 10.20**).

5. In the Select Chapter Owner Track dialog box that appears, select any track from your movie (**Figure 10.21**).

    It doesn't matter which track you choose as long as that track will remain in the movie.

6. Click OK.

    The track you selected in Step 5 is now listed in the Set as Chapter Track panel. In the Player window, the Chapter Control appears to the right of the Time slider (**Figure 10.22**).

7. Disable the text track, following the steps in "Disabling and Enabling Tracks" in Chapter 7.

continues on next page

(This assumes that you don't want to have a visible text track in addition to a chapter list.)

8. Save the movie.

✔ Tips

■ For movies that will be delivered over the Internet, you'll want to set the text track you set as a chapter track to be preloaded. (If you don't do this, the width of the Chapter List button or the Chapter Control gets defined by the width of the chapter defined at the beginning of the movie; this is problematic if you have no chapter or a chapter with few characters defined at the beginning). To preload the text, in the Info window, from the left pop-up menu choose the text track and from the right pop-up menu choose Preload. Then check "Preload". (See "Loading Tracks into Memory" in Chapter 7 for more info.)

■ If you embed a movie with a chapter list on a Web page and find that the Chapter List button doesn't appear in the controller, it's probably because the movie isn't wide enough. How wide the movie needs to be depends on how many characters are in the name of the longest chapter as well as which platform it will be viewed on. You should preview movies with chapter lists on a Web page on both platforms to make sure you can see the Chapter List button. (If the movie's width is smaller than what's necessary to have the Chapter List button appear on a Web page, you can resize it before saving, or you can use the SCALE attribute in your EMBED tag—as we'll describe in Chapter 17—to make it large enough.)

■ Other applications that create or use QuickTime chapters use the terms *cues* or *cue points* rather than chapters.

SPRITE, 3D, AND FLASH TRACKS

Sprite, 3D, and Flash tracks are the tracks with a visual component that we haven't yet covered. While these are very different types of tracks, they have one thing in common: you can't do very much with them in QuickTime Player.

In this chapter we'll cover the few QuickTime Player techniques available to alter these tracks. We'll also cover the limited number of ways to create tracks of these types: You can open 3D or Flash files in QuickTime Player.

Of course, if you have existing movies with sprite, 3D, or Flash tracks you can use many of the techniques covered in Chapters 6, 7, and 8 that apply to all movies, tracks, and visual tracks.

Tools to Create Sprite, 3D, and Flash Tracks

If you want to create sprite, 3D, or Flash tracks, you'll need to use other tools. For creating sprite tracks, look into Electrifier Inc.'s Electrifier Pro, Paceworks' ObjectDancer, and Totally Hip Software's LiveStage. For Mac OS users, there's also the freeware tool Spritz and Apple's free, unsupported Sprite Export Xtra for Macromedia Director. Of these tools, only Electrifier Pro, LiveStage, and Spritz currently can be used to create wired sprites. For creating 3D tracks, Mac OS users can use Strata VideoShop 4.5 or another free, unsupported tool from Apple called 3D Movie Maker; both let you animate 3D objects created with 3D modeling software. Flash tracks are created with Macromedia Flash.

Attaching a Graphic or Video Sequence to a Sprite

ATTACHING A GRAPHIC OR VIDEO SEQUENCE TO A SPRITE

Often, a sprite is a static graphical object that moves across the screen in a particular way. However, QuickTime Player lets you replace a sprite's graphic with data from a QuickTime track. This can be a video track, giving you an animated sprite.

To replace a sprite's graphic with another QuickTime track:

1. Add your replacement track to the movie containing the sprite track. (You'll want the added track to have the same duration as the sprite track, so use the Add Scaled command, as described in Chapter 7. For dynamic tracks, make sure the track is the right duration before adding it, or it will play in fast or slow motion.)

   Don't worry about the track's location in the Movie window (**Figure 11.1**).

2. From the Movie menu, choose Get Info to open the movie's Info window.

3. From the left pop-up menu, choose the sprite track; from the right pop-up menu choose Image Overrides.

4. Select the sprite you want to change, and click the Select Override Track button (**Figure 11.2**).

5. In the Select Override Track dialog box, select the added track, and click OK (**Figure 11.3**).

   The sprite's original graphic is replaced by the data from the added track (**Figure 11.4**).

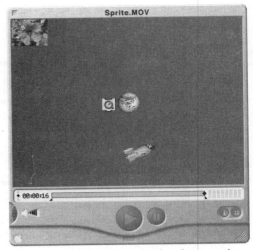

Figure 11.1 Start by adding a visual track to a movie with a sprite track. (Here the added track is a video track of a flower. The sprite track contains three graphics that move around in the window.)

Figure 11.2 In the Image Override panel in the Info window, select a sprite and click the Select Override Track button.

Figure 11.3 Select the track you added.

Figure 11.4 The sprite's graphic is now the track you added. (The flower video now moves around in the window, following the path the QuickTime icon previously followed.)

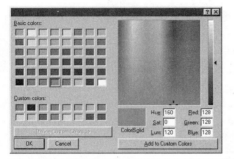

Figure 11.5 Click the Set button in the Sprite Properties panel of the Info window.

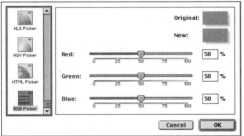

Figure 11.6 Use a Color Picker dialog box to choose a new background color (top is a Windows color picker; bottom is a Mac OS color picker).

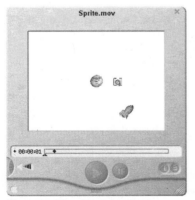

Figure 11.7 The color you select becomes the background color.

Changing the Background Color of a Sprite Track

Sprite tracks have a background color, which is very easy to change if you're so inclined.

To change a sprite track's background color:

1. From the Movie menu, choose Get Info.

2. From the left pop-up menu, choose the sprite track, and from the right pop-up menu choose Properties.

    The current background color appears in the bar below the words *Background Color*.

3. Click the Set button to the right of the colored bar (**Figure 11.5**).

    A Color Picker dialog box appears (**Figure 11.6**).

4. Choose a color, and click OK to close the Color Picker dialog box.

    The color that you selected is now the sprite track's background color (**Figure 11.7**).

Getting Information about Sprites

The Image Format panel contains information about a movie's individual sprites. To access that panel, open the movie's Info window: In the left pop-up menu choose the sprite track; in the right pop-up menu choose Image Format.

You'll be presented with a scrolling list of the movie's sprites: By clicking one of these sprites, you can obtain information about the sprite's width and height (in pixels), the number of colors it contains, the compressor used to compress its graphic, and its registration point. You can also see which sprites have been placed in a group for programming proposes.

Changing Properties of Tracks with Wired Sprites

If you want to alter sprite tracks, it makes sense to use the tools that were employed to create and program their interactivity. However, you can make some minor modifications quickly using QuickTime Player. You can alter a track's visibility. (You might, for example, have interactive sprites overlaying elements in a video track. Although the sprites would be invisible normally, you might wish to make them visible for debugging purposes.) And you can also turn on or off a sprite track's ability to respond to user actions.

To change the visibility of a sprite track:

1. From the Movie menu, choose Get Info.

2. From the left pop-up menu choose the sprite track; from the right pop-up menu choose Properties 2.

   This opens the Properties 2 panel (**Figure 11.8**).

3. Use the Track is Visible checkbox to make a track visible or invisible.

   To make the track visible, make sure the Track is Visible checkbox is selected.

   To make the track invisible, make sure the Track is Visible checkbox is *not* selected.

   Invisible sprite tracks—unlike disabled tracks—can respond to user actions.

To turn on and off a sprite track's ability to respond to user actions:

1. If not already open, open the Properties 2 panel as described in Steps 1 and 2 above.

2. Click the Has Actions checkbox to set if the track will respond to user actions.

   If Has Actions is not selected, the sprite track will not respond to user actions, such as mouse clicks.

Use the Has Actions checkbox to change whether the track will respond to user actions

Use the Track is Visible checkbox to change the visibility of the track

Figure 11.8 The Properties 2 panel allows you to modify wired sprite tracks.

Other Sprite Track Changes

The Properties 2 panel has two buttons that let you make changes to your sprites. Neither, however, is terribly useful.

If you click the Set button located on the Preferred depth line, you can choose the number of colors that will be used to draw the sprites in the sprite track before they get displayed on the screen.

If you click the Set button located on the Idle Frequency line, you can specify how often the system sends an idle message. (An idle message gets sent continuously when the system isn't busy performing other actions, such as responding to user actions. The creator of a wired sprite track will often write a piece of code—called an *idle handler*—that specifies actions that should occur whenever the system sends an idle message. The frequency is measured in *ticks* (one tick equals a 60th of a second).

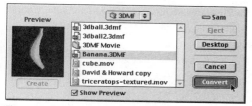

Figure 11.9 From QuickTime Player's File menu, choose Open Movie.

Figure 11.10 Select a 3DMF file, and click Convert.

Figure 11.11 You've created a QuickTime movie with a single 3D track.

Creating a Static 3D Track from a 3D File

QuickTime Player can directly open 3D files in the 3DMF format. Keep in mind, however, that these files have no motion defined for them; they're static 3D objects.

However, if you want to create a track with a still 3D image (perhaps to combine with other data), you would follow the steps used to create many other media files.

To create a 3D track from a 3DMF file:

1. From QuickTime Player's File menu choose Open Movie (**Figure 11.9**).

2. Navigate to and select a 3D file.

   The Open button becomes a Convert button (**Figure 11.10**).

3. Click the Convert button.

   QuickTime opens the file and displays the visual data in a standard QuickTime Player window. The movie contains one 3D track (**Figure 11.11**).

   The original 3D file is not changed unless you save this movie with the same name as the 3D file.

Creating Dynamic 3D Tracks (Mac OS only)

To animate an object in a 3D track, you need a tween track to define the object's motion. You can use an application such as VideoShop to associate a tween track with objects in a 3D track. Or you can use a free tool from Apple called 3D Movie Maker to associate some predefined tween tracks with 3D objects. You can't do this in QuickTime Player, however.

Changing Texture Mapping for a 3D Track

Some QuickTime 3D tracks have 3D objects with a *texture map* defined. (A texture map is an image used to define the surface of the object.)

If you have such a movie, you can use QuickTime Player to replace the texture currently mapped to the 3D object with your own visual track.

To determine if an object in a 3D track has a texture map:

1. From the Movie menu, choose Get Info.

2. In the Info window, from the left pop-up menu choose the 3D track; from the right pop-up menu choose Texture Overrides.

3. If any object is listed (as in **Figure 11.13**), it contains a texture map that you can replace.

To change the image mapped onto a 3D object with a texture map:

1. Add to your movie the visual track you want to map onto the 3D object. Use the Add Scaled command to ensure that the track has the same duration as the 3D track.

   The added track will be layered over or placed next to other tracks (**Figure 11.12**). Don't worry about the added track's positioning; it's temporary.

2. In the Texture Overrides panel (**Figure 11.13**), select the object you want to apply a new texture to and then click the Select Texture Track button.

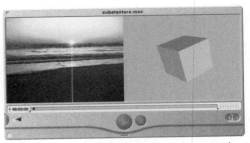

Figure 11.12 Start by adding a visual track to a movie with a 3D track that contains objects with a texture map. (In this case, a beach at sunset is the added video track.)

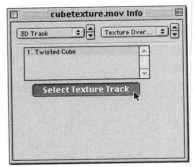

Figure 11.13 Select the object you want to apply a new texture to, and click Select Texture Track.

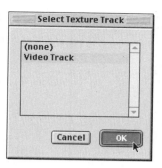

Figure 11.14
Select the track you want to map onto the object (the track you added).

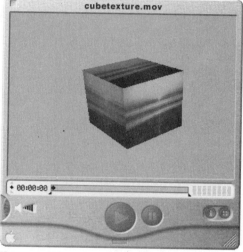

Figure 11.15 The track you selected is mapped onto the object.

3. In the Select Texture Track dialog box that appears, select the track you added in Step 1 and click OK (**Figure 11.14**).

The track selected is now mapped onto the object. The name of the object as listed in the Texture Overrides panel now has the name of the mapped visual track appended to it.

4. If your movie contains a track that was previously being used as a texture, it may become an independent track again, probably layered over other tracks. You can use the Delete Tracks command in the Edit menu to get rid of this extra track.

Now you can see the 3D object with your track mapped onto it (**Figure 11.15**).

Creating 3D Tracks with Texture Maps

You can create a 3D model with a texture map using almost any QuickDraw 3D modeling tool.

If you want to animate it with 3D Movie Maker or open it as a static graphic directly in QuickTime Player but still want to alter the texture (as described here), you'll first need to run it through a tool called 3DMF Optimizer, from Pangea Software.

CHANGING TEXTURE MAPPING FOR A 3D TRACK

Changing the Renderer for a 3D Track

Three-dimensional objects can be rendered using a variety of techniques. By specifying which technique is used to render an object, you determine how it looks. QuickTime Player lets you choose a renderer for objects in 3D tracks.

To change the renderer for a 3D track:

1. From the Movie menu, choose Get Info.

2. In the Info window, from the left pop-up menu choose the 3D track and from the right pop-up menu choose Renderer.

3. In the Renderer panel (**Figure 11.16**), select a renderer.

   The QuickDraw 3D Interactive renderer shows solid surfaces for the 3D objects (**Figure 11.17**). The Default option is the same as the interactive renderer unless the original 3D file specified some other renderer as its default.

   The QuickDraw 3D Wireframe renderer removes any textures from the model, leaving only the wire frame that defines the object's geometry (**Figure 11.18**).

✔ Tip

■ Programmers can create plug-in renderers for QuickDraw 3D, the 3D technology that works with QuickTime. Such plug-ins may be sold on their own; for example, Inklination sells the FineArt 3D renderer which renders 3D models in a pen and ink style. Also, some plug-in renderers are included in 3D modeling software packages (for example, Electric Cafe's ModelShop 3). If you install one of these plug-in renderers, you'll be presented with additional choices in the Renderer panel.

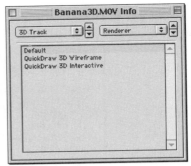

Figure 11.16 Use the Renderer panel in the Info window to choose a renderer.

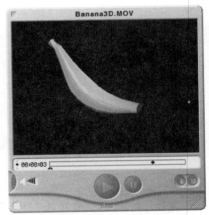

Figure 11.17 A 3D object rendered by the default renderer.

Figure 11.18 A 3D object rendered by the wireframe renderer.

Figure 11.19 You can open a Flash file in QuickTime Player using the Open Movie command.

Figure 11.20 When you select a Flash file, the Open button changes to Convert. Click it to open the file.

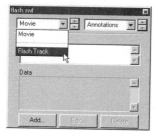

Figure 11.21 When you open a Flash file in QuickTime Player, you create a single Flash track, even if the file also contains audio.

QuickTime in Flash

On this page we've shown how you can open a Flash file using QuickTime. You can also open QuickTime movies using Flash 4, add interactive, vector-based elements, and then export the entire presentation as a QuickTime movie, containing Flash tracks along with the QuickTime tracks that were originally imported.

Creating Flash Tracks from Flash Files

Macromedia Flash is an application for creating interactive, vector-based animations which can contain audio. Flash files are extremely popular on the Web.

QuickTime 4 now opens Flash files. However, rather than going into standard video and audio tracks, the data goes into a special Flash track that contains both audio and video. All interactivity is retained.

Once it's in a QuickTime track, you can combine a Flash track with other track types, and manipulate it in various ways.

To create a Flash track from a Flash file:

1. From the File menu, choose Open Movie (**Figure 11.19**).

2. Locate the Flash file you want to open, and click Convert (**Figure 11.20**).

   The file is opened like any other QuickTime movie. When you check the movie composition in the Info window, however, you'll see that there is a single Flash track (**Figure 11.21**).

✔ Tip

■ If you want to combine a Flash track with other QuickTime tracks, it's best to add the other tracks to the Flash track, rather than vice-versa.

Working with Audio Tracks

Don't forget the audio! Many people are so excited to see the video image that they forget about the audio, making sound an often-overlooked component of multimedia. However, better sound often leads people to believe that the video image is improved as well.

When we use the term *audio*, we're referring to tracks that you can hear. QuickTime has two primary types of audio tracks: There are those that contain digitized sound; the most common of these are *sound tracks*, though *MPEG audio tracks* also contain digitized sound. (Some MPEG tracks and Flash tracks also contain digitized sound.) And there are those that comprise a sequence of commands that tell QuickTime how to play sounds called *instruments*; based on the MIDI standard, these are called *music tracks*.

In this chapter we'll cover techniques that apply to all types of audio tracks—combining them with video or still images and altering the volume and balance, bass, and treble.

In the chapters that follow, we'll discuss sound and music tracks individually.

Adding New Audio to a Movie

If you've read Chapter 7, you may be able to guess how to add new audio to a movie. If not, you needn't worry: We'll show you here anyway. Remember that a QuickTime file can have multiple tracks of the same type, so you can add new audio even if your file already contains an audio track. This technique is often used to add narration or background sound or music to a movie that already contains audio.

Figure 12.1 Use the Add command to add the audio to the video.

To add new audio to a video file:

1. Open a QuickTime file containing a sound or music track, or import an audio file into QuickTime. (Look ahead to Chapters 13 and 14 for details.)

2. Select and copy all or part of the audio movie.

3. Open the movie file you want to add audio to, and move the slider to the point where you want the audio to begin playing.

4. Hold down the Option key (Mac OS) or the Ctrl and Alt keys (Windows), and from the Edit menu choose Add (**Figure 12.1**).

5. Adjust the duration of the audio or video, if necessary:

   If the video is longer than the audio, a portion of the Time slider, representing the length of the audio, is selected and the Current Location indicator is positioned at the end of the selection (**Figure 12.2**). Since the Current Location indicator is positioned at the end of the audio, you can repeat Step 4 one or more times, which will result in the audio repeating when the movie plays.

Figure 12.2 If the audio is shorter than the video, only part of the Time slider is selected after you add audio.

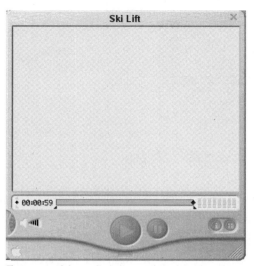

Figure 12.3 If the audio is longer than the video, the window is gray where there's only audio.

If the audio is longer than the video, the image area appears gray during any time that there's no video to go with the audio (**Figure 12.3**). You'll probably want to select and delete the audio-only portion of the track.

✔ Tip

- To quickly get rid of audio that extends beyond the video track, you can move your Current Location indicator to the far right of the Time slider, hold down the Shift key, and press the left arrow key. This selects the audio-only area; you can then simply delete this selection.

ADDING NEW AUDIO TO A MOVIE

Adding a Still Image to an Audio Track

The technique for merging audio with still images differs from the technique for merging audio with an existing movie only in that you can take advantage of QuickTime Player's ability to scale in time; this makes it easy to match the duration of the still image to the duration of the audio.

Figure 12.4 In the audio movie, choose Select All from the Edit menu.

To add a still image to an audio track:

1. In QuickTime Player, open or import your audio file, so you have an audio-only movie.

2. Still in QuickTime Player, open or import your still-image file in a separate window, and from the Edit menu choose Copy. (With nothing selected, the current—and only—frame is copied.)

    Or, in a graphics application, open the image and copy it from there.

Figure 12.5 Use Add Scaled to add previously copied image data. (You'll need to hold down the modifier keys—Shift and Option for the Mac; Shift, Ctrl, and Alt for Windows—to make this choice available.)

3. Click in the window for the audio movie, and from the Edit menu choose Select All (**Figure 12.4**).

4. Hold down the Shift and Option keys (Mac OS) or the Shift, Ctrl, and Alt keys (Windows), and from the Edit menu choose Add Scaled (**Figure 12.5**).

    The audio movie's window expands to fit the graphic (**Figure 12.6**).

5. Save the movie containing both the sound and the graphic as a self-contained file.

Figure 12.6 The graphic is added to the audio movie and appears for the duration of the audio.

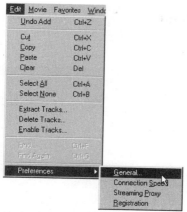

Figure 12.7 Choose General from the Preferences submenu in the Edit menu.

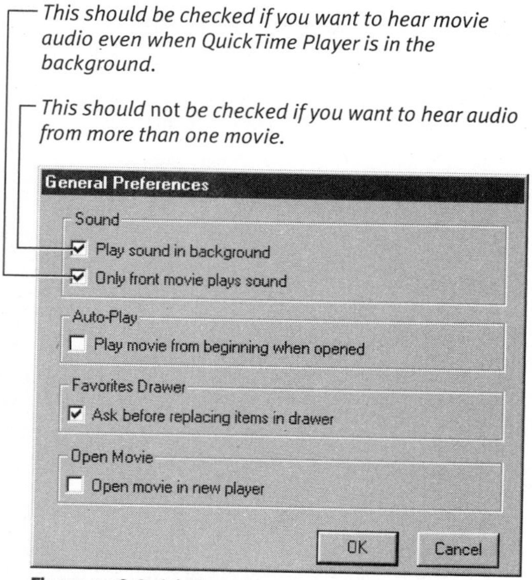

This should be checked if you want to hear movie audio even when QuickTime Player is in the background.

This should not be checked if you want to hear audio from more than one movie.

General Preferences

Sound
☑ Play sound in background
☑ Only front movie plays sound

Auto-Play
☐ Play movie from beginning when opened

Favorites Drawer
☑ Ask before replacing items in drawer

Open Movie
☐ Open movie in new player

OK   Cancel

Figure 12.8 QuickTime Player's General Preferences dialog box contains options that affect whether audio is heard in movies that are not in the front.

Having Audio Play When the Movie Isn't in Front

When your movie file is in the background—either because another application is active or because a different QuickTime Player movie window is active—you can decide whether you want to hear its audio.

To have audio play when a movie is in the background:

1. In QuickTime Player's Edit menu, navigate to Preferences, and from the submenu choose General (**Figure 12.7**).
   The General Preferences dialog box appears (**Figure 12.8**).

2. If you want to hear your movies' audio even when another application is active, check "Play sound in background."

3. If you want to hear multiple movies' audio simultaneously, make sure that "Only front movie plays sound" is not checked.

Changing the Default Volume, Balance, Bass, and Treble of an Audio Track

You can change your audio track's default volume; you can also adjust the balance, making the audio louder on the left or on the right (assuming it's played back in stereo, of course). In addition, you can increase the low frequencies (bass) or high frequencies (treble) of a sound track. (You can make these changes in the Controls tray, as we described in Chapter 4, but the changes remain only as long as the movie is open. On this page, we'll show you how to make the changes in the movie's Info window, in which case the changes to volume and balance get saved when the movie is saved; changes to bass and treble are temporary.)

To change the default volume:

1. From the Movie menu, choose Get Info to open the movie's Info window.

2. From the left pop-up menu choose the sound track you'd like to change the volume of; from the right pop-up menu choose Volume.

   The Volume panel appears (**Figure 12.9**).

3. Drag the bar in the top horizontal rectangle labeled *Volume* (or click in the rectangle to make the bar automatically move to the point clicked). The farther to the right the bar extends, the higher the volume. The number below the bar represents the percentage of normal volume. (If you set the volume beyond 100 percent of normal, the part of the bar to the right of center turns red to warn you that the sound may become distorted.)

   When you play the movie, the sound track's volume level is represented graphically by the small rectangles labeled Level that fill in from left to right. (The Level

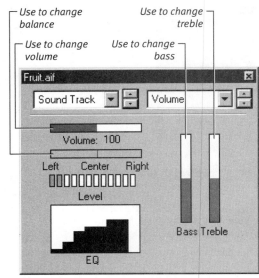

Figure 12.9 This is the Volume panel: Drag in the top horizontal bar to change the track's default volume. Drag in the bar below the Volume bar to change how much sound is directed to each speaker. Drag in the left vertical bar to change bass and in the right vertical bar to change treble.

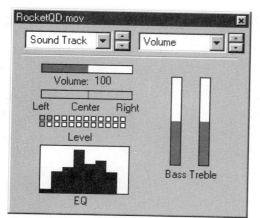

Figure 12.10 As a movie with a stereo sound track plays, the Level indicator breaks into two rows, each of which represents a speaker.

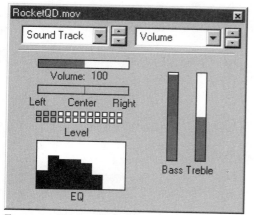

Figure 12.11 The Graphic EQ displays relative frequencies. If you increase the bass, the relative height of the bars to the left of the EQ increases.

display doesn't function for music tracks or MPEG audio tracks.)

To change the balance:

1. Open the Volume panel (see above).

2. Click in the lower horizontal rectangle (labeled *Left Center Right*). Clicking to the right of center directs more sound to the right speaker; clicking to the left of center directs more sound to the left speaker.

   When you play a stereo movie, the volume-level rectangles become two rows of squares (**Figure 12.10**). The top row represents the left speaker, and the bottom row represents the right speaker.

To change the bass or treble:

1. Open the Volume panel (see above).

2. Use the vertical rectangles to change the bass or treble:

   Drag in the left vertical rectangle (or click in the rectangle to move the bar automatically to the point clicked). If you drag the bar up, you add to the low frequencies in the track; if you drag down, you subtract some of the low frequencies.

   Drag in the right vertical rectangle (or click in the rectangle to move the bar automatically to the point clicked). If you drag the bar up, you add to the high frequencies in the track; if you drag down, you subtract some of the high frequencies.

When you play the movie, the large rectangle at the bottom left of the window (called the *Graphic EQ*) displays the relative frequencies in the track (**Figure 12.11**). If you increase the bass, you'll see that the bars on the left side will increase in height. If you increase the treble, the bars on the right side of the Graphic EQ will increase in height as the movie plays.

VOLUME, BALANCE, BASS, AND TREBLE

✔ Tips

■ If you're editing a music or MPEG audio track, you can drag the bass and treble rectangles, but this actually has no effect.

■ Changes to volume and balance are saved when the movie is saved. Changes to bass and treble are not saved when the movie is saved.

■ Hold down the Option key (Mac) or Ctrl and Alt keys (Windows) when you click in the volume rectangle to make the indicator bar snap to numerical values in increments of 25. Hold down the same key or keys when you click in the balance rectangle to make the little green line snap to Left, halfway between Left and Center, Center, halfway between Center and Right, and Right.

■ Some MPEG tracks and Flash tracks contain audio in addition to their visual component; the Volume panel is also available for these tracks.

SOUND TRACKS AND MPEG AUDIO TRACKS

13

QuickTime sound tracks are composed of digitized audio. Like video tracks, sound tracks have certain associated properties—some of which you have a certain amount of control over.

In this chapter, we'll introduce the basic characteristics of digital sound, looking at the dialog box from which you can access these properties and the info panel from which you determine what they are. Then we'll look at various methods for creating sound tracks, including importing MP3 files. (In addition, we'll cover importing MPEG Layer I and II audio files to create MPEG audio tracks; this works only if you have the QuickTime MPEG Extension, which is currently available only on Mac OS.)

Finally, we'll show you how you can use QuickTime Player as a sound-conversion utility.

About Digitized Sound

It helps to think of digitized sound as being analogous to digitized video.

Digitized sound is actually composed of a sequence of individual sound samples. The number of samples per second is called the *sample rate* and is very much like a video track's frame rate. The more sound samples per second, the higher the quality of the resulting sound. However, more sound samples also take up more space on disk and mean that more data needs to be processed during every second of playback. (As we mentioned when discussing video in Chapter 9, the amount of data that must be processed every second is called the *data rate*.)

Sound samples can be different sizes. Just as you can reproduce a photograph more faithfully by storing it as a 24-bit (full-color) image than as an 8-bit image, 16-bit sound samples represent audio more accurately than 8-bit sound samples. We refer to the size of those samples as a sound's *sample size*. As with the sample rate, a larger sample size increases the accuracy of the sound at the expense of more storage space and a higher data rate.

Like video, sound can be compressed using techniques designed to represent the sound data more efficiently and to lower the data rate. You can choose from many sound compressors when you compress a QuickTime sound track (see **Table 13.1**). And as you can for video tracks, you may add additional sound compressors as well.

One additional property of a sound track is the number of channels it contains: one (mono) or two (stereo).

Table 13.1

Audio Compressors Included with QuickTime 4	
COMPRESSOR NAME	**COMMENTS**
24-bit Integer, 32-bit Integer	Increases the sample size to 24 or 32 bits (but will be converted to 8 or 16 bits to play on current hardware).
32-bit Floating Point, Floating Point	Actually increases the sample size of 64-bit audio (to 32 or 64 bits), which allows for more accurate conversion to other sample sizes and for applying effects. (Playback on current systems, however, is still 8 bit or 16 bit.)
ALaw 2:1	Internet standard for compressed audio in Europe and everywhere else except the United States and Japan. Low compression ratio and low quality. Generally not recommended.
IMA 4:1	Very good for music and other audio content. Must be 16 bit; relatively low compression ratio.
MACE 3:1, MACE 6:1	Outdated Macintosh compressors. Low quality. Not generally recommended.
QDesign Music Codec 2	Excellent for music content intended for the Web. Extremely low compression ratio.
QUALCOMM PureVoice	Excellent for voice content intended for the Web. Extremely low compression ratio.
μLaw 2:1	Internet standard for compressed audio in the United States and Japan. Low compression ratio and low quality. Generally not recommended.

This table lists the compressors you can choose when compressing sound tracks; QuickTime uses others internally (such as DV, IMA ADPCM, MP3, and PCM) when importing or exporting certain file formats. You may see one of these listed in the Format panel for the audio track of a DV or AVI file that you've opened in QuickTime Player.

Figure 13.1 The Sound Settings dialog box.

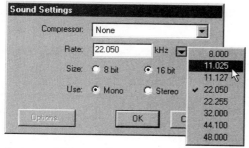

Figure 13.2 It's best to choose your sample rate from the Rate pop-up menu.

About the Sound Settings Dialog Box

You access a sound file's properties via the Sound Settings dialog box (**Figure 13.1**). As with the Compression Settings dialog box for video, you use this dialog box for a few tasks in QuickTime Player as well as in many other QuickTime applications. Your options in the Sound Settings dialog box include:

◆ **Compressor:** Depending on which sound format you select, you'll have various compressors to choose from. When you choose certain compressors, an Options button at the bottom of the dialog box becomes available, providing access to additional compressor features.

◆ **Rate:** You can enter a sample rate or use the pop-up menu to select one (**Figure 13.2**). It's best, however, to choose one of the sample rates presented in the pop-up menu since these rates represent the optimal choices for today's computer sound cards. In general, rates of 22.050 kHz or 11.025 kHz (22,050 samples per second or 11,025 samples per second) usually result in very good quality sound. (It's best to avoid the 11.127 and the 22.125 choices because they may not perform well on Windows computers.)

◆ **Size:** You have a choice of 8 bit or 16 bit, though the 8-bit choice won't be available for some compressors. (Eight-bit sound provides for 256 possible values, and 16-bit sound offers 65,536 possible values.)

◆ **Use:** This refers to the number of channels. You can choose between Mono and Stereo, though Mono is the most common choice since most audio files are recorded in mono, anyway. If you have a stereo file whose quality you wish to retain, it could make sense to select Stereo.

Checking the Characteristics of a Sound Track

If you want to know the properties of a movie's sound track, you can check in the movie's Info window.

To check the characteristics of a sound track:

1. From the Movie menu, choose Get Info to open the movie's Info window.

2. From the left pop-up menu, select the sound track, and from the right pop-up menu, choose Format.

   The Format panel shows the file's sample rate, the number of channels, its sample size, and how it was compressed (**Figure 13.3**).

✔ Tip

■ This panel lists only those characteristics of a sound track that are relevant to digitized sound. Remember that audio tracks have other properties as well; see "Changing the Default Volume, Balance, Bass, and Treble of an Audio Track" in Chapter 12.

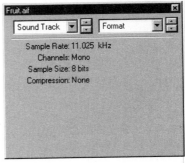

Figure 13.3 The Format panel for a sound track.

The Characteristics of a Streamed Sound Track

If you open an RTSP streaming movie in QuickTime Player, you won't find a separate sound track. However, you can get information about how the sound was originally compressed. Once the movie starts playing, open the Info window. From the left pop-up menu choose the streaming track (probably named "Streaming Track"), and from the right pop-up menu choose Format. You'll see the media types contained in the stream. Look for Sound as a media type, and below it you'll see information about compression, channels, and sample rate.

Figure 13.4 You open most sound files as you would any QuickTime movie.

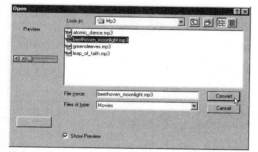

Figure 13.5 The only difference is that when you select the file, the Open button turns into a Convert button.

Figure 13.6 The resulting movie has no visual component.

Creating a Sound Track from a Sound File

You can create a QuickTime sound track from an existing sound file in another audio format by opening it in QuickTime Player. Most audio files—including AIFF/AIFC, MP3, Sound Designer 2, WAV, and μLaw (au) files—open directly in QuickTime Player. Macintosh System 7 sound files need to be imported, however.

To create a sound track from a sound file (in most sound formats):

1. From the File menu, choose Open Movie (**Figure 13.4**) or Import.

2. In the Open dialog box, navigate to the sound file and click the Convert button (**Figure 13.5**).

   A new movie window without an image appears (**Figure 13.6**). The title of the window is the same as the name of the file you opened.

   The sound data in this movie can be combined with other QuickTime movies. However, you have not actually created a QuickTime movie file until you save. If you quit QuickTime Player without saving, the file remains in its original format.

✔ Tip

■ You also create a sound track, along with a video track, when you open DV or AVI files in QuickTime Player. If all you need is the audio, you can simply delete the video track as described in "Deleting Tracks" in Chapter 7.

To create a sound track from a System 7 sound file:

1. From the File menu choose Import (**Figure 13.7**) or Open Movie.

2. In the Open dialog box, locate and select the System 7 sound file, and click the Convert button (**Figure 13.8**).

   A Save dialog box appears (**Figure 13.9**) because QuickTime needs to create a new file to put the System 7 file data into.

3. If desired, change the name and location for the file to be created.

4. Click Save.

   A movie window without an image area appears (**Figure 13.10**).

   Since a new file has already been created, you don't need to save this movie unless you alter it.

✔ Tip

■ If you have problems creating QuickTime movies from System 7 sound files on a Windows computer, we recommend doing it on a Mac OS computer and then copying the resulting QuickTime movies to a Windows computer.

Figure 13.7 For System 7 sound files, choose Import or Open Movie.

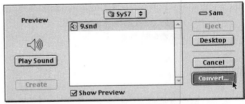

Figure 13.8 The Open button changes to a Convert... button. (The ellipses indicate that there will be another step.)

Figure 13.9 The next step is to save the file.

Figure 13.10 A sound-only movie file appears.

Figure 13.11 Choose Import from the File menu. (Open Movie will work, too.)

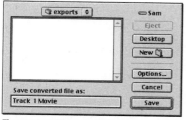

Figure 13.12 Select a file from the audio CD, and click Convert.

Figure 13.13 You can click Save immediately, or you can first click the Options button.

Figure 13.14 If you click the Options button, an Audio CD Import Options dialog box will appear.

Creating a Sound Track from an Audio CD (Mac Only)

On Mac OS computers you can convert audio from a standard audio CD to a QuickTime sound track. You can then incorporate this music into your QuickTime movie.

To import music from an audio CD:

1. Put your audio CD into your CD-ROM drive.

2. From the File menu choose Import (**Figure 13.11**) or Open Movie.

3. Select a file on your audio CD, and click the Convert button (**Figure 13.12**).

4. In the Save dialog box that appears (**Figure 13.13**), you can click the Options button to open the Audio CD Import Options dialog box (**Figure 13.14**), where you can set the sample size, rate, and use (stereo or mono) as you would in a standard Sound Settings dialog box. (See "About the Sound Settings Dialog Box" earlier in this chapter.) You can use the lower part of the window, labeled Audio Selection, to select only a portion of the track by typing start and end times, using the up and down triangles to increase or decrease start and end times or repositioning the sliders to set start and end times; use the Play button to verify your selection. Click OK to return to the Save dialog box.

5. Navigate to the location on your hard disk where you want to save the file, provide a new name if you'd like, and click Save.

✔ Tip

■ It's not legal or ethical to use other people's music in your productions if they are for anything other than personal use.

Creating an MPEG Audio Track from an MPEG Sound File (Mac Only)

MPEG—or Moving Picture Experts Group—sound files are commonly used on the Internet. They come in several flavors (Layer I, Layer II, and Layer III), which are encoded differently. (In theory, the higher the layer number, the better the quality, but this does not always hold true.) You can open MPEG Audio Layer I and Layer II files in QuickTime Player. You do not, however, create a regular QuickTime sound track; instead, you create an MPEG audio track. (MPEG Audio Layer III—more commonly known as MP3—can be converted to a sound track as described in "Creating a Sound Track from a Sound File," earlier in this chapter.)

The process for opening MPEG Audio Layer I and Layer II files is the same as for many other file types.

To create an MPEG audio track:

1. From the File menu choose Open Movie (**Figure 13.15**).

2. Locate and select the MPEG Audio Layer I or Layer II file, and click Convert (**Figure 13.16**).

Figure 13.15 Choose Open Movie from the File menu.

Figure 13.16 Select the file, and click Convert.

Figure 13.17 An audio-only file appears.

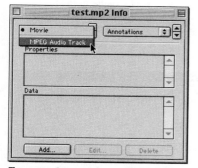

Figure 13.18 It contains an MPEG audio track rather than a sound track.

As with any sound file, a new Player window with no image area appears (**Figure 13.17**). When you check in the Info window, you'll see that the file has a single MPEG audio track (**Figure 13.18**).

3. Make sure to save the file if you want to open it again as a QuickTime movie.

✔ Tips

■ Like regular MPEG tracks (those containing both video and audio), MPEG audio tracks can be copied and pasted into other QuickTime movies. However, when you select and copy a portion, the data from the entire track is copied. You hear only what you selected, but the file you paste into will be increased by the full size of the original MPEG audio track.

■ There is no Format panel in the Info window for MPEG audio tracks, so you can't use QuickTime Player to access information about the sample rate and sample size of these tracks. Remember, however, that you can view and change such properties as volume and balance in the Volume panel.

CREATING AN MPEG AUDIO TRACK

Changing the Characteristics of a Sound Track

You can use QuickTime Player to change the characteristics of a sound track (but not an MPEG audio track). In general, you will want to do this to lower the track's data rate. We'll show you one general technique here. (We cover another technique in "Compressing Selected Tracks" in Chapter 15. We'll also talk about specific choices you might make when we discuss preparing movies for the Web in Chapter 16 and preparing movies for CD-ROMs and kiosks in Chapter 18.)

To change the characteristics of a sound track:

1. From the File menu choose Export (**Figure 13.19**).

   (The only way to get to the Sound Settings dialog box is by exporting.)

2. In the Save dialog box, choose from the Export pop-up menu choose Sound to AIFF and then click the Options button (**Figure 13.20**).

   The Sound Settings dialog box appears (**Figure 13.21**).

Figure 13.19 Choose Export from the File menu.

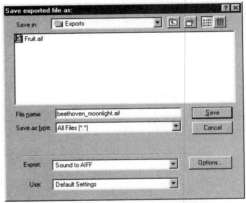

Figure 13.20 Choose Sound to AIFF and click the Options button.

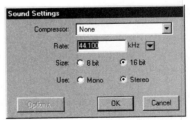

Figure 13.21 In the Sound Settings dialog box, you can change properties of the sound track.

3. In the Sound Settings dialog box, make your choices and then click OK. (See "About the Sound Settings Dialog Box" earlier in this chapter for an overview as well as Chapters 16 and 18 for specific recommendations.)

4. In the Save dialog box click Save to export the file.

5. In QuickTime Player open the exported file.

If the sound track was originally accompanied by other tracks, you'll need to delete the original sound track and add the exported track. (Deleting and adding techniques are covered in Chapter 7.)

✔ Tips

- If you have multiple sound tracks in a movie, this technique will merge them into a single track. See "Compressing Selected Tracks" in Chapter 15 for an alternative technique.

- QuickTime converts sample rates and sizes in a very elementary manner. Thus, if you want to change the rate and size of an audio track, QuickTime Player may not give you the best results. For cleaner-sounding audio, you'll want to use a tool designed for audio editing and conversion, such as MacSourcery's BarbaBatch.

Making Choices in the Sound Settings Dialog Box

It doesn't make sense to pick a higher rate, size, or number of channels than is already in the sound track. You'll only increase the amount of data by duplicating what's already there; you won't increase the quality. It's also not the best idea to compress a sound file that's already compressed; if you have the original, uncompressed file you should compress that instead.

CHANGING THE CHARACTERISTICS OF A SOUND TRACK

Converting a Music Track to a Sound Track

You'll rarely convert a music track into a sound track, but there are a few occasions when this is useful. There may be times, for example, when you want to use a QuickTime editor that doesn't handle music tracks. You also might not like the way QuickTime lets you alter music tracks (see Chapter 14), preferring instead to convert the music into digital sound. A converted music track may also sound better because when exporting, the QuickTime music synthesizer can do a better job since it doesn't have to play the music in real time.

To convert a music track to a sound track, you must first export the music track as a sound file and then open the exported sound file in QuickTime Player.

To convert a music track to a sound track:

1. From the File menu choose Export (**Figure 13.22**).

2. In the Save dialog box, choose from the Export pop-up menu Music to AIFF (**Figure 13.23**).

3. If you want to specify sound format settings, click the Options button.

   A Sound Settings dialog box appears (**Figure 13.24**), where you can select sound format options, such as sample rate and size. (See "About the Sound Settings Dialog Box," earlier in this chapter.) You cannot, however, pick a compressor when exporting a music track as AIFF.

Figure 13.22 Choose Export from the File menu.

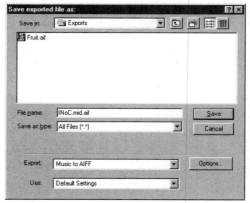

Figure 13.23 Choose Music to AIFF.

Figure 13.24 If you click the Options button, a Sound Settings dialog box appears, allowing you to specify properties of the sound that will be exported.

4. When you've finished setting sound options, click OK to return to the Save dialog box.

5. Click Save.

   It may take a while to export the file.

6. Open the exported sound file as described earlier in this chapter, using the Open Movie command in the File menu.

✔ Tip

■ We generally don't recommend converting a music track to a sound track, since music tracks are so much more efficient. Depending on the settings chosen, the sound track may be hundreds or even thousands of times larger than the original music track and have a correspondingly higher data rate.

CONVERTING A MUSIC TRACK TO A SOUND TRACK

Using QuickTime Player as a Sound Conversion Utility

Because QuickTime Player can open many kinds of sound files, you can use it as a sound conversion utility if you wish to convert between AIFF, WAV, μLaw, or System 7 Sound formats. You can also convert from an MP3 file to one of these other formats. (You cannot, however, convert from or to MPEG Audio Layer I and II.)

To convert a sound file to a different format:

1. In QuickTime Player, open or import the file.

2. From the File menu choose Export (**Figure 13.25**).

3. Choose the format you'd like to convert the file into: AIFF, System 7 Sound, WAV, or μLaw (**Figure 13.26**).

   If you want to compress the sound or change its sample size, rate, or number of channels, click the Options button to open the Sound Settings dialog box. Make your changes, and click OK. (See the section earlier in this chapter explaining the Sound Settings dialog box.)

4. Click Save (**Figure 13.27**).

✔ Tip

■ To export as MP3 from QuickTime Player, you'll need additional software, such as the Fraunhofer MP3 Encoder, which is sold by Terran Interactive.

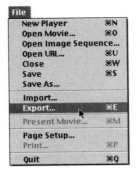

Figure 13.25 After opening or importing your sound file, choose Export from the File menu.

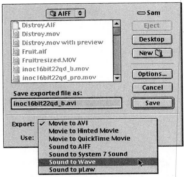

Figure 13.26 Choose the format to which you want to convert the file.

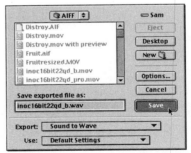

Figure 13.27 Click Save to save the file in the chosen format.

MUSIC TRACKS

Music tracks are very similar to Musical Instrument Digital Interface (MIDI) files—the music-industry standard for representing music.

Both music tracks and MIDI files consist of a sequence of commands specifying what sounds should be played and how they should be played. The sounds (called *instruments*) are not stored in the file. Instead, commands are sent to a hardware or software synthesizer. In music tracks, QuickTime—which contains the instruments—functions as a software synthesizer.

Related to MIDI files are karaoke files, which are essentially MIDI files with textual lyrics.

In this chapter we'll explain how to import or open MIDI and karaoke files, what changes you can make to music tracks within QuickTime Player, and how you can get QuickTime to use an external synthesizer (such as a MIDI keyboard or sound module). We'll also show you how you can convert a music track back to a MIDI file.

Getting MIDI Files

On the Web, you can find MIDI files at http://www.aitech.ac.jp/~ckelly/SMF.html, a comprehensive list of sites with MIDI files. You may also want to try using your favorite search engine to search for .MID and .KAR files.

If you're a musician, you may already know about MIDI music composition tools. A few tools take advantage of QuickTime's built-in instruments to let you compose music without requiring expensive hardware; one of these (for Mac OS) is Uni Software Plus' easy beat.

Converting MIDI Files to QuickTime

QuickTime can import any Standard MIDI file.

To create a music track from a MIDI file:

1. From the File menu choose Import (**Figure 14.1**).

   (Or, you can choose Open Movie from the File menu; everything will work the same way.)

2. Locate and select the MIDI file, and click Convert (**Figure 14.2**).

3. In the Save dialog box that appears, you can click the Options button (**Figure 14.3**) to open the Standard MIDI Import dialog box (**Figure 14.4**), where you can alter certain properties of the resulting music track.

   If you want your music file to play on computers that still use QuickTime 2.0 or QuickTime 2.1 for Mac OS, check the "Compatible with QuickTime 2.0" checkbox.

   Click "Add silence at end" or "Add silence at beginning" to add 1 second of silence to the end or beginning of the movie.

   Click the OK button to return to the Save dialog box.

4. If desired, change the name and location of the file you are about to create, and then click Save.

   A new movie file containing a music track is created.

Figure 14.1 Choose Import from the File menu.

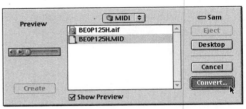

Figure 14.2 Locate a MIDI file and click Convert.

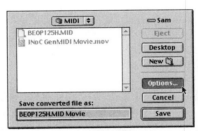

Figure 14.3 Before clicking Save, you may want to click the Options button...

Figure 14.4 ...to open the Standard MIDI Import Options dialog box.

✔ Tips

- MIDI and karaoke files can also be opened directly; in Step 2, before clicking the Convert button, hold down the Command key (Mac OS) or Ctrl key (Windows) so that the ellipses in the Convert button disappear. The file will simply open. The file won't become a QuickTime file, however, until you save it.

- The QuickTime music synthesizer complies with the General MIDI specification, an industry standard. Although you can import Standard MIDI files, the music won't sound the way it's supposed to if the Standard MIDI file doesn't comply with the General MIDI specification.

Converting Karaoke Files to QuickTime

Since karaoke files contain both MIDI and textual data, they become movies with both music and text tracks when converted to QuickTime.

To create a music and text track from a karaoke file:

1. As with MIDI files, from the File menu choose Import or Open Movie, locate the file, and click Convert.

2. You may want to click the Options button and select any of the options available in the top part of the dialog box (as described on the previous page).

   You will notice that the lower portion of the dialog box is not dimmed as it is for MIDI files (**Figure 14.5**). Assuming that you want to import the file's text, make sure that "Import lyrics as karaoke" is checked. You can click the Text options button to open the Text Import Settings dialog box (**Figure 14.6**). See "Specifying Text Track Appearance when You Import" in Chapter 10 for a complete explanation of the options available here.

Figure 14.5 When you import a karaoke file, the lower portion of the Standard MIDI Import dialog box offers you several options.

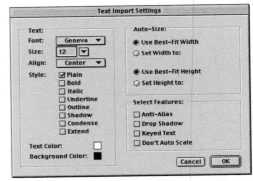

Figure 14.6 If you click the Text Options button in the Standard MIDI Import dialog box, the Text Import Settings dialog box appears so that you can change the properties of the text track that will be created.

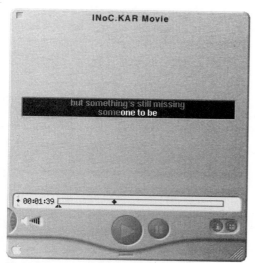

Figure 14.7 An imported karaoke file looks like a text-track movie...

Figure 14.8 ...but it contains both a text track and a music track.

3. In the Text Import Settings dialog box (if you opened it) and the Standard MIDI Import dialog box, click OK to return to the Save dialog box.

4. Click Save.

A window containing a text track appears (**Figure 14.7**). If you check in the Info window, you'll see that the movie contains both a text track and a music track (**Figure 14.8**).

✔ Tip

- There are actually multiple karaoke file formats. QuickTime handles .KAR files, the most popular format.

Changing Instruments in a Music Track

Recall that a music track, like a MIDI file, is composed of a sequence of commands specifying how certain sound samples, or instruments, should be played. Most instruments share the same name and sounds as their real-world counterparts, such as piano, oboe, and bassoon. Some instruments emulate sound effects—for example, a telephone ring or gunshot. In any music track, you can easily switch the instrument used for a certain part of the piece.

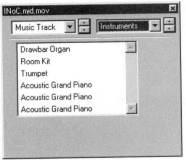

Figure 14.9 The Instruments panel lists the instruments used in the track.

To change instruments:

1. From the Movie menu, choose Get Info to open the movie's Info window.

2. From the left pop-up menu choose the music track, and from the right pop-up menu choose Instruments.

   A list of instruments appears in the window (**Figure 14.9**): These are the instruments currently used in the music track.

3. Double-click an instrument in the list.

   An Instrument Picker dialog box with several pop-up menus appears (**Figure 14.10**).

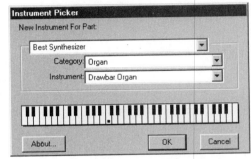

Figure 14.10 When you double-click an instrument in the Instruments panel, this dialog box appears.

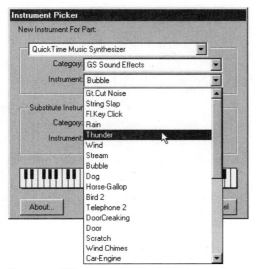

Figure 14.11 When QuickTime Music Synthesizer is chosen, you have some choices that will only work through QuickTime.

4. Leaving Best Synthesizer chosen in the top pop-up menu, pick a new instrument by changing the item chosen in the Category or Instrument pop-up menus (or both).

   For further choices, in the top pop-up menu choose QuickTime Music Synthesizer. The dialog box expands, and the top part of the window presents different Category and Instrument pop-up menu choices than were available when Best Synthesizer was chosen (**Figure 14.11**). These sounds are available as long as the QuickTime music software is installed (part of the normal QuickTime installation). If the file is played on a computer that doesn't have the QuickTime music software (very rare) but is connected to an external synthesizer, the instrument selected in the bottom portion of the window (labeled *Substitute Instrument*) will be used.

✔ Tip

■ If you have an alternate hardware or software synthesizer, it will appear in the top pop-up menu; however, we still recommend choosing Best Synthesizer. See "Playing Music Tracks Through a MIDI Synthesizer" later in this chapter to learn why.

Substituting Your Own Custom Sound for an Instrument in a Music Track (Mac OS Only)

If you've got a music track on a Mac OS computer, you don't have to be satisfied with QuickTime's built-in sound samples. You can use your own sound in place of one of the existing instruments in the music track.

To use one of your own sounds in place of an instrument in a music track:

1. If your sound isn't a System 7 Sound file, open the file in QuickTime Player and export it as a System 7 Sound file. (See "Using QuickTime Player as a Sound Conversion Utility" in Chapter 13 for details.)

2. With your movie containing a music track open in QuickTime Player, choose Get Info from the Movie menu.

3. From the left pop-up menu choose the music track, and from the right pop-up menu choose Instruments.

4. In the Finder, open the folder that contains the System 7 sound file, and position the Info window and the folder window so that you can see both.

5. Drag the sound file to the location in the Info window where the instrument you want to replace is shown (**Figure 14.12**).

   The instrument name is replaced by the name of your sound file (**Figure 14.13**).

   When you play the movie, your sound is used instead of the instrument it replaced.

   The sound data in the sound file becomes part of the QuickTime movie, increasing the size of a music-only file considerably.

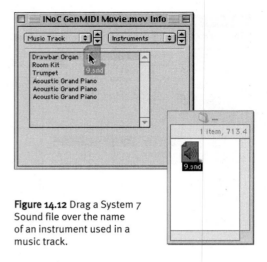

Figure 14.12 Drag a System 7 Sound file over the name of an instrument used in a music track.

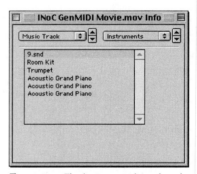

Figure 14.13 The instrument is replaced by your sound.

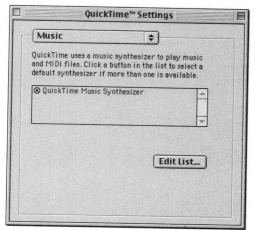

Figure 14.14 The Music panel of the QuickTime Settings control panel lists available synthesizers. If one is missing, click the Edit List button.

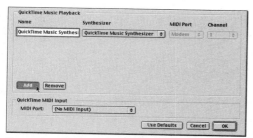

Figure 14.15 If you want to add a new synthesizer, click the Add button.

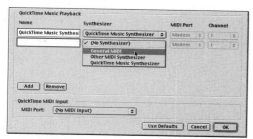

Figure 14.16 When you click the Add button, a new row is created in which you can choose your synthesizer.

Playing Music Tracks Through a MIDI Synthesizer

While QuickTime's built-in music synthesizer is pretty good, you can probably get better audio quality with a hardware synthesizer. If you have a hardware synthesizer that meets the General MIDI specification, you can make QuickTime use it to play a music track. On the Mac, you'll also need MIDI system software, such as Apple's MIDI software, OMS, and FreeMIDI. (See Appendix C for vendor information.) Windows computers normally come with all required MIDI system software.

To tell QuickTime to play music tracks through a MIDI synthesizer connected to your computer:

1. Open the QuickTime Settings control panel, found in your Control Panel(s) folder.

2. From the pop-up menu choose Music to show the Music panel (**Figure 14.14**).

3. Assuming you don't see anything other than QuickTime Music Synthesizer listed in the scrolling field, click the Edit List button. (If your synthesizer is listed, skip to Step 7.)

4. In the QuickTime Music Playback dialog box (**Figure 14.15**), click the Add button. A new row is added.

5. In the pop-up menu in the Synthesizer column for the newly added row, choose your synthesizer (**Figure 14.16**) and then make choices in the MIDI Port and Channel columns (if the pop-up menus are available).

continues on next page

PLAYING THROUGH A MIDI SYNTHESIZER

(The large variety of available software and hardware as well as the many ways it can be configured make it impossible for us to tell you exactly what you'll need to choose here. If your synthesizer doesn't appear, it's likely your MIDI system software is not properly installed or configured.)

6. Click OK.

7. In the QuickTime Settings control panel, your synthesizer should be listed. Select it by clicking the radio button for that line in the list (**Figure 14.17**). (Unlike most radio buttons, this one doesn't get selected when you click the text.)

   Now, when you play movies with music tracks, instruments that are set to Best Synthesizer in the Instrument Picker dialog box will play through your MIDI Synthesizer. (Best Synthesizer is the default.)

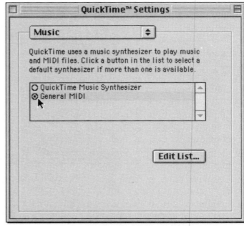

Figure 14.17 The new synthesizer is added to the list of available synthesizers in the Music panel.

✔ Tips

- On Windows computers, a General MIDI synthesizer will usually be available in the list of synthesizers because the sound cards that come in Windows computers normally include a hardware General MIDI synthesizer.

- Even though your synthesizer appears in the pop-up menu in the Instrument Picker dialog box, you should leave Best Synthesizer chosen; this way your synthesizer will be used as long as it's available, but if it's not available, the QuickTime synthesizer will be used.

Figure 14.18 Choose Export from the File menu.

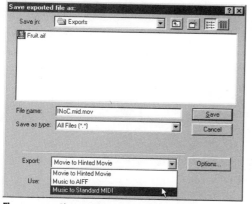

Figure 14.19 Choose Music to Standard MIDI and click Save.

Converting Music Tracks Back to MIDI

Using QuickTime Player's export options, you can save a music track as a standard MIDI file. You'd do this if you wanted to use MIDI editing software to alter the music track.

To export a music track as a MIDI file:

1. From the File menu choose Export (**Figure 14.18**).

2. In the Export pop-up menu in, choose Music to Standard MIDI and click Save (**Figure 14.19**).

✔ Tip

■ If your movie contains more than one music track, when you export as MIDI, QuickTime will export only the first music track listed in the left pop-up menu in the Info window (usually named Music Track 1).

15

DELIVERY BASICS

So you've finished editing your movies, and you'd like to distribute them to the world (or even just to your mother). There are a variety of delivery channels for QuickTime movies, including the Web, CD-ROMs, kiosks, or even such media as Zip disks or—if they're small enough movies—floppies. You may even want to output your movies back to videotape. We'll cover specifics of all these choices in the following chapters.

However, regardless of how you want to distribute your movies, there are some basic concepts you'll need to understand and some tasks you'll want to know how to accomplish. In this chapter we'll explain such concepts as *data rate* and go over methods for preparing movies for final distribution. We'll also talk about incorporating movies into media presentations created with multimedia tools.

About Data Rate and Size

A movie's data rate is the average amount of data per second it contains. We mentioned the concept of a video track's data rate in Chapter 9 and a sound track's data rate in Chapter 13. Of course, all tracks have a data rate—it's just that data rates for video and audio tracks are typically the largest and thus the ones to worry about. A movie's data rate comprises the sum of the data rates of all of its tracks.

The channel through which your movie is delivered has what's called a *bandwidth*—the amount of data per second that particular hardware and software is capable of delivering.

You need to consider how your movie's data rate compares with the bandwidth of the system on which you plan to present your movie. For example, a 4x CD-ROM drive has a theoretical maximum bandwidth of 600 kilobytes per second. If your movie's data rate exceeds that, it will skip and likely be unwatchable.

Internet bandwidths are quite narrow—less than 2 kilobytes per second, in fact, for the slowest modem lines. You want your movie's data rate to be as close to the network bandwidth as possible. The amount you can deviate from this will depend on how long you're willing to make viewers wait before viewing your movie or how much you're willing to sacrifice in terms of playback smoothness. (We'll go into more detail in the next chapter.)

You may also need to be concerned with the *data size* of your movie—the total size of the data it contains (that is, the data rate multiplied by the movie's duration). This is because every storage medium—floppy disks, hard drives, CD-ROMs, DVD-ROMs—has a finite amount of space.

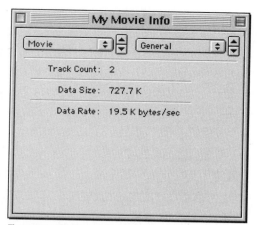

Figure 15.1 The General panel for a movie shows both the data size and the data rate for the movie.

Checking Data Rate and Data Size

Because knowledge of your movie's data size and rate can help you predict how well it will play on a particular platform, we'll show you how to check these. You may also want to know the data size or rate of individual tracks so that you can determine which tracks need to be compressed.

To check the data size and data rate of a movie:

1. From the Movie menu choose Get Info to open the Info window.

2. From the left pop-up menu choose Movie, and from the right pop-up menu choose General.

   The General panel (**Figure 15.1**) shows the data size in bytes, kilobytes (K), or megabytes (MB) and the data rate in bytes per second (bytes/sec), kilobytes per second (Kbytes/sec), or megabytes per second (MB/sec).

To check the data size and data rate of individual tracks:

1. From the Movie menu choose Get Info to open the Info window.

2. From the left pop-up menu choose the track you're interested in, and from the right pop-up menu choose General.

   The General panel for each track shows the data size and data rate.

✔ Tip

- When you compare the data rate of your file to the bandwidth of your delivery platform, you'll need to be careful about your units of measurement: You may have to do some conversions. Kilobytes, for example, are eight times the size of kilobits.

Saving Movies for Distribution

In some cases all you need to do to prepare a movie for distribution is save it. (We described saving in Chapter 6.) In general, if your movie's data rate is as low or lower than your target bandwidth—as is often the case with text, sprite, 3D, and music-track movies—and you are not preparing the movie for RTSP streaming you only need to save it.

Whether you're working on a Mac OS or Windows computer, as long as you use the Save As command, QuickTime automatically saves files so that they are playable on both platforms and are *fast start* (a format good for HTTP Web delivery, which we describe in the next chapter).

You also usually want to save your movie as a self-contained file (**Figure 15.2**). If you're saving a movie on a Mac, you should give it a .mov extension so that Windows computers and Web browsers will recognize it as a QuickTime movie. (When you save a movie on a Windows computer, the .mov extension is added automatically.)

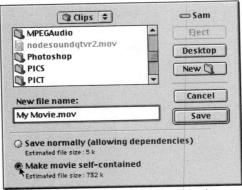

Figure 15.2 In QuickTime Player's Save dialog box, you should save a movie as self-contained unless you have an explicit reason for saving with dependencies.

✔ Tips

- Previous QuickTime versions (prior to 3) didn't automatically save movie files in a format playable on both platforms. If you wish to distribute older QuickTime movies created on a Mac OS computer on both platforms, you may want to open and save them (with the Save As command) using QuickTime Player and the current version of QuickTime. (QuickTime Player doesn't provide any way to check whether your movies are cross-platform.)

- There's no way to guarantee that your movie will play well on all computers. The only way to really be certain is to test it on as many computer systems as possible.

Saving Double-Sized

If you double a movie's window size using the Double Size command in the Movie menu and then save, the movie's file size and data rate don't increase—your movie just *looks* twice as large. QuickTime does a good job of playing back movies at double-size—an effective technique for outputting movies to videotape or putting them on CD-ROMs, kiosks, or the Web.

Exporting Movies as QuickTime Movies

In some cases, you'll want to export your movie rather than simply save it. One of QuickTime Player's export options—called Movie to QuickTime Movie—allows you to do the following things that you can't do by merely saving a file:

◆ **Apply compression to video and sound tracks.** If your movie contains video and sound tracks, you'll probably want to compress them to achieve a desired data rate. (This includes changing such characteristics as frame rate and key frame rate for video, and sample rate and sample size for audio.)

◆ **Combine data in all visual or sound tracks into a single video or sound track.** If you have lower-data-rate visual tracks (3D, sprite, or text) in a movie that also contains a video track, and you don't need any of those tracks' special features (for example, searchable text), you may want to make that data part of the video track. This way, you improve your chances of achieving smooth playback. In addition, if your movie has multiple video or sound tracks, combining them into a single video or sound track will almost definitely smooth playback. (We're referring specifically to QuickTime sound tracks here rather than other audio track types, such as music tracks.)

◆ **Apply visual filters.** Although this may seem like a task you'd want to do earlier— say, while you're editing the file—this is, in fact, where you do so in QuickTime Player.

◆ **Permanently reduce a movie's frame size.** If you reduce the size of a movie's window and then save it, the movie's data size doesn't change because its default "normal" window size remains the same. (That is, when you choose Normal from the Movie menu, the movie will return to its original size.) When you export a movie, however, you can specify a new size, which results in a permanent change and a reduction in data size. After exporting, you can reopen the movie in QuickTime Player, double its size, and resave if you want it to appear big. (See the "Saving Double-Sized" sidebar, earlier in this chapter.) You can also scale it larger for playback on a Web page, as we describe in the next chapter.

◆ **Format the file for Internet streaming.** Depending on whether you plan to use HTTP streaming or RTSP streaming, you can choose different formats to properly structure your file for streaming playback.

To export a movie as a QuickTime movie:

1. From the File menu Choose Export (**Figure 15.3**).

2. From the Export pop-up menu choose Movie to QuickTime Movie (**Figure 15.4**).

3. Click Options.

Figure 15.3 Choose Export from the File menu.

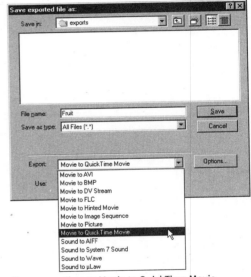

Figure 15.4 Choose Movie to QuickTime Movie.

4. In the Movie Settings dialog box (**Figure 15.5**), make sure that both the Video and Sound checkboxes are selected (unless your movie doesn't contain visual or sound tracks, or you actually want to make a movie that doesn't include video or audio).

5. Click the Settings button in either the Video or Sound areas if you want to change any of the settings to the right of those buttons. (The default settings are rarely appropriate. We'll offer specific compression recommendations in the following chapters.) When you've chosen new settings, click OK to return to the Movie Settings dialog box.

continues on next page

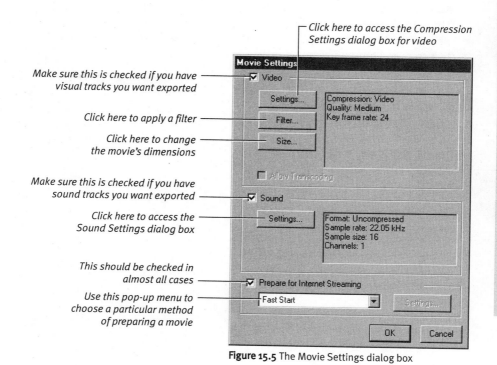

Click here to access the Compression Settings dialog box for video

Make sure this is checked if you have visual tracks you want exported

Click here to apply a filter

Click here to change the movie's dimensions

Make sure this is checked if you have sound tracks you want exported

Click here to access the Sound Settings dialog box

This should be checked in almost all cases

Use this pop-up menu to choose a particular method of preparing a movie

Figure 15.5 The Movie Settings dialog box

EXPORTING MOVIES AS QUICKTIME MOVIES

233

6. If you want to apply a video filter, click Filter in the Video area of the Movie Settings dialog box, (See "Applying Filters," later in this chapter for more information about filters.) When you're done picking and configuring a filter, click OK to return to the Movie Settings dialog box.

7. If you want to change the size of the movie, click Size in the Video area of the Movie Settings dialog box. In the Export Size Settings dialog box, click "Use custom size," type in your desired width and height (**Figure 15.6**), and then click OK to return to the Movie Settings dialog box.

8. In most cases, make sure that the Prepare for Internet Streaming checkbox at the bottom of the Movie Settings dialog box is selected. Then choose one of the options in the pop-up menu: Fast Start, Fast Start-Compressed Header, or Hinted Streaming (**Figure 15.7**). (The next chapter describes the concepts of fast start and hinted streaming in detail.)

Only choose Fast Start-Compressed Header if you are sure the movie will be played with QuickTime 3 or later. (Although movies compressed in this fashion will load somewhat faster, they will not work with earlier versions of QuickTime.)

9. Click OK.

10. Specify a file name (with a .mov extension) and location; then click Save.

Figure 15.6 When you click Size in the Movie Settings dialog box, this Export Size Settings dialog appears. This is where you specify new dimensions for your movie.

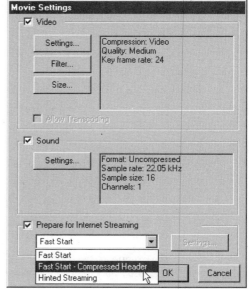

Figure 15.7 In most cases, you'll check Prepare for Internet Streaming and then choose one of the options in this pop-up menu. (See Chapters 16 and 18 for more details.)

✔ **Tips**

■ Once you've chosen Movie to QuickTime Movie (in Step 2 above), you may be able to employ the Use pop-up menu to choose a preconfigured group of settings and then skip right to Step 10. (Note that all the streaming choices are for RTSP streaming.)

■ Be aware that the default settings in the Movie Settings dialog box do not reflect the current status of the video or sound track; to determine those, use the Format panel of the Info window as described in Chapters 9 and 13.

■ If possible, you should avoid recompressing already-compressed video because compressors create visual artifacts (blocky, noisy, or hard-to-discern areas), which are considerably worsened the second time a clip is compressed. By the same token, you should avoid recompressing audio. You always want to use your least compressed movie version.

■ It's actually a good idea to check Prepare for Internet Streaming and to select Fast Start even for CD-ROM and other non-Internet distribution platforms. The only disadvantage to doing so would be that it might take slightly longer to export; however, files exported as Fast Start work just fine in non-Internet contexts and load slightly faster.

■ Many QuickTime compressors work best if the width and height of the movie image are multiples of four. So, in the Export Size Settings dialog box described in Step 7 above, it's best to enter values that are multiples of four.

When Not to Export as a QuickTime Movie

If your movie contains only 3D, music, sprite, or text tracks (and no video or sound tracks), don't export it as a QuickTime movie. Exporting 3D, sprite, or text tracks this way only converts them to video tracks, which have much higher data rates. Music tracks are ignored if you export as a QuickTime movie; they're not even converted to sound tracks, as you might expect. You also can't export MPEG tracks, even though the choice is there in the pop-up menu: You get an error message as soon as you hit Save. If your movie includes a combination of tracks, some of which you'd like to export and some of which should be left alone, see "Compressing Selected Tracks" later in this chapter. If you are preparing a movie for RTSP streaming that has no video or sound tracks, or that has already-compressed video and sound tracks, you'll use the Export to Hinted Movie option. (For more details, see the following chapter.)

Applying Filters

QuickTime includes filters that can be used to alter the appearance of a video track. Using QuickTime Player, you can apply any one of these filters when you export a movie as a QuickTime movie. In the following section, we'll cover the general process for applying a filter as well as provide some examples. In addition, see Table 15.1 for a list of the filters you can access from QuickTime Player.

To apply a filter:

1. From the Movie menu choose Export and then Movie to QuickTime Movie before clicking the Options button to open the Movie Settings dialog box. (These are the steps you would normally follow to export a movie.)

2. Click the Filter button (**Figure 15.8**).

3. In the Choose Video Filter dialog box (**Figure 15.9**), click on a filter in the list on the left.

   Depending on which filter you've selected, you'll be provided with controls and fields (on the right) to vary properties of that filter. (See "Some Example Filters" below.)

4. Adjust the settings using the image sample in the lower left corner of the window to ensure that you're achieving your desired effect.

5. Click OK to return to the Movie Settings dialog box.

   Make any necessary additional changes in the Movie Settings dialog box. (See "Exporting Movies as QuickTime Movies" previously in this chapter for information about the other changes you can make.)

6. Click OK to return to the Export dialog box, specify a file name and location, and click Save.

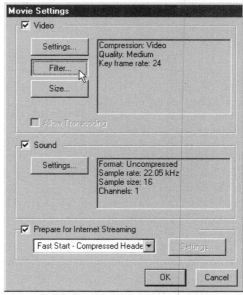

Figure 15.8 In the Movie Settings dialog box, click the Filter button.

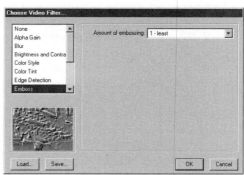

Figure 15.9 The Choose Filter dialog box has a number of filters to choose from. Each has different settings.

Table 15.1

Video Filters	
FILTER	COMMENTS
None	Lets you undo any of the other filters in this table.
Alpha Gain	Lets you manipulate an image's alpha channel.
Blur	Fuzzes the image. You can adjust the amount of blurring and the brightness.
Brightness and Contrast	Brightness lets you make the image lighter or darker. Contrast adjusts an image's color intensity.
Color Style	Lets you add solarization and posterization effects.
Color Tint	Lets you change the image to black and white, tint it any color, and invert colors.
ColorSync (Mac OS only)	Lets you link the movie's image to a ColorSync profile. You can link to a source and a destination profile. Only available if ColorSync system files are installed.
Edge Detection	Finds an image's edges, allowing you to set the edge width and colorize the results.
Emboss	Gives the image a raised, metallic look. You can choose the amount of embossing.
Film Noise	Adds noise to the image so it looks like movie film. You can set various parameters relating to hairs, scratches, dust, and fading.
General Convolution	Lets you enter values in a grid to specify a brightness pattern for the pixels in the image. (Based on a mathematical process called *convolution*.)
HSL Balance	Lets you alter the look of an image by setting its hue, saturation, and lightness.
Lens Flare	Lets you simulate the effect of a bright light (such as the sun) on an image.
RGB Balance	Lets you alter the look of the image by setting its red, green, or blue values.
Sharpen	Sharpens the image. You can set the degree of sharpening and brightness.

✔ Tip

- If you think you'll want to use the same filter settings again, you may want to save those settings. Once you have adjusted settings in the way you desire in Step 4 above, click the Save button in the lower left corner of the dialog box, and you'll be prompted in a standard Save dialog box to save the settings as a file. When you need to reuse those settings, simply click the Load button and select your previously saved file that contains the settings.

APPLYING FILTERS

Some Example Filters

Figure 15.10 shows an original, unfiltered movie image. **Figures 15.11, 15.12,** and **15.13** show this same image after certain filters have been applied as well as how the filters were configured in the Choose Video Filter dialog box.

Figure 15.10 Here's an original unfiltered movie image.

Figure 15.11 The image after applying the Emboss filter with these settings.

Figure 15.12 Here's the image after applying the Color Style filter with these settings.

Figure 15.13 Here's the image after applying the Blur filter with these settings.

Figure 15.14 Choose Extract Tracks from the Edit menu and extract the tracks that you want to compress.

Figure 15.15 Export the movie created by the extraction in order to compress it.

Cloud, Ripple, and Fire

You may have seen examples of the three special effects—Cloud, Ripple, and Fire—included in QuickTime 3 and later. These translucent, ever-changing images seem to float over the underlying movie, and one of them—the Ripple effect—is even interactive: By clicking the image, you can make new ripples appear.

Although these effects resemble filters, the QuickTime architecture doesn't consider them such, and you can't access them via QuickTime Player. You can, however, access them via other tools, such as Electrifier Pro.

Compressing Selected Tracks

There will be times when you want to designate that selected tracks in a movie be compressed while other tracks be left alone. For example, if you have a movie with text and video tracks, you might want to compress the video track but not the text track. Or, you might just want to lower the data rate of your sound track, leaving other tracks as they are.

While other, more expensive tools (such as Media Cleaner Pro) provide simple methods for designating a hands-off approach to certain tracks, there's no correspondingly simple way to do this using QuickTime Player. You'll need to use some combination of techniques covered in this book—copying, pasting, adding, extracting, deleting, exporting, and importing—to achieve the desired result. We'll cover one possibility here. (See "Changing the Characteristics of a Sound Track" in Chapter 13 for an alternative technique.)

To compress only selected tracks in a movie:

1. In the Edit menu use the Extract Tracks command to open the Extract Tracks dialog box and extract the tracks you want to compress (**Figure 15.14**).

   This creates a new movie containing only the extracted tracks.

2. In the File menu use the Export command (**Figure 15.15**) to export the movie created by the extraction. Apply appropriate compression settings. (See "Exporting Movies as QuickTime Movies" earlier in this chapter for details about this process.)

continues on next page

3. Back in the original movie (the one containing all the tracks), in the Edit menu use the Delete Tracks command to access the Delete Tracks dialog box (**Figure 15.16**) so that you can delete the tracks you extracted in Step 1.

4. Open the movie that you exported in Step 2, and select and copy the entire movie. (Be careful not to confused the *extracted* movie with the *exported* movie.)

5. In the original movie, move the Current Location indicator to the far left of the Time slider, hold down the Option key (Mac OS) or Ctrl and Alt keys (Windows), and from the Edit menu choose Add (**Figure 15.17**).

The tracks you extracted are now added back in their compressed form.

✔ Tip

■ We recommend making a copy of your original movie before following this procedure because you can't restore deleted tracks once the movie has been saved.

Figure 15.16 Choose Delete Tracks from the Edit menu and delete the same tracks you extracted.

Figure 15.17 Open the exported movie, copy it all and add it back into the original movie file. (To access the Add command in the Edit menu, Windows users need to hold down the Alt and Ctrl keys; Mac users need to hold down the Option key.)

Better Tools

Although we'll show you the basics of preparing your movies for distribution using QuickTime Player, it's important to know that you can use other tools to accomplish the same tasks. In particular, Media Cleaner Pro from Terran Interactive is generally considered a must-have by most multimedia developers who are processing QuickTime movies for final delivery. (Media Cleaner Pro does an optimal job of compression, and it includes a wizard that can help you make decisions. You can also use it to do a number of things you can't with QuickTime Player, such as cropping movies before compressing them and batch processing movies.)

Table 15.2

Some Authoring Tools That Support QuickTime		
TOOL	AUTHORING PLATFORM	COMPANY
Director	Mac/Windows	Macromedia
Flash	Mac/Windows	Macromedia
HyperCard	Mac	Apple
SuperCard	Mac	IncWell
PowerPoint	Mac/Windows	Microsoft
HyperStudio	Mac/Windows	Roger Wagner Publishing
Katabounga	Mac	Abvent
IShell	Mac/Windows	Tribeworks
ClickWorks	Mac	Pitango
ToolBook	Windows	Asymetrix
Authorware	Mac/Windows	Macromedia
MovieWorks	Mac	Interactive Solutions
MetaCard	Windows (also Unix)	MetaCard Corporation
Special Delivery	Mac	Interactive Media Corp.

The information in this table is accurate at the time of writing. Some products may have added support for additional platforms since the time of writing. See Appendix C for contact information.

Exporting as an AVI File

Because some Windows authoring and presentation tools can't use QuickTime files, you may need to turn your QuickTime movie into an AVI file.

You can use QuickTime Player's Export command (in the File menu), and choose Movie to AVI. Be aware, however, that this export won't work if your movie contains music, wired sprite, Flash, or MPEG tracks.

Overview of Authoring and Presentation Tools That Support QuickTime

Although QuickTime Player works fine as a movie player, many people want to use QuickTime movies as part of larger presentations or applications that include other elements, such as text and graphics. Some also want to create interactive programs.

While QuickTime movies can contain different types of media as well as interactivity, a large set of tools for creating multimedia applications exists; these often provide different advantages or meet specific business requirements.

On the Macintosh, just about all presentation tools (such as PowerPoint) and multimedia authoring tools provide some level of QuickTime support—ranging from simply allowing you to include a QuickTime movie in the presentation to providing extensive methods for interactively controlling the movie. On Windows computers, however, only a select set of tools (Macromedia Director among them) support QuickTime 4—a situation we expect to change soon (many tools support older versions of QuickTime). In the meantime, you can export your QuickTime movies as AVI files (see sidebar).

In the following paragraphs we'll summarize the QuickTime support available in Macromedia Director, Tribeworks iShell, and Apple HyperCard (since these offer the most extensive support). **Table 15.2** lists some other tools that support QuickTime.

QuickTime in Macromedia Director

It's easy to include QuickTime and QuickTime VR movies in projects created with the current version of Macromedia Director 7. You typically choose Import from the File menu, and then choose your movie or movies (**Figure 15.18**) and import them into Director's cast. Once in the cast, QuickTime movies can be included in your presentation, just like any other media element.

With the movie selected in the cast, you can click the *i* button to open the Xtra Cast Member dialog box. Here you can click the Options button (**Figure 15.19**) to open a dialog box in which you can specify various settings for the movie (**Figure 15.20**).

In Director, you can use the chapters in a QuickTime movie to synchronize the movie with other media elements. (Macromedia calls chapters *cue points*.)

In addition, Director's scripting language, Lingo, contains commands that can be used to control the movie interactively, such as those for enabling and disabling tracks, starting and stopping the movie, reading the text in a text track, changing the volume of an audio track, and controlling the view in a VR movie. If you take advantage of Macromedia's free update to Director 7.02, you can also include streaming RTSP movies in your presentation.

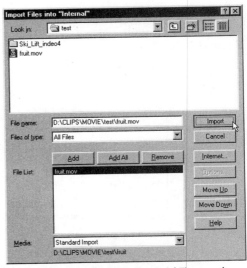

Figure 15.18 In Director 7, import QuickTime movies as you would any media element: From the File menu choose Import, and then use this dialog box to select your QuickTime movie or movies.

Figure 15.19 In Director's Xtra Cast Member dialog box (which you can access by selecting the movie in the cast and clicking the *I* button), click the Options button...

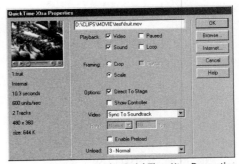

Figure 15.20 ...to open the QuickTime Xtra Properties window where you can specify settings for the movie.

Figure 15.21 In iShell, you can set some basic properties of a movie in the Root window.

Figure 15.22 Without any scripting, iShell allows you to trigger actions when certain events occur, such as when the movie reaches a specific time.

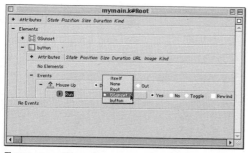

Figure 15.23 Other elements, such as buttons, can control movies. Here a button is programmed to play a movie.

QuickTime in Tribeworks iShell

Tribeworks' iShell is a relative newcomer to the authoring tools market. As a full-featured cross-platform multimedia tool, it naturally includes support for QuickTime movies. In fact, adding QuickTime movies to an iShell project can be as easy as dragging a movie file from your desktop onto the iShell Layout window. Basic properties can be set in the Root window (**Figure 15.21**).

With iShell, you can easily (and without scripting) recognize various events, such as user interactions or specific times in movie playback. For example, you can trigger an action to occur (**Figure 15.22**) when the movie reaches a certain QuickTime chapter (or *cue* as iShell calls it). You can also have other objects, such as buttons, control QuickTime movies (**Figure 15.23**).

AUTHORING AND PRESENTATION TOOLS

Using iShell, you can apply built-in QuickTime filters and effects. And you can also include streaming RTSP movies in your presentation.

The model for using iShell is different than for most other software tools. Rather than purchase or license iShell, you become a Tribeworks member to use it; you may want to check out the free membership option to start (details are at the Tribeworks Web site). As a member, you're qualified to purchase iShell plug-ins, some of which provide additional control over QuickTime movies.

QuickTime in Apple HyperCard

HyperCard is a Mac-only application. A movie can be added to a HyperCard stack in a number of ways, one of the easiest of which is to add a button to a card, click Task in the button's Info window, and assign a Movie task (**Figure 15.24**).

The current version of HyperCard (2.4) includes a huge number of scripting elements for controlling and testing just about every aspect of a movie's appearance and behavior. Using HyperTalk (HyperCard's scripting language), you can do many of the things you can do to a movie in QuickTime Player—as well as some that you can't. Some examples include exporting a movie, finding text in a text track, rotating and skewing a movie, specifying actions to occur when the movie reaches a certain point, specifying a graphics mode and transparency color, accessing copyright information, specifying a language for a track, and moving sprites in a sprite track.

✔ Tip

■ Note that you may also be able to present what you need as a Web page or series of Web pages. The next two chapters cover the use of QuickTime movies on Web pages.

Figure 15.24 You can attach a Movie task to a button in a HyperCard stack.

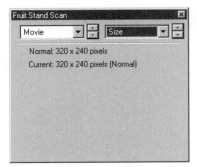

Figure 15.25 The Size panel for the movie displays the movie's width and height. The width for this movie is 320 pixels. The height for this movie is 240 pixels; including the controller, it's 256 pixels.

Checking the Dimensions of a Movie

Whether you intend to put your movie on a Web page or use it in an interactive presentation created with a multimedia authoring tool, you'll probably need to know your movie's frame size. (This will help you plan screen layout and write your HTML code.)

To determine the dimensions of a movie:

1. From the Movie menu, choose Get Info.

2. In the left pop-up menu choose Movie, and from the right pop-up menu choose Size.

   The Size panel (**Figure 15.25**) tells you the dimensions of the movie (width by height) at its normal size as well as the dimensions at which it is currently set. (The second line will only differ from the first if the window size has been altered. See "Changing Window Sizes" in Chapter 3.) The word *none* appears for movies with no visual track.

✔ Tip

■ The dimensions listed don't include the height of the standard controller, which is 16 pixels. To determine the height of the movie including the controller (which you will often need to do), add 16 to the height stated in this panel.

QuickTime
on the
Internet: Basics

If you've decided to deliver your QuickTime movies over the Internet, you're not alone: There are more QuickTime movies on the Web than movie files in any other video format.

In this chapter, we'll start by explaining the concept of *streaming video* and what it means in the context of QuickTime movies. In particular, we'll discuss the two types of streaming QuickTime allows: RTSP and HTTP. We'll then get into some specifics about how to best prepare QuickTime files for streaming using QuickTime Player.

Finally, we'll detail the HTML you use to put a movie on a Web page. In the following chapter we'll explore some special techniques for additional Internet delivery options.

About Streaming

As digital video becomes more popular on the Web, *streaming* is a term heard with increasing frequency.

Although the term has a number of definitions, many people understand it to mean that the media plays immediately rather than waiting for the file to be downloaded.

QuickTime now offers two types of streaming: *HTTP streaming* and *RTSP streaming*.

HTTP streaming has been available since the introduction of QuickTime 2.5 several years ago. With HTTP streaming, you simply put your movie files on a Web (HTTP) server as you do Web pages and image files. Movies are downloaded in their entirety to the user's computer, where the QuickTime plug-in plays them. This is considered streaming because the movie can start playing before its file has been completely downloaded. The QuickTime plug-in determines when enough of an HTTP streaming movie has been downloaded to enable it to play continuously to the end. Movies with very low data rates—such as those that can be achieved with QuickTime's low-data-rate track types or its excellent compression technologies—can begin playing immediately. (This technique is sometimes generically referred to as *progressive downloading*; Apple uses the term *fast start* to refer to movies that are formatted for HTTP streaming.)

New to QuickTime 4 is RTSP streaming: In this method, a dedicated media server sends out movie data on an as-needed basis; no file is stored on the viewer's computer. If the network is congested, preventing portions of the movie from arriving on time, RTSP will ignore the fact that there's data missing. Viewers may not see or hear all the data, but what they do experience occurs at the intended time. This is how traditional streaming technologies work.

No Browser Required

In previous versions of QuickTime, the ability to access movies over the Internet was built into the QuickTime browser plug-in, so the only way to view Internet video was with a Web browser.

With QuickTime 4, Internet video is now a function of QuickTime (not just the plug-in), so movies you put on the Internet can be accessed from just about any application that supports QuickTime.

We've already shown you how QuickTime Player does this (using the Open URL command). Tools such as word processing, presentation, and email applications can also open movies residing just about anywhere on the Internet. (At this time many more applications supporting QuickTime are available for Mac OS computers than for Windows machines. For example, a QuickTime Web movie can be opened and displayed inside a PowerPoint presentation or a Microsoft Word document on a Mac OS computer but not a Windows computer.)

RTSP Vs. HTTP Streaming

Your decision about whether to use HTTP or RTSP streaming may be determined simply by whether you have access to a QuickTime streaming server—a requirement for RTSP streaming (see "QuickTime Streaming Servers" sidebar). However, even if you have access to a QuickTime streaming server, you need to consider other factors.

Reasons to use HTTP streaming

One advantage of HTTP streaming is that if the viewer wishes to replay the data, it doesn't need to be served over the network again—it's already on their hard drive. With RTSP streaming, in contrast, the data needs to be served over the network again if the viewer wishes to replay the movie.

With HTTP streaming, you can also provide higher-data-rate (and thus higher-quality) files—if you're willing to make users wait for enough of the file to be downloaded. (HTTP guarantees delivery of all the movie data—no matter how long it takes. With RTSP streaming, users will experience dropouts if the network can't deliver all of the data on time.)

In addition, only video, audio, text, music, and tween tracks can be streamed via RTSP. If you have other track types (sprites or 3D, for example), you must use HTTP. (You can, however, deliver a movie in which some tracks are streamed via HTTP and others via RTSP; see "Preparing Movies for Mixed RTSP and HTTP Streaming" later in this chapter.)

Reasons to use RTSP streaming

HTTP streaming can be a problem for lengthy movies since viewers must have enough room to store the file. HTTP streaming prevents users from randomly accessing portions of the clip until the file has been downloaded. Finally, use RTSP streaming if you want to broadcast video live.

About Live Streaming

Because QuickTime 4 supports RTSP streaming without files, it's possible to do live broadcasts, where all viewers see the same movie data at the same time. (This contrasts with *stored streaming*, also called *on-demand streaming*, where each viewer can view any portion of a movie at any time.)

To broadcast live, you need special software, usually called a *broadcaster*. The broadcaster captures, compresses, and formats the media for broadcast. High-volume broadcasting usually requires two machines—one with the broadcaster software and a second to act as the RTSP streaming server.

Currently, the only QuickTime streaming broadcaster is the Sorenson Broadcaster.

Preparing Movies for HTTP Streaming

In preparing a movie for HTTP streaming, it's important to get the movie's data rate relatively close to the bandwidth of the network connection you expect users to have. If the movie's data rate is higher than the available bandwidth, users will have to wait until a certain amount of the file has downloaded before it starts playing (**Figures 16.1** and **16.2**). If a movie's data rate is only slightly higher, this wait may be quite short—perhaps no more than a few seconds, which for all intents and purposes would be considered streaming.

If your movie contains video and sound tracks, you'll want to follow the process we described in the previous chapter for compressing video and sound tracks using QuickTime Player's Export command. We'll review those steps below.

If your movie contains low-data-rate tracks (music, sprite, 3D, or text), you generally only need to save the file with the Save As command, as described in "Saving Movies" in Chapter 6 (**Figure 16.3**).

Besides ensuring that the data rate is low enough, you need to save the movie in a fast-start format. (Fast start is what enables QuickTime to begin playing the movie before it has been completely downloaded.) This occurs automatically when you save as a self-contained file and is an option when you export a movie to compress it.

Figure 16.1 When an HTTP movie is being downloaded for viewing on a Web page, the shaded portion of the slider represents the amount of the movie that has been downloaded. The higher the data rate and the longer the movie, the more data that needs to be downloaded before the movie will play.

Figure 16.2 When an HTTP movie is being downloaded in QuickTime Player, the frame around the Time slider is dotted to represent the portion of the movie that has yet to be downloaded.

Figure 16.3 If your movie has a low enough data rate, you need only save it using the Save As command; it will automatically be saved as a fast-start movie.

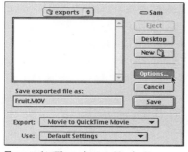

Figure 16.4 If your movie has high data–rate video and audio tracks, you need to compress it. Start by choosing Export in the File menu.

Figure 16.5 Then choose Movie to QuickTime Movie and click the Options button in the Export pop-up menu.

Figure 16.6 The Settings buttons open dialog boxes in which you can choose compression settings for your video and sound tracks.

To compress a movie and make it fast start:

1. From the File menu, choose Export (**Figure 16.4**).

2. In the Export pop-up menu, choose Movie to QuickTime Movie and then click the Options button (**Figure 16.5**) to open the Movie Settings dialog box.

3. By clicking the Settings buttons in the Video and Sound areas (**Figure 16.6**), you can access the dialog boxes where you make video and sound compression choices. (In "Choosing Video Compression Settings" and "Choosing Sound Compression Settings" later in this chapter, we'll examine the appropriate compression choices for Web video and sound tracks.)

4. After making choices in each of these dialog boxes, click OK to return to the Movie Settings dialog box.

5. In the bottom of the Movie Settings dialog box, check Prepare for Internet Streaming.

continues on next page

PREPARING MOVIES FOR HTTP STREAMING

251

6. In the pop-up menu below the Prepare for Internet Streaming checkbox, choose either Fast Start or Fast Start-Compressed Header (**Figure 16.7**).

Only choose Fast Start-Compressed Header if you are sure the movie will be played with QuickTime 3 or later. Although movies compressed this way will load a bit faster, they will not work with earlier versions of QuickTime.

7. Click OK to close the Movie Settings dialog box.

8. Specify a new file name and location for your movie (if desired), and click Save.

✔ Tips

■ One mistake people often make is placing movie files created for CD-ROM on the Web. Because such files have relatively high data rates, users often have to wait minutes or even hours before the movie begins to play.

■ It's even a bad idea to recompress for the Web movies that were originally compressed for CD-ROM. To get the best-looking video, you'll want to track down the originally captured files (which should have light or no compression), and reedit and recompress them.

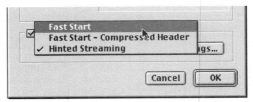

Figure 16.7 Check Prepare for Internet Streaming, and select one of the Fast Start options.

What's the Right Data Rate?

When trying to estimate a good target data rate for your movie, be certain you know what units are being used: *bytes* or *bits*. QuickTime Player reports data rates in bytes, kilobytes, or megabytes per second. Network bandwidths are usually expressed in kilobits per second. A byte is 8 bits. So, a 28.8 modem theoretically moves data at 3.6 (28.8 divided by 8) kilobytes per second.

A quick way to estimate a data rate (in kilobytes) that will provide a good-quality streaming experience (that is, one that won't require a long wait for HTTP movies or cause dropouts for RTSP movies) is to simply divide the bandwidth by ten and round down. (Dividing by ten rather than eight is faster; plus, it gives you a lower, more conservative estimate that usually ends up being more accurate because networks rarely reach their theoretical speeds.)

So, if you're creating a movie to be played over 33.6 modems, a good target data rate is about 3 kilobytes per second. (It may also help you to know that single-channel ISDN lines are 56 kilobits per second, dual-channel ISDN lines are 112 kilobits per second, and T1 lines are 1.5 megabits per second.)

And don't forget that the total data rate is the sum of the data rates of all of a movie's tracks—including the audio data rate.

Figure 16.8 If a movie needs to be hinted *and* compressed, choose Export from the File menu.

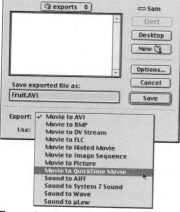

Figure 16.9 Choose Movie to QuickTime Movie from the Export pop-up menu.

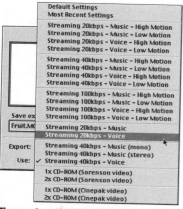

Figure 16.10 Check the Use pop-up menu to determine whether there's a preset that might work for you. If so, choose it.

Preparing Movies for RTSP Streaming

As with HTTP streaming, you'll need to make sure that the data rate of your RTSP movie is low enough. In fact, with RTSP streaming, it's even more important that the data rate be as low or lower than the lowest-bandwidth connection through which you intend the movie to be viewed (see sidebar on previous page). Otherwise, the movie will appear to skip and jump, and viewers may miss portions of it.

You also need to *hint* the movie—that is, add information to the movie that the streaming server uses to determine how to break movie data into packets and then send out that data.

If your movie needs to be compressed *and* hinted, you'll follow one technique. If your movie already has a low data rate, you'll follow a slightly different technique.

To compress and hint a movie:

1. From the File menu, choose Export (**Figure 16.8**).

2. From the Export pop-up menu, choose Movie to QuickTime Movie (**Figure 16.9**).

3. Pull down the Use pop-up menu (**Figure 16.10**) and see whether any of the options listed there describe what you want for your final movie. (All the choices listed as Streaming are for RTSP streaming and will hint your movie.) If any option applies, choose it. You can then skip to Step 9. If an option appears close to what you're looking for, choose it but continue with the following steps to fine-tune or verify the settings.

continues on next page

PREPARING MOVIES FOR RTSP STREAMING

4. Click the Options button.

The Movie Settings dialog box appears (**Figure 16.11**).

5. In the Video and Sound areas click the Settings buttons to specify compression settings for the resulting video and audio track. (See "Compressing Video for the Web" and "Compressing Sound for the Web," later in this chapter for some specific compression choices.)

6. In the bottom of the Movie Settings dialog box, check Prepare for Internet Streaming.

7. In the pop-up menu below the Prepare for Internet Streaming checkbox, choose Hinted Streaming (**Figure 16.12**).

You can click the Settings button to the right of this pop-up menu to further specify some settings; however, see "Hinting Options" sidebar first.

8. Click OK to close the Movie Settings dialog box.

9. Specify a new file name and location for your movie, if desired, and click Save.

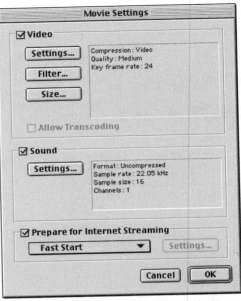

Figure 16.11 If none of the preset choices in the Use menu seems appropriate, or if you want to fine-tune a preset, click the Options button to open the Movie Settings dialog box, where you can click the Settings buttons to access dialog boxes for setting video and sound compression options.

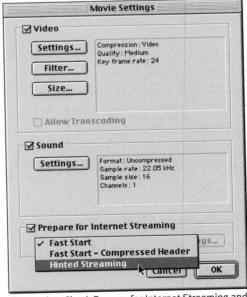

Figure 16.12 Check Prepare for Internet Streaming and choose Hinted Streaming.

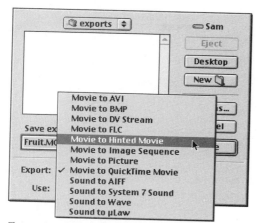

Figure 16.13 If a movie only needs to be hinted, use the Export command but choose Movie to Hinted Movie.

To hint a movie without compressing it:

1. From the File menu, choose Export.

2. From the Export pop-up menu, choose Movie to Hinted Movie (**Figure 16.13**). (You can click Options, but the default settings are recommended. See "Hinting Options" sidebar.)

3. Click Save.

✔ Tip

■ If you have a movie in which some tracks need to be compressed and others don't, you can use the Extract Tracks and Delete Tracks commands (see "Extracting Tracks" and "Deleting Tracks" in Chapter 7) to split the movie into two separate movies—one that needs to be hinted and another that needs to be both hinted and compressed. Follow the appropriate set of steps (above) for each of these movies, and then put them back together as described in "Combining Tracks with the Add and Add Scaled Commands" in Chapter 7.

Hinting Options

If when exporting to a QuickTime movie, you click the Settings button to the right of the pop-up menu where you chose Hinted Streaming, the Hint Exporter Settings dialog box appears. Alternatively, if when exporting to a Hinted Movie, you click Options, you'll also get the Hint Exporter Settings dialog box.

In the Hint Exporter Settings dialog box, you can click Optimize Hints For Server to allow the server to support more viewers. However, this sort of optimization is only useful for certain streaming servers (the Mac OS X server is one), and it doubles the movie's file size.

You can also click the Track Hinter Settings button to specify certain details about how the tracks will be prepared for streaming. Unless you understand the intricacies of your server and network, as well as how packet networks work, these settings should be left as they are.

Preparing Movies for Mixed RTSP and HTTP Streaming

You may have a movie in which you want some tracks served using RTSP (for example, video and audio tracks) and other tracks that can only be served using HTTP (for example, 3D or sprite tracks). You can use QuickTime Player to prepare such a movie for streaming.

To prepare a movie in which some tracks will be served via RTSP and some tracks will be served via HTTP:

1. Split the movie into two separate movies: one containing the tracks you want streamed via RTSP and the other containing the tracks you can serve only through HTTP.

    To do this, use the Extract Tracks and Delete Tracks commands as described in "Extracting Tracks" and "Deleting Tracks" in Chapter 7. For example, you can extract all the tracks intended for HTTP serving (**Figure 16.14**) and then delete them from the original movie (**Figure 16.15**), leaving a movie with only the tracks you want served via RTSP.

2. Prepare the movie you want to stream via RTSP as described in "Preparing Movies for RTSP Streaming" earlier in this chapter.

3. Prepare the other movie as described in "Preparing Movies for HTTP Streaming" earlier in this chapter.

4. Upload the RTSP movie to your streaming QuickTime server.

5. In QuickTime Player, from the File menu choose Open URL, and in the Open URL dialog box, enter the URL of the RTSP movie you uploaded in Step 4. Then click OK (**Figure 16.16**).

    QuickTime Player starts receiving the RTSP stream.

Figure 16.14 To split your movie into two separate movies, you can extract the tracks intended for HTTP serving (or those intended for RTSP serving).

Figure 16.15 You should then delete whatever tracks you extract, leaving only the other type of tracks.

Figure 16.16 Once the movie with the tracks for RTSP streaming is properly prepared (hinted) and uploaded to a QuickTime Streaming server, use the Open URL command in the File menu to open it over the network.

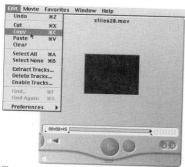

Figure 16.17 Select all the data in the movie opened over the network and choose Copy from the Edit menu.

Figure 16.18 Open the movie with the tracks for HTTP streaming and add the data from the RTSP movie that you opened over the network. The Add command appears in the Edit menu when you hold down the Option key (Mac OS) or Ctrl and Alt keys (Windows).

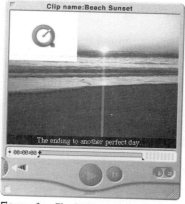

Figure 16.19 The RTSP movie is added to the HTTP movie. Immediately after adding the data you'll see only the QuickTime logo as the connection is being made.

6. Select all the data (by choosing Select All from the Edit menu, and then from the Edit menu, choose Copy (**Figure 16.17**).

7. Open the movie prepared for HTTP streaming, and move the Current Selection indicator to where you want the RTSP tracks to start playing (usually the beginning).

8. Hold down the Option key (Mac OS) or Ctrl and Alt keys (Windows), and from the File menu choose Add (**Figure 16.18**). The visual portion of the RTSP movie is placed in the upper left of the window (**Figure 16.19**). If you want to change the location of the visual portion of the RTSP movie, use the Size and Layer panels, as described in Chapter 8.

9. From the File menu, choose Save As, and save the movie as a self-contained file with a new name.

10. Upload the movie you saved in Step 9 to your HTTP server.

11. If you want to embed this movie on a Web page, follow the instructions found later in this chapter in "Embedding an HTTP QuickTime Movie" on a Web Page.

   When a viewer opens this movie over the Internet, it will automatically link to your RTSP server and play the tracks from the RTSP movie you uploaded in Step 4.

✔ Tip

- In Step 9, you can save the movie allowing dependencies. However, if you do so, in Step 10 you must upload both the newly saved movie and the movie consisting of the tracks you want streamed over HTTP (that is, the one you opened in Step 7). Don't change the time scale of the RTSP data when add. (In other words, use the Add command rather than the Add Scaled command.)

Choosing Video Compression Settings

Unfortunately, it's impossible to provide the one thing everybody wants: a precise recipe for compressing your video for the Web. The settings you choose should depend on the content of your video, your personal aesthetics, your audience, and many other factors.

We can, however, give you some tips and guidelines that will help you make appropriate choices, whether you're doing HTTP or RTSP streaming. (Use this information only as a starting point, though; even professionals experiment with different setting combinations to achieve the proper balance of data rate, frame rate, and image quality.)

To compress video for the Web using QuickTime Player, use the Compression Settings dialog box (**Figure 16.20**), which you access during the compression process outlined in both "Preparing Movies for HTTP Streaming" and "Preparing Movies for RTSP Streaming" earlier in this chapter. Here, we'll comment on each choice you're required to make in that dialog box. Remember that other applications provide the same choices, so the information we provide here applies no matter what QuickTime tool you use to do the compression.

Making Web-appropriate choices in the Compression Settings dialog box:

◆ **Compressor**: In general, the best of the built-in QuickTime compressors for Web video is *Sorenson Video*. This compressor does an excellent job of delivering good quality at the very low data rates required for streaming Web delivery. Alternatively, you may want to try with *H.263* if you need very low data rates and your video has a good deal of motion.

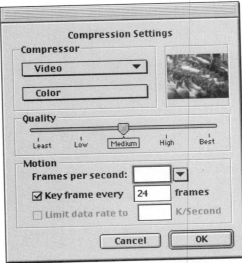

Figure 16.20 The Compression Settings dialog box is where you specify various settings for the video track.

Cinepak is yet another choice, though it won't achieve very low data rates. It should be used when you know that some of your viewers won't have version 3 or later of QuickTime; neither Sorenson Video nor H.263 decompressors were included in QuickTime prior to that. It's also a good choice if your viewers have very slow computers; both Sorenson and H.263 require Pentiums or Power Macs, and Sorenson doesn't work well on computers with processors slower than 120 MHz. (However, there's a way to create a movie that will work for pre-QuickTime 3 users but still provide the advanced features of QuickTime 3 or 4; see "Creating Alternate Movies" in Chapter 17.) For computer-generated imagery, if you don't like the results you're getting with Sorenson Video or Cinepak, you might also want to try the *Graphics* compressor or the *Animation* compressor. (The former achieves lower data rates but only works in 256 colors and decompresses more slowly. So, it may not perform well on old computers.)

◆ **Colors**: Some compressors don't let you choose the number of colors, but when they do, we generally recommend that you opt for the greatest number available. Decreasing the number of colors doesn't usually lower your data rate enough to warrant the resultant loss in quality. Of course, if your movies only use, say, 256 colors, there's no reason to choose more than that.

◆ **Quality**: Remember, the higher the quality, the lower the amount of compression and thus the higher the data rate. We recommend picking a value in the middle of the scale on your first test.

◆ **Frame rate**: The fewer the frames, the lower the data rate. Most current streaming Web video has frame rates of 2 to 10 frames per second. Try to stick to the

Can It Be Smaller?

If you reduce the window size when you export (by clicking the Size button in the Movie Settings dialog box), you'll get a correspondingly smaller file and lower data rate. Although this isn't acceptable for all video clips, it will often help you achieve a lower data rate while retaining more of your image and motion quality. You can later stretch the frame size for playback, either by changing its size in QuickTime Player and then saving again, or by scaling it on your Web page; neither of these techniques increases file size or data rate.

bottom of that range for RTSP streaming. Either way, try a low number to start. And to get the best results, use a number that divides evenly into the movie's frame rate before compression. (For example, if your movie currently has 30 frames per second, try 2, 3, 5, 6, 7.5, or 10.)

◆ **Key-frame rate**: The higher the number here, the lower the data rate. The best choice will depend on which compressor you choose. Sorenson Video works well with a key-frame rate that's about ten times the frame rate; so try a key frame every 50 frames if your chosen frame rate is 5, and then see if you can get away with even fewer key frames (that is, a higher number). Most Cinepak movies, however, play best with a key frame every second or two; so for a frame rate of 3, try 3 or 6 in this field, and then try higher numbers.

◆ **Data rate**: Not all compressors let you set a data rate, but Sorenson Video, Cinepak, and H.263 will. Specifying a number here limits the data rate to that number of kilobytes per second, increasing the compression and lowering the quality to achieve that rate.

The correct number here will depend on the connection speed of your target audience, how much compression your movie can stand, and the type of streaming experience you wish to provide. With Sorenson Video or H.263, you can usually get data rates that approach modem bandwidths—as long as you have a small frame size and a low frame rate. With Cinepak, don't even try to get a data rate low enough for streaming over modem lines; even with quarter-screen movies, about 40 kilobytes per second is as low as you can go if you want something that's recognizable as video. It's important to realize that the data rate you specify here doesn't include the data rate of your audio.

Spending More to Get Better Results

Although the compressors that come with QuickTime are quite good and will be sufficient for most users, those who want the absolute best-looking video may want to consider purchasing the Sorenson Developer Edition compressor, which costs $500 for unlimited use.

You can obtain other compressors to use with QuickTime, too; however, the advantage of Sorenson Developer Edition is that movies compressed with it can be played back with the standard Sorenson compressor included with QuickTime 3 or 4. With other compressors, anyone who views your movie must have the same compressor, or at least a compatible decompressor, installed on their system. And even if you tell them where they can get the necessary decompressor free of charge, Web users generally don't like to download and install extra files.

No matter which compressor you use, you'll get better results if you access it via Media Cleaner Pro, which includes lots of built-in tricks and optimizes compression in such a way that image quality is retained.

Figure 16.21 Use the Sound Settings dialog box to specify sound settings, including compressor.

Choosing Sound Compression Settings

Even though sound isn't as data-heavy as video, you'll still want to compress it for Web playback.

You make your sound compression choices from the Sound Settings dialog box (**Figure 16.21**), which you access during the general export and compression process described in "Preparing Movies for HTTP Streaming" and "Preparing Movies for RTSP Streaming" earlier in this chapter. Here we'll provide some Web-specific guidance for making your sound compression choices. (See Chapter 13 for more in-depth coverage of this dialog box.)

Making choices in the Sound Settings dialog box:

◆ **Compressor:** Two sound codecs that were new to QuickTime 3 provide very high compression ratios while maintaining good-quality sound. For sound tracks containing only voice, use *Qualcomm PureVoice*. For most other types of sound, use *QDesign Music*. For HTTP streaming, *IMA 4:1* is a good choice if you believe that some of your viewers won't have QuickTime 3 installed. (Another consideration: You need a Power Mac or Pentium-based machine to compress using QDesign or PureVoice.)

◆ **Rate:** In general, we recommend choosing 8 kHz or 11.025 kHz for the rate. With Qualcomm PureVoice, you might even want to go as high as 22.050 kHz to get acceptable quality.

◆ **Size:** Choose 8-bit if it's available; however, some compressors only work in 16-bit.

◆ **Use:** Mono is best unless it's crucial that your track play back in stereo.

Professional Sound Compression

Just as you can purchase a professional versions of the Sorenson Video compressor, you can also buy a professional version of the QDesign Music compressor when you need to get the lowest data rate while still retaining high-quality sound. (The professional version of QDesign Music also compresses considerably faster.)

You can also purchase professional software tools for QuickTime sound compression.
One of these is MacSourcery's BarbaBatch, which provides optimal sound conversion and compression as well as the ability to process many files simultaneously.

✔ Tip

■ If you use QDesign Music with QuickTime 4 to compress, users must have QuickTime 4 to play back your movie. (QuickTime 3 shipped with version 1 of QDesign Music, and QuickTime 4 shipped with version 2 of QDesign Music; version 1 can't decompress version 2 files.)

About MP3

MP3 is a popular file format for delivering music. Just because it's popular, however, doesn't mean it's always the right choice. If you don't have a specific need to deliver MP3 files (for example, for playback on MP3 devices), you're much better off exporting as a QuickTime movie and using the QDesign Music compressor: You can get much lower, more appropriate Web data rates with QDesign than with MP3 while achieving comparable audio quality.

If you do have a specific need to distribute your sound-only movies using MP3, you can convert them with Terran's Media Cleaner Pro (which comes with an MP3 encoder), or you can purchase this same MP3 export component from Terran for $99 so that you can use it with QuickTime Player (or any other tool that exports QuickTime movies). Mac users can also download the MPecker MP3 encoder free of charge (from http://www.anime.net/~go/mpeckers.html). To use MPecker, you must export the file from QuickTime Player as an AIFF file—in the Export dialog box, choose Sound to AIFF—which MPecker can then encode. (Note that some people think MPecker-encoded MP3 files don't sound as good as those created with the encoder included with Media Cleaner; you should judge for yourself.)

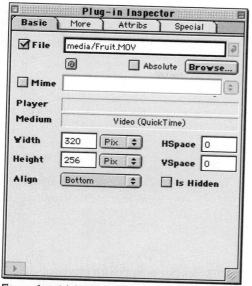

Figure 16.22 Adobe GoLive lets you insert a QuickTime movie and then specify settings in this dialog box.

Embedding an HTTP QuickTime Movie on a Web Page

If a QuickTime movie is to appear on a Web page, that page's HTML must include an EMBED tag—the standard tag for embedding content on Web pages. You can type the EMBED tag yourself or use a WYSIWIG Web authoring tool that supports QuickTime.

If you are using a WYSIWIG tool you generally insert the QuickTime file (in much the same way you'd insert a graphic), and then choose specific settings in a dialog box. The EMBED tag is automatically generated; in most cases, you don't even need to look at it if you don't want to. We can't cover the precise methods used in all tools, but see **Figure 16.22** for an example.

The following explains how to write the simplest EMBED tag using only the required attributes; in the next chapter we discuss some additional attributes that you can add.

✔ Tip

- If you have no previous experience writing your own HTML, we recommend Peachpit's *HTML 4 for the World Wide Web: Visual QuickStart Guide*.

To write the minimal HTML necessary for embedding an HTTP streaming QuickTime movie on a Web page:

1. If your movie name doesn't already end in .mov, rename it so it does.

   The .mov extension enables servers and browsers to recognize the file as a QuickTime file.

2. Place your cursor in the location of the HTML body of the Web page where you want the movie to appear.

3. Type `<EMBED SRC="mymovie.mov"`, replacing "`mymovie.mov`" with your movie file location. (You can use relative or absolute URLs.)

4. Type a space and then `WIDTH=w HEIGHT=h`, replacing `w` with the width of your movie and `h` with the height of your movie. (See "Checking the Dimensions of a Movie" in Chapter 15 if you're not sure what these values are.)

5. Type a final `>` to close the EMBED tag. (See **Figure 16.23** for the full tag.)

When this page is opened in a browser, viewers will see a QuickTime logo (**Figure 16.24**) and then the movie itself (**Figure 16.25**).

✔ Tip

■ If you're using a WYSIWYG editor that doesn't directly support QuickTime, you may find that it does include a menu choice that allows you to insert an HTML tag. Netscape Composer, for example, has an HTML Tag command in its Insert menu. When you choose this, a dialog box appears in which you can simply type the EMBED tag as described above—simpler than having to switch to editing your HTML source code.

Figure 16.23 When writing your own HTML, use the EMBED tag to insert a movie into a Web page.

Figure 16.24 The QuickTime logo appears for a second or less...

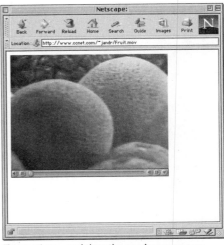

Figure 16.25 ...and then the movie appears on the page.

Configuring a Web Server for QuickTime

The MIME Types configuration file in the HTTP Web server that holds your QuickTime movie must include a listing for QuickTime files. Most companies and educational institutions, as well as most Internet service providers (ISPs) set this correctly on their Web servers. However, if your QuickTime movie isn't appearing, and you're certain you typed the HTML correctly, uploaded the file properly, and installed QuickTime the right way, there's a chance your server has been improperly configured for QuickTime. Contact your Webmaster. He or she should know what to do, but you can mention that the MIME type should be "video/quicktime" and the suffix should be "mov."

Telling Your Viewers to Get QuickTime

While millions of people have already installed QuickTime and the QuickTime plug-in on their computers, it's always a good idea to alert visitors to your Web site or page that they'll need QuickTime 4 to play the movies found there. The notice should include a link to http://www.apple. com/quicktime/, where they can get QuickTime.

Using HREF links

A less elegant alternative to embedding your movie on a Web page is to use a standard link. On your Web page you'd type something like <A HREF="mymovie. mov"><IMG SRC = "oneframe.jpg"> Click here to play mymovie </A>, replacing "mymovie.mov" with the location of your movie, "oneframe.jpg" with the name of a still-image file representing the movie, and the text string with whatever text you desire. (If you wish, you can omit either text or image.)

When users who have the QuickTime plug-in click the link, a new page opens containing the movie. Or, if they've configured their browser to use a helper app (like QuickTime Player) to play QuickTime movies, the helper app will open and play the movie.

Embedding an RTSP QuickTime Movie on a Web Page

Things get slightly trickier when you want to embed an RTSP streaming movie on a Web page. You can't use an RTSP address as the value for the SRC attribute in the EMBED tag, so you have to use a workaround. There are a number of methods for doing this: Two involve creating a file that points to the RTSP movie—you can then write a standard EMBED tag and use the URL of this pointing movie as the SRC. The third method requires a new attribute, the QTSRC attribute.

To embed a movie that points to your RTSP movie:

1. Upload your properly prepared RTSP movie (see "Preparing Movies for RTSP Streaming" earlier in this chapter) to your RTSP streaming server.

2. In QuickTime Player, from the File menu, choose Open URL (**Figure 16.26**).

3. In the Open URL dialog box, enter the URL of your RTSP movie (**Figure 16.27**), and click OK.

4. From the File menu, choose Save As (**Figure 16.28**).

5. In the Save dialog box, click the "Make movie self-contained" radio button, enter a file name with a .mov extension, specify a new location (if desired), and click Save (**Figure 16.29**).

   This newly saved movie does not contain the movie data but rather the *address* of your RTSP movie.

   When a user opens it, a connection will be made to the RTSP server and the movie data will be streamed.

Figure 16.26 First upload the RTSP movie to an RTSP streaming server and then choose Open URL from the File menu.

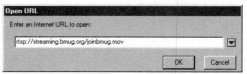

Figure 16.27 Enter the URL of the movie you uploaded and click OK.

Figure 16.28 Then choose Save As...

Figure 16.29 ...to save to your hard drive the file containing a pointer to your RTSP movie. Make sure to give it an .mov extension.

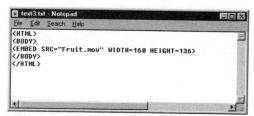

Figure 16.30 Then write an EMBED tag in which the movie you just saved is the value for the SRC attribute.

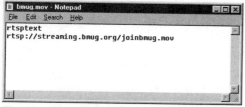

Figure 16.31 Another technique involves creating a text file that contains the address of your RTSP movie. (Save the text file with an .mov extension.)

Figure 16.32 Write an EMBED tag in which the text file is the value for the SRC attribute.

6. In your Web page HTML, write a standard EMBED tag. For example: `<EMBED SRC="mymovie.mov" WIDTH=160 HEIGHT=120>` where "`mymovie.mov`" is replaced by the name of the file you saved in Step 5, and the proper values are inserted for the WIDTH and HEIGHT attributes. (See **Figure 16.30** for an example.)

7. Upload both your Web page and the movie saved in Step 5 to your HTTP Web server.

To embed a movie that's really a text file pointing to your RTSP movie:

1. Upload your properly prepared RTSP movie (see "Preparing Movies for RTSP Streaming" earlier in this chapter) to your RTSP streaming server.

2. In a text editor, create a new document and type `rtsptext` on the first line.

3. On the second line type the URL of your RTSP movie (**Figure 16.31**).

4. Save the file, with a .mov extension.

5. In the HTML of your Web page, write a standard EMBED tag. For example: `<EMBED SRC="textpointer.mov" WIDTH=160 HEIGHT=120>` where `textpointer.mov` is replaced by the name of the file you saved in Step 4, and the proper values are inserted for the WIDTH and HEIGHT attributes (**Figure 16.32**).

6. Upload both your Web page and the movie saved in Step 4 to your HTTP Web server.

   When a Web browser encounters the EMBED tag you wrote in Step 5, the QuickTime plug-in opens the text file and immediately reads the RTSP movie URL and opens a connection to it.

To write an embed tag that uses QTSRC:

1. Upload your properly prepared RTSP movie (see "Preparing Movies for RTSP Streaming" earlier in this chapter) to your RTSP streaming server.

2. You need to have a movie, any movie, on an HTTP server somewhere. (The only reason to have this movie is to trick the Web browser into thinking that it's the file that will be opened. In reality, this movie won't get opened as long as your RTSP movie can be opened. We typically use a small, single-frame movie that we call dummy.mov. However, see Tip below.)

3. In your HTML, type <EMBED SRC= "any.mov", replacing "any.mov" with the name of the movie identified in Step 2.

4. Type a space and then QTSRC="rtsp:// streaming.bmug.org/ joinbmug.mov", where "rtsp://streaming.bmug.org/ joinbmug.mov" is replaced by the address of the movie that you really want to appear on the Web page.

5. Type a space and then WIDTH=w HEIGHT=h, replacing w with the width of your movie and h with the height of your movie.

6. Type a final > to close the EMBED tag (see **Figure 16.33** for the complete tag).

7. Save and upload this Web page to an HTTP server.

✔ Tip

- If you use the last technique, involving the QTSRC attribute, users will see the movie specified by the SRC attribute if they have a version of QuickTime earlier than QuickTime 4. You can create a simple movie (perhaps a single frame) that tells them they'll need QuickTime 4 to view the streaming movie.

Figure 16.33 A third technique involves writing an EMBED tag in which a different movie is the value for the SRC attribute, but the RTSP movie you really want opened is the value for the QTSRC attribute.

QUICKTIME ON THE INTERNET: ADVANCED

Now that you've mastered the basics and can deliver a movie over the Internet, let's explore the QuickTime features that allow you to do some more sophisticated things with Internet movies.

We'll discuss additional attributes for the EMBED tag, and then show a few special techniques, such as those for *poster movies* (small movies that stand in for larger ones until a user clicks), *HREF tracks* (text tracks that call up Web pages), and hyperlinks in text tracks. We'll also demonstrate how you can force a movie to show up in QuickTime Player rather than directly on a Web page.

Then we'll cover some tasks that require additional tools—all of which Apple provides free of charge. (As of this writing, some of these tools were not yet available on the Windows platform; however, they're worth checking for on Apple's Web site when you read this.) Some of the tasks you can accomplish with these tools include creating a set of movies so users get the right one for their system, inserting Web-specific data directly into movies, and creating low-resolution previews and thumbnails for QuickTime VR movies.

Adding Attributes to Your EMBED Tag

In addition to the SRC, HEIGHT, WIDTH, and QTSRC attributes covered in the last chapter, you can use other attributes to specify appearance or playback characteristics of your movie. Some, such as VOLUME, LOOP, and PLAYEVERYFRAME, merely do things that you can do in QuickTime Player (for example, change the volume or set the movie to loop or play every frame; see Chapter 4). Others, such as PAN, TILT, FOV, NODE, CORRECTION, and HOTSPOT, are intended for QuickTime VR movies and allow you to specify properties that can also be specified when the VR movies are created. Still other attributes have Web-specific qualities. A complete list of known attributes is provided in **Table 17.1**; however, we'll also examine some of the most useful attributes and discuss why you might want to use them after we show you how to add additional attributes.

To add additional attributes:

1. Insert your cursor before the closing angle bracket in the EMBED tag.

2. Type the attribute name, followed by = (the equal sign) and a valid value for that attribute.

   Although many browsers can interpret these attributes if there are spaces before or after = (the equal sign), we recommend not leaving any spaces. **Figure 17.1** shows the HTML for a QuickTime EMBED tag with additional attributes.

```
my.html
<HTML>
<BODY>
<EMBED SRC="mymovie.mov" WIDTH=200 HEIGHT=200 AUTOPLAY="true" LOOP="true">
</BODY>
</HTML>
```

Figure 17.1 Here's an EMBED tag with additional attributes.

Table 17.1

EMBED Tag Attributes for QuickTime Movies

Attribute	Use	Example
AUTOPLAY	If set to "true", movie begins playing when enough data has been downloaded. If set to "false", movie won't start playing even if browser plug-in is configured to autoplay by default.	AUTOPLAY=true
BGCOLOR	Specifies color in space defined by WIDTH and HEIGHT tags but not taken up by movie. Value is a hexadecimal number. (Can also do HTML color names.)	BGCOLOR="#FFFFFF"
CACHE	Can be set to "true" (tells browser to cache the movie if possible) or "false" (tells it not to cache the movie). Doesn't work for all browsers.	CACHE=true
CONTROLLER	Indicates whether the controller should be shown. Value can be "true" or "false".	CONTROLLER=true
CORRECTION	For QuickTime VR movies. Value can be "none", "partial", or "full".	CORRECTION=none
DONTFLATTENWHENSAVING	When movies are saved from a Web page using the Save As QuickTime movie choice, the movie is actually saved as though Save As Source had been chosen. (References not resolved.) Useful for QuickTime VR movies with directional sound.	DONTFLATTENWHENSAVING
ENDTIME	Indicates the time location in the movie where play should stop. Value is in hours:minutes:seconds.thirtieths of a second.	ENDTIME= "1:23:17.15"
FOV	For QuickTime VR movies only. Specifies initial field of view.	FOV=60.0
HEIGHT	Required attribute unless HIDDEN is used. Indicates height (in pixels) to be reserved in the document for the movie.	HEIGHT=256
HOTSPOTn	For QuickTime VR movies only. Replace n with ID of hot spot. Value should be the URL of page to load when hot spot is clicked.	HOTSPOT28="http://www.peachpit.com"
HREF	Indicates page to load if movie is clicked. Value should be a valid URL.	HREF="http://www.bmug.org/quicktime"
KIOSKMODE	Value can be "true" or "false". When true, removes the pop-up menu that shows on the right side of the controller when a movie is played on a Web page.	KIOSKMODE="true"
LOOP	Value can be "true", "false", or "palindrome". Has the same effect as Loop (if set to "true") and Loop Back and Forth (if set to "palindrome") commands in QuickTime Player's Movie menu.	LOOP=true
MOVIEID	A number used to identify a movie so another wired sprite movie can control it.	MOVIEID="3"
MOVIENAME	A name used to identify a movie so another wired sprite movie can control it.	MOVIENAME="gamemovie"
NODE	For QuickTime VR movies only. Specifies which node of a multinode movie should open first. Value is an integer less than or equal to the number of nodes in the movie.	NODE=2
PAN	For QuickTime VR movies. Indicates initial pan angle. Value usually can be between 0 and 360, but depends on the movie.	PAN=90
PLAYEVERYFRAME	Value can be "true" or "false". If "true", has the same effect as the Play All Frames command in QuickTime Player's Movie menu.	PLAYEVERYFRAME=true

continues on next page

ADDING ATTRIBUTES TO YOUR EMBED TAG

Table 17.1 *continued*

EMBED Tag Attributes for QuickTime Movies

ATTRIBUTE	USE	EXAMPLE
PLUGINSPAGE	Tells viewers without the plug-in where to go to get it. Value should be set to http://www.apple.com/quicktime.	PLUGSINSPAGE= "http://www.apple.com/quicktime"
QTNEXTn	Used to specify the URL of a movie that should be loaded nth in a sequence of movies, after the previous in the sequence is played. Value can be a URL of a movie or "GOTOn" where n is the number in the sequence. (GOTO 0 will play the movie designated by the SRC attribute.)	QTNEXT1="http://www.bmug.org/bestmovie.mov" QTNEXT="GOTO0"
QTSRC	Indicates the file that should be opened by the QuickTime Plug-in rather than that designated by the SRC attribute. (For example uses, see "Embedding an RTSP QuickTime Movie on a Web Page" in Chapter 16 and "Forcing QuickTime to Open Non-QuickTime Files on Web Pages" later in this chapter.).	QTSRC="rtsp://streams.bmug.org/mymovie.mov"
QTSRCCHOKESPEED	Allows you to specify that file designated by QTSRC attribute should be downloaded in chunks. Value can be a number (in bytes per second) or "movierate" (to match the movie's data rate). See sidebar "What's Choke?" later in this chapter for more information.	QTSRCCHOKESPEED=5000
SCALE	Scales movie dimensions. Can be set to "tofit", "aspect", or a number.	SCALE = 1.5
STARTTIME	Indicates the time location in the movie where play should begin. Value is in hours:minutes:seconds.thirtieths of a second.	STARTTIME="00:00:09.10"
TARGETn	Indicates window or frame in which to load URL specified in HREF or HOTSPOT attributes. Leave off the n for an HREF. For HOTSPOT, n should be the same as the following HOTSPOT.	TARGET="_blank"
TARGETCACHE	Specifies the CACHE value for a movie that is called by a poster movie. (See "Writing the HTML for a Poster Movie" later in this chapter.) Value can be "true" or "false".	TARGETCACHE="true"
TILT	For QuickTime VR movies. Indicates initial tilt angle. Value usually can be between -42.5 and 42.5, but depends on the movie.	TILT=15.5
VOLUME	Sets the volume of an audio track. Can be set to a number between 0 and 100.	VOLUME=50
WIDTH	Required attribute. Indicates width (in pixels) to be reserved in the document for the movie.	WIDTH=320

See http://www.apple.com/quicktime/authoring/embed.html for complete and current documentation of the known QuickTime EMBED tag attributes.

Figure 17.2 If you specify CONTROLLER=false, the movie appears without the controller.

Figure 17.3 You can put a colored frame around a movie image by specifying a value for BGCOLOR. Here we've specified BGCOLOR=black.

Some sample attributes and values and their uses:

♦ AUTOPLAY=true

This attribute/value ensures that the movie (as long as it's saved as a fast-start movie) will begin playing automatically when enough of it has been downloaded so that it can play smoothly to the end. (The currently installed QuickTime plug-in is configured by default to play movies automatically—regardless of what the EMBED tag contains. However, some viewers may have changed this default or have an older version of QuickTime: In either case, the movie will not play until the viewer starts it manually if you don't include AUTOPLAY=true.)

♦ CONTROLLER=false

This attribute/value is useful when you don't want a controller to appear for your movies (**Figure 17.2**). (The controller appears by default for regular QuickTime movies, though not for QuickTime VR movies or Flash files opened by QuickTime on a Web page. If you *do* want a controller for VR movies or Flash files, you'll need to type CONTROLLER=true.)

♦ BGCOLOR=black

If the HEIGHT and WIDTH attributes specify a height and width that exceed your actual movie size and you haven't used the SCALE attribute to enlarge the movie, the above attribute and value place a black frame around the movie on the Web page (**Figure 17.3**). You can use a wide range of colors as the value for the BGCOLOR attribute. Certain colors can be specified with words: black, green, silver, lime, gray, olive, white, yellow, maroon, navy, red, blue, purple, teal, fuchsia, and aqua. Other colors require hexadecimal values (see http://www.prgone.com/colors/ for a color-to-hex table).

ADDING ATTRIBUTES TO YOUR EMBED TAG

273

◆ HIDDEN=true

You can use this attribute/value for an audio-only movie whose background soundtrack you don't want users to be able to control. The movie downloads and plays, but there's nothing on the page that viewers can see.

◆ HOTSPOT47="http://www.bmug.org/"

This attribute and value would cause the page located at http://www.bmug.org/ to be loaded when a viewer clicked the hot spot with an ID of 47 in the embedded QuickTime VR movie. (Hot spot IDs are defined when the hot spot is created; you will need to know what these IDs are.) This overrides any URLs already associated with that particular hot spot in the movie. If you want the page loaded into a frame or a window other than the current window, you can use the target attribute with a number identical to the hot spot ID number. (In this case, you could include TARGET47="text" to have the page loaded into a frame called "text.")

◆ HREF="http://www.apple.com/"

Using this attribute/value causes the page located at http://www.apple.com/ to be loaded when a viewer clicks in the movie. If you want the page loaded into a frame or a window other than the current window, you can use the TARGET attribute. (The HREF attribute can also be used to load another movie in the same location; see pages about poster movies later in this chapter.)

◆ SCALE=tofit

This attribute and value will scale the movie to fit the values provided for the HEIGHT and WIDTH attributes. Many movies look good and perform reasonably well when scaled to fit a HEIGHT and WIDTH twice the movie's true height and width (**Figure 17.4**).

Figure 17.4 If you specify a WIDTH and HEIGHT double the size of your movie, and include SCALE=tofit in your EMBED tag, you can double the size of your movie on playback. (Here we show the movie in QuickTime Player and then the same movie embedded double-size on a Web page.)

◆ STARTTIME=4.0, ENDTIME=22.5

You can use these attributes to make QuickTime begin playing the movie 4 seconds past its true beginning and stop playing the movie 22.5 seconds after its true beginning. Note, however, that the entire movie is still downloaded. Viewers can use the Step buttons and the indicator in the time slider to see frames outside the range defined by STARTTIME and ENDTIME, but they can only *play* what's inside the range.

◆ KIOSKMODE=true

Use this to eliminate the plug-in pop-up menu that normally appears on the right side of the standard controller. (See Chapter 2 and Appendix B for details about this pop-up menu.) This is one technique you can use to make it difficult for users to save a movie. (See "Putting Movies on the Internet That Can't Be Saved" later in this chapter for more details.)

◆ CACHE=true

You can use this attribute and value if you want to ensure that the movie stays in the user's browser cache even after they've left the page on which the movie is embedded. You'd want to do this if you expect the user to return to the page and you don't want them to have to wait while the movie downloads again. If you don't specify a cache value, the value is determined by the settings in the user's QuickTime Plug-in Settings; see Appendix B, "Configuring QuickTime." The TARGETCACHE attribute works in the same way but sets a cache value for a movie called by an HREF attribute in the EMBED tag. (See pages about poster movies later in this chapter.)

Specifying a Value for the TARGET Attribute

If you want the new page to load in a frame when you're using the HREF attribute, use the frame's name as the value for the TARGET attribute. The frame's name is specified by the NAME attribute in the FRAME tag in your HTML (for example, use "text" as the name of your target if the HTML used to create your frame is <FRAME SRC="moreinfo.html" NAME="text">).

Use _blank if you want the Web page to appear in a new browser window. Once a window is opened with this name, you can use the same _blank with subsequent URLs to load additional pages into that browser window.

The TARGET attribute is not specific to the QuickTime EMBED tag. If you want to find out more about how to specify valid values for the TARGET attribute, you can go to http://home.netscape.com/eng/mozilla/2.0/relnotes/demo/target.html.

ADDING ATTRIBUTES TO YOUR EMBED TAG

Creating a Small Movie to Use as a Poster Movie

One of the newer features of the QuickTime plug-in is its ability to handle *poster movies*—one- or several-frame QuickTime movies that serve as stand-ins for larger, "full-length" movies. When you click a poster movie embedded on a Web page, the larger movie file begins to either download (in the case of HTTP movies) or stream (in the case of RTSP movies). Creating a poster movie is typically a matter of creating a movie containing a subset of the information in the full-length movie. You can use various combinations of copying, pasting, extracting, deleting, exporting, and importing movie data to create a poster movie; we'll show you the most commonly used methods here.

To create a still-image poster movie:

1. Move the Current Location indicator so that the image you wish to use for the poster is visible, and from the File menu choose Export (**Figure 17.5**).

2. In the pop-up menu at the bottom of the Export dialog box choose Movie to Picture (**Figure 17.6**).

3. If you wish, click the Options button to open a dialog box where you choose new compression settings for the image.

   We generally recommend that you choose Photo-JPEG as your compressor because it can compress the image to a very small size. Medium as your quality choice often works fine, too. And if you don't like the results, you can always repeat the process.

4. After choosing your settings, click OK.

5. Click Save.

   The file is exported as a still image.

Figure 17.5 Position the Current Location indicator at the image you wish to use as a poster and choose Export from the File menu.

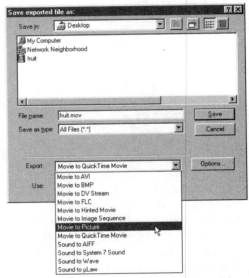

Figure 17.6 Choose Movie to Picture, and then click Save. (Before clicking Save you can click the Options button to access a compression settings dialog box.)

Figure 17.7 Then import the exported still image to create a single-frame movie that can be used as a poster movie.

Figure 17.8 Or, start by copying the frames you want to appear in your poster movie.

Figure 17.9 Paste the frames into a new, empty movie.

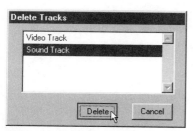

Figure 17.10 Delete tracks that shouldn't be in the poster.

6. In the File menu use the Import command (**Figure 17.7**) to turn the still image back into a single-frame QuickTime movie.

   As part of the import process, you'll need to provide the new movie file with a name that includes an .mov extension. (For more on importing a still image, see "Creating a Video Track from a Single Still Image" in Chapter 9.)

To create a multiple-frame poster movie:

1. Select the frames you wish to use as your poster movie, and from the Edit menu choose Copy (**Figure 17.8**).

2. From the File menu choose New to create an empty movie file; then from the Edit menu choose Paste (**Figure 17.9**).

3. In the Edit menu use the Delete Tracks command to delete any audio or other tracks that you don't want to appear in the poster movie (**Figure 17.10**).

4. Save the file as a self-contained file with an .mov extension.

✔ Tips

- Poster movies made up of just a few frames can remain very small and serve as a better advertisement for your movie than a still image.

- The method for creating a multiple-frame poster movie can also be used to create a still-image poster, if you select only a single frame.

- If you like the dynamic nature of multiple-frame posters but are dealing with QuickTime VR panoramic movies, you may be interested in dynamic thumbnails for VR panoramas. See "Creating Panorama Thumbnails with QTVR PanoToThumbnail" later in this chapter.

CREATING A POSTER MOVIE

Writing the HTML for a Poster Movie

Once you have a full-length movie and corresponding poster movie, you'll need to write your EMBED tag so that everything works correctly.

To write the HTML for a poster movie:

1. Place your cursor in the HTML body of the Web page in the location where you want the movie to appear.

2. Type `<EMBED SRC="myposter.mov"`, replacing "myposter.mov" with the location of your poster movie file.

3. Type `CONTROLLER=false`. (You generally don't want the controller to appear for a poster.)

4. Type `WIDTH=w HEIGHT=h`, where w is the width of your full-length movie window and h is the height of your full-length movie window. (See "Checking the Dimensions of a Movie" in Chapter 15 if you're not sure of your movie's width and height.)

   The reason for specifying the dimensions of the full-length movie is that you need to make space on the page for that movie.

5. Type `HREF="myreal.mov"`, replacing "myreal.mov" with the location of your real movie.

   If the full-length movie resides in a different folder than the poster movie, you must specify the path after the HREF relative to the poster movie—not relative to the Web page.

```
test.html
<HTML>
<BODY>
<EMBED SRC="myposter.mov" CONTROLLER=false WIDTH=320
HEIGHT=256 HREF="myreal.mov" TARGET="myself">
</BODY>
</HTML>
```

Figure 17.11 Here's a full EMBED tag for a poster movie.

6. Type TARGET="myself".

   This ensures that the full-length movie appears in the same location on the Web page as the poster movie.

7. Type the final > to close the EMBED tag. (See **Figure 17.11** for the full tag.)

   When the page with this tag is opened in a Web browser, the poster movie appears. When the poster movie is clicked, the full-length movie replaces it.

✔ Tips

■ The poster movie will be centered in the space provided by the HEIGHT and WIDTH tags. With no controller, its bottom and top edges won't match those of the full-length movie. If you're bothered by this, you might want to use image-processing software or QuickTime Player to add to the bottom of the poster image a 16-pixel-high rectangle, perhaps matching your Web page's background pattern or color or containing text such as "Click to see the movie."

■ The full-length movie automatically appears according to the defaults for the EMBED tag attributes (for example, with a controller for regular QuickTime movies). If you want to change any of these attributes, you'll need to include them in the full-length movie itself, using Plug-In Helper, which is described later in this chapter. The one exception occurs if you want to specify a cache value. You can set a cache value for your full-length movie using the TARGETCACHE attribute; see "Adding Attributes to Your EMBED Tag" earlier in this chapter.

WRITING THE HTML FOR A POSTER MOVIE

Making an Internet Movie Appear in QuickTime Player

In the previous chapter we covered basic techniques for embedding movies in Web pages. However, you may want your Web page viewers to watch your QuickTime movies in QuickTime Player. Here's the basic technique to cause this to occur.

To make a movie open in QuickTime Player:

1. Create a poster movie (as described in "Creating a Small Movie to Use as a Poster Movie" earlier in this chapter).

   The poster movie doesn't need to have the same dimensions as the movie you wish to play in QuickTime Player. In fact, a commonly used technique involves creating a still-image poster movie from a small graphic, such as that shown in **Figure 17.12**. Position your cursor in the HTML body of the Web page where you want the poster movie to appear.

2. Type <EMBED SRC="myposter.mov" CONTROLLER=false WIDTH=w HEIGHT=h HREF="myreal.mov", replacing "myposter.mov" with the location of your poster movie file, w with the width of your poster movie, h with the height of your poster movie, and "myreal.mov" with the location of the movie you want to appear in QuickTime Player.

3. Type TARGET="QuickTimePlayer".

   This special value for the TARGET attribute (new to QuickTime 4) specifies that the movie should open in QuickTime Player.

4. Type the final > to close the EMBED tag. (See **Figure 17.13** for the full tag.)

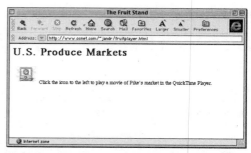

Figure 17.12 When you intend for a movie to appear in QuickTime Player, it's often appropriate to use a small graphic as a poster movie. Here's how Apple does it.

Figure 17.13 Here's an EMBED tag that will open the movie "myreal.mov" in QuickTime Player.

✔ Tips

- See "Checking the Dimensions of a Movie" in Chapter 15 if you're not sure of the width and height of your poster movie.

- If you want to use relative path names to specify the location of the movie you want to appear in the Player, you must specify the path in the HREF attribute relative to the poster movie—not relative to the Web page.

Figure 17.14 In a word processor, type and enclose in angle brackets the full URL of a Web page, followed by a T and a frame or window name in angle brackets. Then select and copy this text.

Using HREF Tracks to Make Movies Load Web Pages

By including a special text track—called an *HREF track*—in your movie, you can make Web pages load at specified times during movie playback.

The simplest type of HREF track loads a Web page into the current browser window when a user clicks at the specified time. Variations allow you to specify another browser window or a frame into which the Web page should load, or to specify that the page be loaded automatically rather than only if the user clicks.

To create an HREF track that loads a Web page if a user clicks on the movie:

1. In any text editor, type and enclose in angle brackets the full URL of the Web page you wish to load—for example, `<http://www.bmug.org/quicktime/>`.

2. If you want the Web page to load in a window or frame other than that in which the movie is playing, type `T` (for *target*) after the closed angle bracket, followed by the name of the window or frame in angle brackets.

   For example, type `T<_blank>` to make the URL in Step 1 load in an empty browser window (**Figure 17.14**). (See the sidebar "Specifying a Value for the TARGET Attribute" earlier in this chapter for information about how to specify targets.)

3. Select and copy the text you've typed.

4. In QuickTime Player, select the portion of the movie during which you'd like the URL fired if the user clicks, and then hold down the Shift and Option keys (Mac OS) or the Shift, Ctrl, and Alt keys (Windows), and from the Edit menu choose Add Scaled (**Figure 17.15**), to add a new text track.

5. From the Movie menu, choose Get Info; in the Info window's left pop-up menu choose the added text track and in the right pop-up menu choose General. (If the movie already contained a text track before you added the text in Step 4 the added track will be the last text track to appear in the list.)

6. Click the Change Name button (**Figure 17.16**).

7. In the Change Track Name dialog box that appears, type HREFTrack and click OK (**Figure 17.17**).

   The name of the track, as listed in the left pop-up menu in the Info window, is now HREFTrack.

8. Unless you want the HREF track to be visible, use the Enable Tracks command in the Edit menu to disable the track.

9. Save the file using the Save As command and embed it on a Web page, as described earlier in this chapter.

Figure 17.15 Select the portion of the movie during which you wish the URL to be active, and then use the Add Scaled command to add the copied text.

Figure 17.16 Open the General panel in the Info window for the text track you've just added, and click the Change Name button.

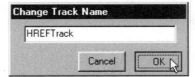

Figure 17.17 Type HREFTrack and click OK.

USING HREF TRACKS

Figure 17.18 You can make the page load automatically (rather than when a user clicks) by putting an A before the text string.

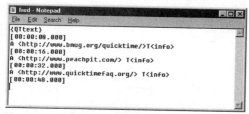

Figure 17.19 If you plan to have multiple URLs, create a text file like this and import it.

To specify that a Web page be loaded automatically:

◆ Follow the steps for creating an HREF track that plays when a user clicks but type an A in front of the text you copy from the word processor (**Figure 17.18**).

✔ Tips

■ If you want different URLs to be fired at various times, you can create and import a text file with time stamps (as described in Chapter 10) rather than individually copy and paste multiple lines of text. To create the file, you may want to use the technique described under "Creating a Text Track That's Synced to Other Tracks" (also in Chapter 10). **Figure 17.19** shows an example text file with URLs that can be imported.

■ It's best to save files containing an HREF track as self-contained; otherwise, you'll need to make sure to upload the imported text movie file along with the movie file.

■ When you test your movie that contains an HREF track, don't assume it's not working if the Web page doesn't load as quickly as you think it should. Be patient: It may take a few seconds.

Creating Hyperlinks in a Text Track

Just as you can have hyperlinks (clickable text that opens a Web page) on a Web page, you can have hyperlinks in a movie's text track.

To create a hyperlink in a text track:

1. Start with a text file that contains all of your text track's text as well as time stamps and a first line of {QTtext} (**Figure 17.20**).

   You can create this file by typing it yourself as described in "Specifying the Duration and Appearance of Individual Frames of Text" in Chapter 10 or by exporting an existing track from a movie as described in "Exporting a Text Track with Text Descriptors and Time Stamps" in Chapter 10.

2. In the text file, directly before any text you wish to be clickable, type {HREF: "http://www. myurl.com"} where "http://www.myurl.com" is replaced by the address of the page you want to open when the text is clicked.

3. At the point where you'd like clickable text to end, type {endHREF} (**Figure 17.21**).

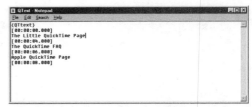

Figure 17.20 Start with a text file that contains time stamps.

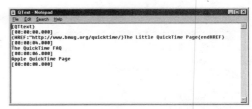

Figure 17.21 Place an HREF descriptor in front of any text you wish to make clickable; then type {endHREF} after the text.

Figure 17.22 The text you specified with the HREF and endHREF descriptors is highlighted and clickable.

4. Save this text file and import it into QuickTime Player, as described in "Creating a Text Track by Importing a Text File" in Chapter 10.

You now have a text-track movie with a text hyperlink (shown as blue, underlined text). (**Figure 17.22**).

5. You can then add the text track to a movie in which you want this clickable text to appear, as described in "Combining Tracks with the Add and Add Scaled Commands" in Chapter 7.

6. If the movie previously contained a version of the text track without hyperlinks, delete that text track, as described in "Deleting Tracks" in Chapter 7.

✔ Tip

- On Windows, a bug in the current version prevents you from creating working hyperlinks in a text track. We expect this bug to be fixed in a future update.

Forcing QuickTime to Open Files

The real magic of using the QTSRC attribute (which we discussed in earlier chapters) in an EMBED tag is that it in essence tricks Web browsers. A browser's job is to look at the extension of the file designated by the SRC attribute and hand it over to the plug-in designated in its MIME types table. The browser also passes on the attributes listed in the EMBED tag. The plug-in then takes over and does what it's supposed to do, which in most cases is play or display the SRC file. However, if the QuickTime plug-in sees that QTSRC is an additional attribute, it will ignore the SRC value and handle what's listed as QTSRC instead. In Chapter 16 we showed how this can be useful for playing RTSP movies, since a browser doesn't know how to handle an RTSP file. It's also useful if you want to force QuickTime to open a file that has an extension that the QuickTime plug-in is not normally associated with. This allows you, as a Web page author, to pass control of files (such as Flash and MP3) to QuickTime.

To force QuickTime to open a file:

1. You'll need to have a movie, any movie, on an HTTP server somewhere.

   This movie will serve as a dummy file so that the browser, seeing the .mov extension, hands control to the QuickTime plug-in. It won't get opened as long as the file you designate using the QTSRC attribute can be opened. We typically use a small, single-frame movie.

2. In your Web page, type <EMBED SRC= "any.mov", replacing "any.mov" with the name of the movie you identified in Step 1.

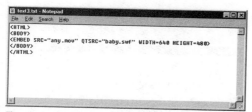

Figure 17.23 Here's an EMBED tag that forces QuickTime to open a file it normally wouldn't.

3. Type a space and then QTSRC= "myflash.swf", where "myflash.swf" is replaced by the address of the file you really want to show up on the Web page.

4. Type a space and then WIDTH=w HEIGHT=h, replacing w with the width of the file you want to open and h with the height of the file.

5. Add any other attributes and values you wish.

6. Type a final > to close the EMBED tag. (See **Figure 17.23** for the final tag.)

   When the Web page containing this EMBED tag is opened in a browser, the file you designated for the QTSRC attribute will be embedded on the Web page.

✔ Tip

■ In contrast to most files opened by the plug-in, Flash files don't show the standard controller. While this is usually fine, if you do want it to show, include CONTROLLER=TRUE in the EMBED tag.

Obtaining Important Utilities

Apple has made available some special tools you can use to exploit QuickTime capabilities. (While many software developers plan to support these capabilities in future versions of their software, the free Apple utilities described here will serve in the meantime. Be aware, however, that these tools are not supported.)

To find these tools go to http://www.apple.com/quicktime/developers/tools.html.

While you'll find of number of interesting tools on this page (**Figure 17.24**), the following are those you should download to perform the activities described in this chapter:

◆ MakeRefMovie

◆ Plug-In Helper

◆ QTVR Flattener

◆ QTVR PanoToThumbnail

Available for both Mac OS and Windows computers, **MakeRefMovie** and **Plug-In Helper** are small applications that you can store anywhere on your hard drive.

QTVR Flattener and **QTVR PanoTo-Thumbnail** are Mac-only extensions to QuickTime that work in conjunction with QuickTime tools (such as QuickTime Player) that have QuickTime export functionality. Put these extensions into your Extensions folder within your System Folder, and then restart your computer. They will make their presence known when you choose Export from QuickTime Player's File menu: You'll see additional choices for formatting your exported movies in the Export pop-up menu at the bottom of the dialog box (**Figure 17.25**).

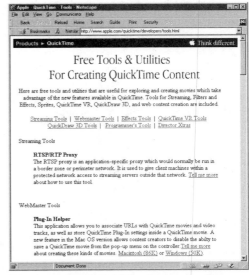

Figure 17.24 Apple's QuickTime Tools page offers a number of free, interesting utilities.

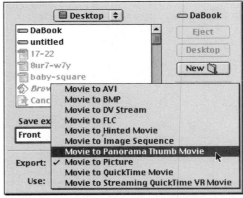

Figure 17.25 You'll find that some of the utilities add extra choices to QuickTime Player's export options for QuickTime VR movies.

Creating Alternate Movies

The QuickTime plug-in has a feature that allows something often called *smart streaming*. The general idea is that although Web viewers see only a single movie on your Web page, you can actually have a set of alternate movies on your Web server: Only the movie that's appropriate for the viewer downloads. (Factors that determine what's appropriate include the viewer's connection speed, QuickTime version, preferred language, and CPU speed.) You need to first generate the movies with the different specifications, called *alternate movies*. Then you use the MakeRefMovie tool to create the movie (called a *reference movie*) that you'll embed on your Web page; the reference movie contains pointers to the various alternate movies.

To create alternate movies:

◆ Generate two or more versions of the same movie, each of which is appropriate for some segment of your movie's audience. You can prepare these movies for either RTSP streaming or HTTP streaming.

Generally, if you're concerned with connection speed, you'll want to create one movie for 28.8-Kbps modems, another for 56-Kbps modems, and perhaps another for ISDN lines, T1 lines, or faster connections. (See Chapter 16 for guidelines concerning creating movies for these bandwidths.)

You may also want to create a movie that doesn't depend on QuickTime 3 or 4 compressors. (See the sidebar "Built-In QuickTime 3- and 4-Only Compressors" for a list.)

In some cases you may want different movies for different CPU speeds. (For example, since the Sorenson codec does not work well on slow machines, you may want to provide a movie using a different codec for the slowest computers.)

What's *Choke*?

Adding an HTTP movie via the Add URL command in MakeRefMovie makes a Choke pop-up menu available; you can also use the QTSRCCHOKESPEED attribute in your EMBED tag.

Choke pertains to the way data is moved from HTTP servers to the browser over the network. When a server copies a movie's data to the network, it normally copies the entire file—fine for small files but problematic with large ones because every request for the file spurs it to send an entire copy, potentially flooding the network and leading to network performance problems. By specifying a choke value, you are restricting (or choking) the amount of data the server sends to the network at any one time, essentially telling it to send the data out in chunks.

For large movie files that many people will access simultaneously, it's usually best to choose Choke to Movie Data Rate in MakeRefMovie or to use QTSRCCHOKESPEED="movierate" in your EMBED tag. (You can also specify a specific rate. You may want to confer with your Webmaster about what's recommended for your particular Web server.)

Conversely you might have different movies for different languages—for example, one for English, one for Spanish, one for French.

To generate a reference movie:

1. Put any alternate movies intended for HTTP streaming into the folder or folders that match the directory or directories where you plan to place them on your Web server. (To keep things simple, it's best to put them all in the same folder.)

   Or, upload them now to your HTTP Web server. (See sidebar "What's Choke" to see why you might want to do this.)

2. Upload any alternate movies intended for RTSP serving to your QuickTime streaming server.

3. Open the MakeRefMovie application.

   A Save dialog box appears.

4. Enter a name with an .mov extension for your reference movie (**Figure 17.26**); then navigate to the folder that maps to the server folder where you want the reference movie to reside. (Again, to keep things simple, place the movie in the same folder that contains your alternate movies.)

5. Click Save.

   An empty window appears (**Figure 17.27**).

6. If you have any HTTP alternates on your local hard drive, from the Movie menu choose Add Movie File (**Figure 17.28**), locate one of your HTTP alternate movies, and click Open.

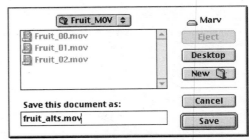

Figure 17.26 When you first open the MakeRefMovie application, you're immediately asked to save the file for your reference movie.

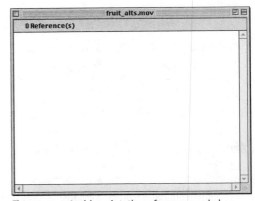

Figure 17.27 At this point, the reference movie has nothing in it.

Figure 17.28 Choose Add Movie File from the Movie menu to add one of your alternate movies to your reference movie. (Choose Add URL to add files residing on the Internet.)

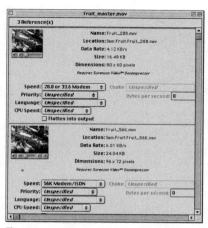

Figure 17.29 As you add your alternate movies, they are listed in the window.

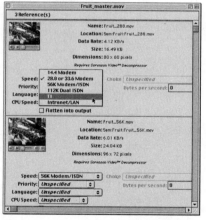

Figure 17.30 Use the Speed pop-up menu to specify the speed at which you intend each movie to be played.

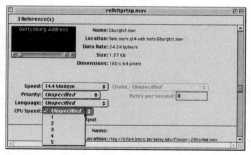

Figure 17.31 Use the CPU Speed pop-up menu if some movies are appropriate for faster or slower computers.

7. If you have RTSP alternates or any HTTP alternates that have already been uploaded to your Web server, from the Movie menu choose Add URL to specify the location of one of these movie files on the Internet. Then click OK.

8. Repeat Steps 6 and 7 for each of the alternate movies, until they are all listed in the window (**Figure 17.29**).

9. In the Speed pop-up menu for each movie, choose your intended connection speed for that movie (**Figure 17.30**).

10. If some of your movies are appropriate only for computers of a certain power, use the CPU Speed pop-up menu (**Figure 17.31**) to indicate this.

While the algorithm QuickTime uses to determine which systems match what numbers is rather complicated (taking into consideration CPU speed, multimedia capabilities, and processor cache), you can assume that the lowest number on the scale should be used for the oldest and slowest computers and the highest number should be used for the newest and fastest computers.

continues on next page

CREATING ALTERNATE MOVIES

11. If you wish to have different movies for different languages, use the Language pop-up menu to choose the language for each of your alternates (**Figure 17.32**). QuickTime will use the language set in a viewer's QuickTime Plug-in Settings dialog box to pick the appropriate alternate. By default the language is the same as the language of the viewer's operating system.

12. If one of your movies is one that you have created specifically to be compatible with versions of QuickTime prior to QuickTime 3, pick a value in the Speed pop-up menu identical to one of the other movies intended for QuickTime 3 or later. In the Priority menu select Last Choice and click the Flatten into Output checkbox. Set the priority of the movie with the identical speed to First Choice (**Figure 17.33**).

Figure 17.32 Use the Language pop-up menu to designate which movies should appear, depending on which language is specified in the viewer's plug-in settings.

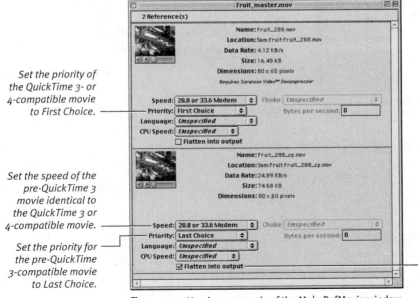

Set the priority of the QuickTime 3- or 4-compatible movie to First Choice.

Set the speed of the pre-QuickTime 3 movie identical to the QuickTime 3 or 4-compatible movie.

Set the priority for the pre-QuickTime 3-compatible movie to Last Choice.

Click this checkbox for the pre-QuickTime 3 movie.

Figure 17.33 Here's an example of the MakeRefMovie window when it's been set to include an alternate movie compatible with versions of QuickTime prior to 3.

A movie designated as Last Choice will not be chosen if there are other, higher-priority movies that are appropriate in terms of connection speed and compressors installed on the viewer's computer. Checking Flatten into Output causes the reference movie to actually contain the data for this movie; this is necessary because previous versions of QuickTime don't know how to interpret reference movies on Web pages.

13. From the File menu choose Save.

14. Embed the reference movie on your Web page (as described in "Embedding an HTTP QuickTime Movie on a Web Page" in Chapter 16).

15. Make sure to upload any HTTP alternate files that haven't yet been uploaded, along with the reference file, placing them in the same directory structure as that which existed on your hard drive.

✔ Tips

■ Rather than use the Add Movie File command, you can drag files from the Macintosh Finder or the Windows desktop directly to the MakeRefMovie window.

■ If you have Media Cleaner Pro, we suggest you use it, rather than the above techniques, to create your alternate movies and reference movie. This tool automates the process. Version 4 also lets you specify additional criteria (such as QuickTime version) for QuickTime to use when picking an alternate movie.

■ Don't change the names or relative locations of your alternate movies after creating a reference movie. If you do, the reference movie won't be able to locate them.

■ Don't edit the reference movie using QuickTime Player or any other editor.

Built-In QuickTime 3- and 4-Only Compressors

- Alaw 2:1
- DV-NTSC
- DV-PAL
- H.263
- Indeo 4.4 (only available as a built-in compressor on Windows)
- QDesign Music
- Qualcomm PureVoice
- Sorenson Video
- 24-bit Integer, 32-bit Integer
- 32-bit Floating Point, 64-bit Floating Point

Storing Plug-In Settings in a Movie

The Plug-In Helper tool allows you to store information normally stored in an EMBED tag directly in the movie itself. You generally want to do this if the movie is not the one embedded on the Web page (for example, it is called by a poster movie). It's also a way to specify default settings for your movie's Web playback characteristics. (Note, however, that if attributes set for the EMBED tag contradict the values set by Plug-In Helper, the values in the EMBED tag take precedence.)

To use Plug-In Helper to put EMBED tag attributes in a movie:

1. Download Plug-In Helper (if you haven't already done so).

2. Open the application, PlugInHelper.

   You'll notice that the name of the application contain no spaces or hyphens.

3. From the File menu choose the Open command (**Figure 17.34**) and open the movie in which you want to store plug-in settings.

   The Plug-In Helper window appears (**Figure 17.35**). A preview area located below an Open and an Export button shows your movie. (Don't be concerned if the proportions are not correct. For display purposes, Plug-In Helper squeezes your movie into the space available in the preview area, but it won't save the file this way.)

4. Click the Add button in the upper right area of the Plug-In Helper window labeled *Plugin Settings ('plug')*. In the Edit User Data dialog box that appears, type a valid EMBED tag attribute followed by an equal sign and a valid value for that attribute (**Figure 17.36**). Make sure that there are no spaces on either side of the equal sign.

Figure 17.34 Choose Open from the File menu to open a movie in which you want to store plug-in settings or URLs.

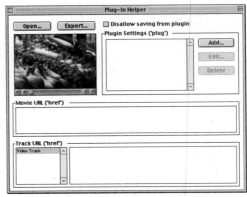

Figure 17.35 The Plug-In Helper window shows your movie in the preview area.

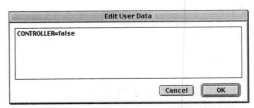

Figure 17.36 Click the Add button in the Plug-In Helper window, and type a valid EMBED tag attribute in the Edit User Data dialog box.

STORING PLUG-IN SETTINGS IN A MOVIE

Figure 17.37 You'll see all your properties in the scrolling list in the Plug-In Helper window.

You can use any valid attributes for the QuickTime EMBED tag except CACHE, WIDTH, HEIGHT, and HIDDEN. See "Adding Attributes to Your EMBED Tag" earlier in this chapter for more information on the attributes you can use. (If you need to set a cache value, use the TARGETCACHE attribute, also described earlier in this chapter.)

Click OK or press the Return key when you have finished adding the attribute.

5. Repeat Step 4 until you've added each attribute you want included (**Figure 17.37**). Use the Edit and Delete buttons to alter these attributes.

6. Click the Export button above the preview area.

7. In the Save dialog box that appears, specify a file name (ending in .mov) and location; then click Save.

✔ Tip

■ If the Plug-In Helper window is already open, you can use the Open button in the upper left portion of the window, or you can drag a movie from the Macintosh Finder or the Windows Desktop to the preview area rather than use the Open command in the File menu.

Specifying Web Pages to Load When a User Clicks in a Movie

Plug-In Helper also allows you to specify a URL to go to when a user clicks in the movie. You can enter a URL for the entire movie or different URLs for different video tracks. (You might want different URLs for different video tracks if a video track contained a logo for a company and you wanted people to go to the company's home page when they clicked on that logo. Or, you might have side-by-side video tracks and want different pages to load depending on which side they click.)

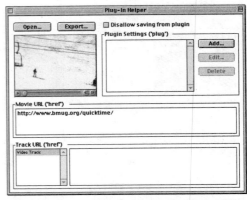

Figure 17.38 Type a URL directly into the Movie URL ('href') area of the Plug-In Helper window. The page designated by this URL will be opened when the movie is clicked.

To specify that a Web page be loaded when the movie image is clicked:

1. In Plug-In Helper open the movie.

2. Type the URL of the Web page you want to load in the Movie URL ('href') area (**Figure 17.38**).

   Typing the URL here provides the same effect as using the HREF attribute in the Plugin Settings ('plug') area. The advantage to the latter is that a target window or frame can be specified.

3. Unless you want to make other changes using Plug-In Helper, click the Export button, and in the Save dialog box that appears, specify a file name (ending in .mov) and location, and click Save.

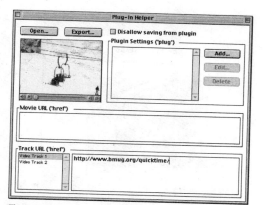

Figure 17.39 You can also specify a URL to open when a specific video track in the movie image is clicked.

To specify a Web page to load when a specific video track is clicked:

1. In Plug-In Helper open the movie.

2. In the list on the left side of the Track URL ('href') area, select the video track for which you want to specify a URL.

3. Type the URL of the Web page you want to load in the text box on the right side of the Track URL ('href') area (**Figure 17.39**).

4. Repeat Steps 2 and 3 for any additional video tracks you want to assign a URL to.

5. Unless you want to make other changes using Plug-In Helper, click the Export button, and in the Save dialog box that appears, specify a file name (ending in .mov) and location. Then click Save.

Putting Movies on the Internet That Can't Be Saved

In most cases, any QuickTime Pro user can save a movie embedded on a Web page: All one has to do—as described in Chapter 2—is simply pull down the plug-in menu and choose Save As QuickTime Movie (**Figure 17.40**).

However, there are methods of *preventing* people from saving movies embedded on Web pages: On the Mac (and, we hope, soon on Windows), you can use Plug-In Helper to turn your movie into one that can't be saved. And on either platform, you can simply remove the entire plug-in menu so that users can't access the Save As QuickTime Movie option.

To disallow saving of a movie (Mac OS only):

1. Open Plug-In Helper.

2. From the File menu, choose Open.

3. In the Open dialog box, locate the movie you don't wish people to save, and click Open.

4. Check "Disallow saving from plugin" (**Figure 17.41**).

5. From the File menu, choose Export.

If someone views this movie on a Web page, the Save As QuickTime Movie and Save As Source menu items will be disabled in the plug-in pop-up menu (**Figure 17.42**).

Those who open this movie in QuickTime Player will find that if they try to save, export, cut, or copy from the movie, a dialog box appears explaining that the operation cannot be completed "because this movie does not allow saving." If a user tries to drag from the movie window or extract a track, nothing will happen.

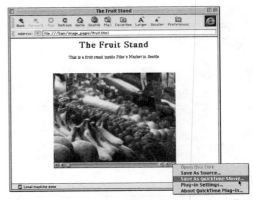

Figure 17.40 Normally, QuickTime Pro users can pull down the plug-in menu and choose Save As QuickTime Movie to save a movie to their hard drive.

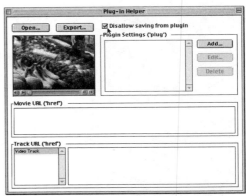

Figure 17.41 To make a movie that can't be saved, open the movie in Plug-In Helper, check "Disallow saving from plugin," and then export it.

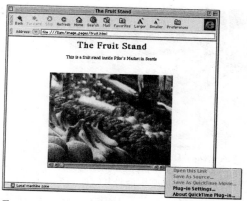

Figure 17.42 On a Web page, the Save as QuickTime Movie and Save as Source menu items will be disabled.

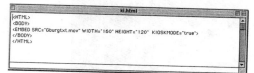

Figure 17.43 Add the KIOSKMODE attribute to your EMBED tag.

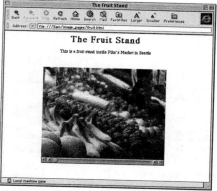

Figure 17.44 When the KIOSKMODE attribute is set to true, the plug-in menu is removed from the embedded movie.

✔ Tips

- Make sure not to trash the original file. Once you export with saving disallowed, you can't reverse the action using Plug-In Helper.

- The reason you can't disallow saving if you're authoring on Windows is simply that Apple hasn't updated the Windows version of Plug-In Helper to include the "Disallow saving from plugin" choice. However, by the time you read this, the company may have updated the tool—it's worth downloading a copy to find out.

To remove the plug-in menu on a Web page:

- ◆ In the EMBED tag you write to embed the movie on a Web page, type KIOSKMODE=true (See **Figure 17.43**). Now anyone who views this Web page will not see a plug-in menu button on the right side of the standard controller (**Figure 17.44**), nor will you be able to drag and drop from the Web page.

✔ Tips

- Users may still be able to save a copy of your HTTP movie on their hard disks even if you use the above options. Savvy Web users can find the movie in the Netscape cache folder and copy the file before it's erased from the cache. However, if you've used the first method (designating the movie as one which can't be saved), the cached movie will also be one that users won't be able to save, export, cut, or copy from.

- With RTSP movies, the movie's data is never downloaded to the user's computer, so even when Save as QuickTime Movie is chosen, the user gets only a file that points to the location on the Internet where the movie resides.

Creating Streaming VR Movies with QTVR Flattener

QTVR Flattener creates QuickTime VR movies that viewers can explore before the movies have finished downloading. These streaming VR movies either have a low-resolution preview that gets replaced by the full-resolution image as it's downloaded (**Figure 17.45**) or are structured in such a way that they are downloaded a vertical strip (or *tile*) at a time (**Figure 17.46**). In either case, a viewer can start clicking and dragging in the movie before the full VR movie has been downloaded. (If you are also adding settings to your movie using Plug-In Helper, use Plug-In Helper first and then use QTVR Flattener—otherwise, the settings may not work.)

To create a streaming QTVR movie:

1. If you haven't already done so, download QTVR Flattener, place it in your Extensions folder within your System Folder, and restart your computer.

2. In QuickTime Player, open your QTVR movie.

   Currently, only single-node panorama movies will work.

3. From the File menu choose Export.

4. In the pop-up menu at the bottom of the Save dialog box, choose Movie to Streaming QuickTime VR Movie (**Figure 17.47**).

5. Click the Options button.

   A dialog box appears (**Figure 17.48**).

6. If you want your movie to have a tiled effect, make sure the Create Preview checkbox is not selected, and then skip to Step 10.

   If you want to create a low-resolution preview, click the Create Preview checkbox to select it.

Figure 17.45 A QuickTime VR movie with a low-resolution preview shows the full-resolution portions as they're downloaded.

Figure 17.46 QuickTime VR movies can also be downloaded a tile at a time.

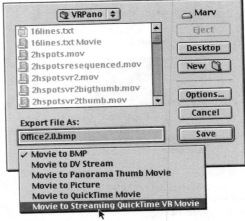

Figure 17.47 To create a streaming VR movie, choose Export from the File menu and Movie to Streaming QuickTime VR Movie in the pop-up menu. (This choice will only be available if you have installed QTVR Flattener in your Extensions folder in your System Folder.)

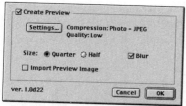

Figure 17.48 After you click the Options button in the Save dialog box, this dialog box appears.

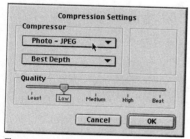

Figure 17.49 Click the Settings button to get a Compression Settings dialog box. Photo-JPEG is usually the best choice.

Figure 17.50 If you don't check the Blur checkbox, the image will be pixelated. (Compare this image with **Figures 17.45** and **17.46**.)

Preview Vs. Tiling

Whether you add a preview image or use the tiling really boils down to personal preference. A preview's one functional advantage is that the viewer can click on hot spots before the movie is completely downloaded; without the preview, the hot spots won't work until the entire movie has been downloaded.

7. Although the default settings—Photo-JPEG at low quality—work fine for most purposes, you can click the Settings button if you want to change them for the preview you're creating.

A Compression Settings dialog box appears (**Figure 17.49**). Good compressors to choose for this purpose are Photo-JPEG or Sorenson Video because they can achieve the highest compression ratios. (The Read Me file that is currently downloaded with this tool states that the only choices that will work are Component, Graphics, Motion JPEG, None, Photo-JPEG, Planar RGB, and Video, but we've found that Sorenson Video works just fine.)

When you're done choosing your settings, click OK to return to the previous dialog box.

8. To get the smallest and fastest-downloading preview, choose the Quarter radio button for Size.

This will create an image with one-quarter the resolution of the movie image. Half creates an image with half the resolution. The lower the resolution, the more pixelated the preview image will be.

9. Check the Blur checkbox if you want the image to be blurry (**Figure 17.50**) rather than pixelated.

10. Click OK.

11. Give the file a new name, specify a location, and click Save.

There's no way to remove or change the information added with QTVR Flattener, so make sure not to overwrite your original file.

If embedded on a Web page, this movie will show either the low-resolution preview or a tile at a time while the movie is being downloaded.

Creating Panorama Thumbnails with QTVR PanoToThumbnail

Poster movies (which we covered earlier in this chapter) provide a nice method of previewing a full-length movie. For QuickTime VR panorama movies, another method involves creating a *thumbnail,* or miniature self-playing version, of the full panorama (**Figure 17.51**), which can be placed on a Web page.

The tool you'll use, QTVR PanoToThumbnail, currently works only with single-node movies created with QuickTime VR 2 (the version that's installed with QuickTime 3 and 4).

To create a thumbnail version of a QuickTime VR panorama movie:

1. If you haven't already done so, download QTVR PanoToThumbnail and place it in your Extensions folder within your System Folder.

2. Open your QuickTime VR single-node panorama in QuickTime Player.

3. From the File menu choose Export.

4. In the pop-up menu at the bottom of the Save dialog box, choose Movie to Panorama Thumb Movie (**Figure 17.52**).

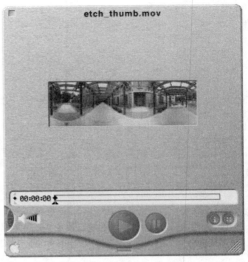

Figure 17.51 A thumbnail version of a panorama, particularly if it's self-playing, can be a great enticement for people to explore your movie.

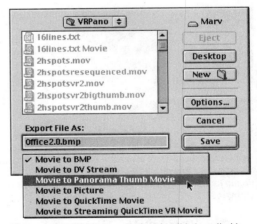

Figure 17.52 If QTVR PanoToThumbnail is installed in your Extensions folder, the Movie to Panorama Thumb Movie choice is available when you choose Export from the File menu.

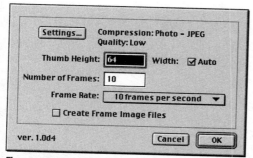

Figure 17.53 The default settings for the thumbnail produce good results.

5. Click the Options button.

A dialog box appears (**Figure 17.53**).

We've found that the default settings— Photo-JPEG compression at Low quality, with a height of 64 pixels, Auto width, 10 frames, and a frame rate of 10 frames per second—work quite well; however, you can change any of these, if you'd like. (Clicking the Settings button gives you access to a standard Compression Settings dialog box in which you can change the compressor, color depth, and quality.)

6. Click OK to return to the Save dialog box, and then click Save to begin exporting the file.

When you embed the exported file on a Web page, you probably want to add the following to your EMBED tag: CONTROLLER=false LOOP=true AUTOPLAY=true.

✔ Tip

- If you want to make a thumbnail for a QuickTime VR 1.0 movie, you'll need to first convert it to a VR 2.0 movie. You can do this easily with the QTVR Converter utility, located on the same Web page as the other tools we covered in this chapter. Put it in your Extensions folder, restart, and when you choose Export from QuickTime Player's File menu, you'll find an additional option in the pop-up menu: Movie to QuickTime VR Movie 2.x.

CREATING PANORAMA THUMBNAILS

Movies on CD-ROM, Kiosk, and Videotape

18

While vast numbers of people distribute QuickTime movies over the Internet and World Wide Web, QuickTime is also the best choice for CD-ROM as well as an excellent choice for video kiosks. You can even use it to produce traditional videotape.

In this chapter, we'll cover the basics of preparing QuickTime video for CD-ROMs and kiosks and then address specific compression options. (Be sure also to read Chapter 15, which examines issues common to all delivery platforms.)

We'll also talk about the licensing requirements for distributing QuickTime.

And finally, we'll outline some techniques for putting QuickTime movies onto videotape.

Preparing Movies for CD-ROM and Kiosk

As with Web video, the most important thing you need to do to prepare your movies for CD-ROM or kiosk playback is ensure that their data rates are sufficiently low.

Because CD-ROM and kiosk video don't have the same bandwidth constraints as the Web, you generally don't need data rates anywhere near as low as required for Web playback. For 2x CD-ROM (the low end of what's commonly available), the data transfer speed is 300 kilobytes per second; movie data rates can approach 200 kilobytes per second—tens to hundreds of times the practical data rates for streaming Web video. Hard drives (on which you may store video for kiosks) can transfer data at multiple megabytes per second.

For many people, these higher data rates open the door for better-quality images, larger frame sizes, and higher frame rates. However, other issues may deter you from trying to achieve the maximum possible data rate. For example, you still have the problem of the total data size of your movie running up against the storage limits of your chosen medium. In addition, at the high end, factors other than drive speed can slow down a computer's ability to deliver video, so don't assume that you can pick a data rate in the megabytes simply because a computer's hard drive can transfer data at those speeds. And finally, there's often no reason to take advantage of such high data rates when compressors like Sorenson Video can provide high quality at lower data rates.

We'll provide a quick review here of how to use QuickTime Player to compress video for CD-ROM or kiosk; the following pages provide recommendations for settings.

Figure 18.1 To compress a movie for CD-ROM in QuickTime Player, start by choosing Export from the File menu.

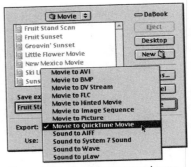

Figure 18.2 In the Export menu choose "Movie to QuickTime Movie."

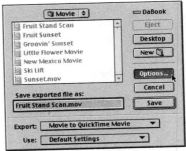

Figure 18.3 Click the Options button...

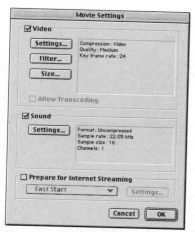

Figure 18.4 ...to open the Movie Settings dialog box in which you'll click the Settings buttons to access dialog boxes where you can make compression choices for the video and sound tracks.

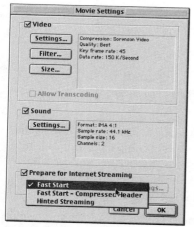

Figure 18.5 Check Prepare for Internet Streaming and choose Fast Start.

To compress a movie for CD-ROM or kiosk:

1. From the File menu, choose Export (**Figure 18.1**).

2. In the Export pop-up menu, choose Movie to QuickTime Movie (**Figure 18.2**).

3. Click the Options button (**Figure 18.3**) to open the Movie Settings dialog box (**Figure 18.4**).

4. In the Video and Sound areas, click the Settings buttons to access the dialog boxes in which you make video and sound compression choices. (We'll cover specific compression choices in the following pages.) After making choices in each of these dialog boxes, click OK to return to the Movie Settings dialog box.

5. In the bottom of the Movie Settings dialog box, check Prepare for Internet Streaming, and in the pop-up menu below the Prepare for Internet Streaming checkbox, choose Fast Start (**Figure 18.5**).

   (Yes, do this even though you're not preparing for Internet streaming. Movies will load more quickly.)

6. Click OK to close the Movie Settings dialog box.

7. Specify a new file name and location for your movie (if desired), and click Save.

continues on next page

✔ Tips

- In Step 3, it may be helpful to know that in the Use pop-up menu, the 1x choices set data rates at 90 kilobytes per second and the 2x choices set data rates at 150 kilobytes per second.

- If you want QuickTime Player to use a predetermined set of compression settings for your movie, after Step 2 use the Use pop-up menu to choose one of the CD-ROM options (**Figure 18.6**) and then skip to Step 7. However, we recommend that you don't rely on the presets in the Use pop-up menu; the key frame rate that these select will rarely be right.

Figure 18.6 If you're compressing for CD-ROM, you can pull down the Use pop-up menu and select a preconfigured group of settings.

PREPARING MOVIES FOR CD-ROM AND KIOSK

About DVD

DVD (an acronym that doesn't actually stand for anything, although many people believe it to mean *digital video disc*) is the next-generation compact disc. It can store as much as 17 gigabytes of data on a disc that looks just like a compact disc (which holds only 650 megabytes).

Like compact discs, DVD comes in several forms. *DVD-ROM* discs are like CD-ROM discs: Both hold data just as hard drives and other storage devices do. Because QuickTime movies are just files, they can be put on DVD-ROM discs as part of any standard multimedia production.

Related to DVD-ROM are *DVD-R*, which is recordable, and *DVD-RAM*, which is recordable and erasable.

Video Compression Choices for CD-ROM

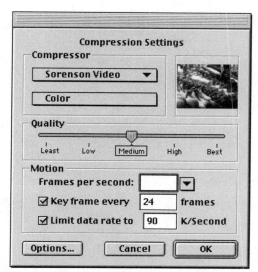

Figure 18.7 You make video compression choices in the Compression Settings dialog box.

When you compress your video for the higher data rates enabled by CD-ROM, you will make somewhat different selections in the Compression Settings dialog box (**Figure 18.7**) than for Web delivery. The following explains those choices. And remember: Other applications provide the same choices, so the information we provide here will apply to whichever QuickTime application you use to do the compression—not just QuickTime Player.

As with Web video, we can't give you one specific recipe for preparing QuickTime video for CD-ROM. You'll need to experiment to come up with the best combination of settings. Here are some ideas to get you going.

Making CD-ROM–appropriate choices in the Compression Settings dialog box:

- **Compressor:** Of the codecs included with QuickTime, you will again probably choose either Cinepak or Sorenson Video. Because Sorenson Video provides better quality at lower data rates, you can put more hours of video on a single CD-ROM or hard drive with it than you can if you use Cinepak to achieve similar quality. However, at high data rates Sorenson Video doesn't play well on slower computers (those running at less than about 150 MHz). So, for CD-ROMs targeted at the lowest common denominator, Cinepak may be a better choice.

- **Colors:** As with any other delivery method, you should choose the highest possible number of colors—unless your video truly requires the lower bit depth.

◆ **Quality:** You can probably leave the quality slider at its default position for your first test. (Remember that the higher the quality, the better the image will look, but the less compressed the movie will be.)

◆ **Frame rate:** If your uncompressed video has a high frame rate (even as high as 30 frames per second), it's reasonable to keep the same frame rate; if you don't enter a value in this field, the frame rate will be left alone. However, high frame rates result in high data rates; if you want a lower frame rate (perhaps because you're willing to sacrifice motion quality for image quality or frame size), pick a value that is a fraction of your original frame rate.

◆ **Key frame rate:** As with Web video, the compressor and frame rate you've selected will determine the appropriate entry here. For Sorenson Video, we recommend that you start with a number ten times the frame rate. For Cinepak, start with a number one or two times the frame rate.

◆ **Data rate:** If this field is enabled, you can enter a target data rate in kilobytes per second. If you're compressing with Cinepak, you generally want to pick a high value to ensure decent quality. The highest number you should enter will depend on the speed of the slowest drive that you expect your movie to be played from. For movies to be played on 2x CD-ROM drives, 180 is usually a safe maximum value. For 4x CD-ROMs, 300 is a good place to start. If you're targeting even faster CD-ROM drives or hard drives for kiosk use, you can choose a higher value here. However, it may work best to simply turn this choice off and let the other variables determine the data rate. If you're using the Sorenson Video compressor, you can get very good quality at much lower data rates; we recommend starting with a number less than 100, regardless of your target drive's speed.

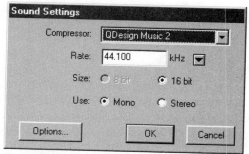

Figure 18.8 The Sound Settings dialog box is where you specify sound settings.

Sound Compression Choices for CD-ROM

When you're preparing movies for CD-ROM or kiosk, you can also be somewhat more liberal in the choices you make in the Sound Settings dialog box (**Figure 18.8**).

◆ **Compressor:** You should choose among IMA 4:1, QDesign Music 2, or Qualcomm PureVoice. However, Qualcomm PureVoice is only appropriate if your audio consists solely of spoken word. IMA provides very good sound quality and compresses faster than the other two, but its data rates are higher. However, since you're not compressing for the Web, those ultra-low data rates aren't as important. QDesign Music provides very good quality at very low data rates. If you have the Pro version of QDesign Music 2, it will almost certainly give you the best quality of the three. (See "About Additional Compressors" later in this chapter.)

◆ **Rate:** Here also you may want to try settings that give you better quality rather than go for the lowest number. A good place to start is 22.050 kHz.

◆ **Size:** 16-bit audio will sound better than 8-bit audio. The IMA 4:1, QDesign Music 2, and Qualcomm PureVoice compressors only work in 16-bit anyway.

◆ **Use:** You generally don't need to use stereo unless your original source is stereo and it's important for your presentation to have stereo sound.

✔ Tip

■ If you compress with QDesign Music 2, users must have QuickTime 4 to play back your movie. (QuickTime 3 shipped with version 1 of QDesign Music, which can't decompress version 2 files.)

Compression Choices for Kiosk

Because kiosks usually consist of a single computer whose media reside on the local hard drive, your movies' data rates are of even less concern here than they are with CD-ROM. Hard drives can transfer data at multiple megabytes per second (though you don't necessarily want to create movies with data rates this high without first testing on your kiosk system.)

If you don't want to spend much money, you can use any old computer and choose one of the standard video compressors included with QuickTime. (Read the preceding sections for general guidance on the compression dialog boxes, but assume that you can go for the high range of the settings.)

If you're willing to spend more, some video cards use specialized hardware for compression and decompression: Because they contain a dedicated chip for compression and decompression rather than rely on the computer's processor, these cards can deliver more video to the screen faster, allowing for full-screen, full-motion video. (Most such cards are based on a Motion JPEG compressor and are often referred to as *M-JPEG cards.*) The compressor you choose will be a proprietary one that works specifically with that card and is installed with the software for the card. For other settings, refer to the documentation that comes with the card—and make sure to test on your kiosk system.

An in-between solution can be provided by one of the third-party (software-only) compressors described in About Additional Compressors on the next page. Because you're setting up the playback computer, you simply need to make sure that the appropriate codec is installed.

Embedding Movies on a Web Page

If your movies will be embedded on Web pages, you may want to use the KIOSKMODE attribute in your EMBED tag to eliminate the plug-in settings menu. See "Adding Attributes to Your EMBED Tag" in Chapter 17.

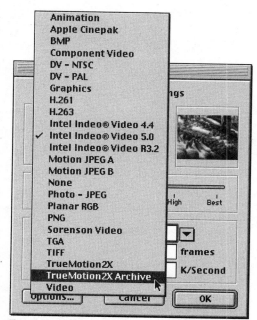

Figure 18.9 Additional video compressors can show up on your list of compressors if you've added them to your system. (Here we've added *TrueMotion* and *Intel Indeo* compressors.)

About Additional Compressors

Some additional codecs that can be used to compress QuickTime movies for CD-ROM or kiosk often result in higher-quality audio and video than QuickTime's built-in compressors can provide.

For video compression, Sorenson Developer, described in Chapter 16, is one of the most commonly used. Movies compressed with it will play back on any computer that includes QuickTime 3 or 4—there's no need for any additional files. For sound compression, the QDesign Music Codec Professional Edition will also provide higher-quality audio than the basic version that comes with QuickTime, and movies compressed with it will play back on any computer that includes QuickTime 4.

Other video compressors you can purchase that might provide better quality include Eidos Escape (from Eidos Technologies) and TrueMotion 2x (from Duck Corp.). For these, your viewers must have the corresponding decompressor, but this is less of an issue than it is with Web video. For CD-ROM, you include the decompressor on the disc—users don't generally have a problem if this extra file is installed during the installation process. For kiosks, you simply install the decompressor on the hard drive.

Some people have found Intel's Indeo to be a good choice for video compression—and they appreciate that it's free. (See "Indeo Compressors and Decompressors" sidebar.)

For most of these compressors, once you've installed them, they will appear in any QuickTime pop-up menus in which you choose compressors. (See **Figure 18.9**.)

continues on next page

✔ Tip

- If you purchase and install Sorenson Video Developer Edition, you won't see anything different in the video compression pop-up menu; it says Sorenson Video regardless of whether you have the Basic or Developer Edition. On the other hand, if you purchase the professional edition of QDesign Music, the item listed in the compressors pop-up menu in the Sound Settings dialog box changes from QDesign Music 2 to QDesign Music Pro 2.

Indeo Compressors and Decompressors

One additional compressor choice is Indeo, Intel's video compression technology, which is available in three versions: Indeo 3, Indeo 4, and the shipping version, Indeo 5. With QuickTime, it's possible to compress *and* play back all three versions on Mac OS and Windows computers. However, no versions are built in to the Mac version of QuickTime, and only the Indeo 4 compressor and decompressor and the Indeo 3 decompressor are built into the Windows version. You'll need to get and install an extra file to make any of the non-built-in versions work. (See Appendix C, under Apple Computer, to find out where to get these.)

In general, we don't recommend Indeo—not only because it's not fully built into QuickTime but because it requires more powerful computers to play back and compress than does Cinepak. (Indeo 3 can actually run on slower computers, but the resulting quality typically isn't any better than what you can get with Cinepak.) You may want to experiment with versions of Indeo yourself, however.

Licensing Requirements for Distributing QuickTime

You can distribute QuickTime movies (as long they're yours) without getting anyone's permission or paying a fee.

However, usually when you create any kind of disc for distributing your movies, you want to include the QuickTime software (in case the user doesn't have QuickTime or has an older version that won't show your movies to their best advantage). And for that, you must get legal permission from Apple. You can find Apple's QuickTime software distribution agreement at http://developer.apple.com/mkt/swl/agreements.html#Quicktime.

In essence, the agreement states that to distribute QuickTime, you must include Apple's QuickTime installer on your disc and use it during your installation process. There is no cost to distribute the Standard Edition of QuickTime. QuickTime Pro (which costs end-users $30) is $2 per distributed unit.

✔ Tip

- We're authors, not lawyers. If you're worried about signing legal documents that you don't fully understand, you should talk to a lawyer.

Outputting to Videotape

If you want to distribute a QuickTime movie to viewers without access to a QuickTime capable computer, outputting to videotape may provide the solution.

Your computer will need extra hardware—*video-out*—to translate the QuickTime movie into something a videotape machine can understand. On some computers these capabilities are built in. In addition, many inexpensive video cards also include this feature. Once you've installed and configured this hardware—read the user manual for the computer or card—you can use the Present Movie command in QuickTime Player.

To output a movie to videotape:

1. In QuickTime Player, open the movie.

2. From the File menu choose Present Movie (**Figure 18.10**).

   The Present Movie dialog box appears (**Figure 18.11**).

3. From the Movie Size pop-up menu choose an appropriate size for your movie.

   You may need to test to see which size setting provides the optimal combination of performance, visual quality, and size. For 320-by-240 movies, Double often works well. If your movie is smaller than 320 by 240, you may have a hard time getting full-screen video that looks good and plays well.

Figure 18.10
Choose Present Movie from the File menu.

Figure 18.11 Choose Normal as the mode, pick a size, and then press record on your VCR and click Play in the Present Movie dialog box. As long as the video from the computer is going into your VCR, the movie will be recorded to tape.

4. For mode, choose Normal.

5. When your settings are correct, press Record on your VCR and then click Play in the Present Movie dialog box.

✔ Tip

■ If you have high-resolution movies, you've probably made them with a hardware and software digital video solution that should also be used for doing the output.

Outputting to DV

DV (short for *digital video*) is many manufacturers' format of choice for their new DV camcorders. (In Chapter 9 we discussed how you can open DV files.)

If you want to output your QuickTime movie to DV tape rather than to analog tape, you'll have to follow different steps.

To start, you need a computer equipped with a *IEEE 1394* (also called *FireWire* by Apple and *iLINK* by Sony) port. This high-speed port enables the transfer of DV data as well as other types of data. You can purchase such cards for most newer computers, and many of Apple's most recently introduced machines come with FireWire ports.

It's possible to use QuickTime Player to export the movie in DV format. To do this, you choose Export from the File menu, and then in the Export pop-up menu choose Movie to DV Stream. In theory, you can then copy the DV-formatted movie from your computer to your DV camcorder or DV video deck. Currently, however, no software tools enable this copying.

In practice, outputting QuickTime video to DV is commonly done with software other than QuickTime Player. Most IEEE 1394 hardware cards that you may purchase, such as Digital Origin's MotoDV, come with software to output the video to a DV device. For Mac users, Apple's Final Cut Pro has an export to DV option and Apple's FireWire-equipped computers come with Adobe Premiere plug-ins that allow you to output video to a DV device when using Premiere.

Mouse and Keyboard Tricks

Tables **A.1** through **A.4** list various keyboard and mouse actions that perform useful functions in QuickTime Player or when using the standard controller. Although we mentioned many of these in the book, we've consolidated them here for your convenience. (We haven't listed the keyboard equivalents that appear in QuickTime Player's menus.) When you see the standard controller, it will normally be within some other application, which may already use some of the key combinations described here (in **Tables A2** and **A4**). So, all of the key combinations won't necessarily work.

Table A.1

Mac OS Mouse and Keyboard Shortcuts and Enhancements That Work in QuickTime Player

SHORTCUT/ACTION	WHAT IT DOES
Ctrl Play button	Plays all frames
Option drag Resize control	Scales to next "good" size
Shift drag Resize control	Scales movie disproportionately
Up or down arrow keys	Raises or lowers volume
Left or right arrow keys	Steps back or advances active indicator one frame
Return or spacebar	Plays if paused; pauses if playing
⌘ . (period)	Stops playing
Double-click movie image	Plays
Single-click playing movie image	Stops playing
⌘ right arrow key	Plays
⌘ left arrow key	Plays the movie backward
Shift double-click movie image	Plays the movie backward
Option Right Arrow key, Current Selection Indicator active	Jumps to end of movie or end of selection
Option Left Arrow key, Current Selection Indicator active	Jumps to beginning of movie or beginning of selection
Shift pointer over image in VR movie	Zooms in
Ctrl pointer over image in VR movie	Zooms out
Option pull down File menu	Open Movie in New Player replaces Open Movie (or vice-versa if Preferences are set differently)
Option pull down Edit menu	Trim replaces Clear, Add replaces Paste
Shift pull down Edit menu	Replace replaces Paste
Shift Option pull down Edit menu	Add Scaled replaces Paste

continues on next page

MOUSE AND KEYBOARD TRICKS

Table A.1 *continued*

SHORTCUT/ACTION	WHAT IT DOES
(Ctrl) Paste, Add, or Add Scaled*	Brings up Text Import Settings dialog box or Compression Settings dialog box
(Option) click image sample in Compression Settings dialog box	Zooms in
(Shift) (Option) click image sample	Zooms out
(Option) click close box of Player window	Closes all open Player windows

When pasting or adding text copied from editor or graphic copied from graphics application.

Timecode Mode Selector
(tells which indicator
is active)

Current Location indicator

Selection Start indicator

Selection End indicator

Resize control

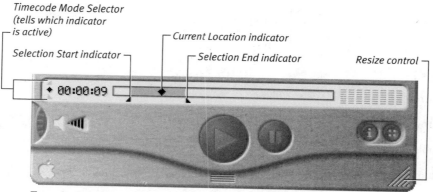

Figure A.1 QuickTime Player interface elements used in mouse and keyboard shortcuts and enhancements.

Table A.2

Mac OS Mouse and Keyboard Shortcuts and Enhancements That Work with the Standard Controller

SHORTCUT/ACTION	WHAT IT DOES
Ctrl Step buttons	Shows scratching slider
Option right Step button	Jumps to end of movie or selection
Option left Step button	Jumps to beginning of movie or selection
Option Volume Control button	Turns audio on/off
Up or down arrow keys	Raises or lowers volume
Left or right arrow keys	Steps back or advances one frame
Return or spacebar	Plays if paused; pauses if playing
⌘ . (period)	Stops playing
Double-click movie image	Plays
Single-click playing movie image	Stops playing
⌘ right arrow key	Plays
⌘ left arrow key	Plays the movie backward
Shift double-click movie image	Plays the movie backward
Shift Volume Control button	Overdrives audio
Shift pointer over image in VR movie	Zooms in
Ctrl pointer over image in VR movie	Zooms out

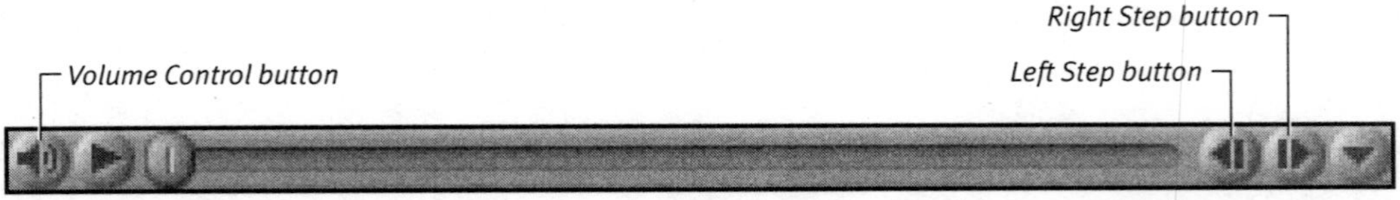

Figure A.2 QuickTime standard controller elements used in mouse and keyboard shortcuts and enhancements.

Table A.3

Windows Mouse and Keyboard Shortcuts and Enhancements That Work in QuickTime Player

SHORTCUT/ACTION	WHAT IT DOES
Alt Play button	Plays all frames
Ctrl Alt drag Resize control	Scales to next "good" size
Shift drag Resize control	Scales movie disproportionately
Up or down arrow keys	Raises or lowers volume
Left or right arrow keys	Steps back or advances active indicator one frame
Enter or spacebar	Plays if paused; pauses if playing
Double-click movie image	Plays
Single-click playing movie image	Stops playing
Ctrl right arrow key	Plays
Ctrl left arrow key	Plays the movie backward
Shift double-click movie image	Plays the movie backward
Ctrl Alt right arrow key, Current Selection Indicator active	Jumps to end of movie or end of selection
Ctrl Alt left arrow key, Current Selection Indicator active	Jumps to beginning of movie or beginning of selection
Shift pointer over image in VR movie	Zooms in
Ctrl pointer over image in VR movie	Zooms out
Ctrl Alt pull down Edit menu	Trim replaces Clear, Add replaces Paste
Ctrl Alt pull down File menu	Open Movie in New Player replaces Open Movie (or vice-versa if Preferences are set differently)
Shift pull down Edit menu	Replace replaces Paste
Shift Ctrl Alt pull down Edit menu	Add Scaled replaces Paste

continues on next page

Table A.3 *continued*

Shortcut/Action	What It Does
Alt Paste*	Opens Text Import Settings dialog box or Compression Settings dialog box
Ctrl Alt click image sample in Compression Settings dialog box	Zooms in
Shift Ctrl Alt click image sample	Zooms out
Ctrl Alt click close button of Player window	Closes all open Player windows and quits QuickTime Player

When pasting text copied from editor or graphics copied from graphics program.

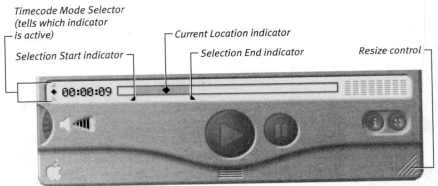

Timecode Mode Selector
(tells which indicator
is active)

Current Location indicator

Selection Start indicator

Selection End indicator

Resize control

Figure A.3 QuickTime Player interface elements used in mouse and keyboard shortcuts and enhancements.

Table A.4

Windows Mouse and Keyboard Shortcuts and Enhancements That Work with the Standard Controller

SHORTCUT/ACTION	WHAT IT DOES
[Alt] Step buttons	Shows scratching slider
[Ctrl] [Alt] right Step button	Jumps to end of movie or end of selection
[Ctrl] [Alt] left Step button	Jumps to beginning of movie or beginning of selection
[Ctrl] [Alt] Volume Control button	Turns audio on/off
Up or down arrow keys	Raises or lowers volume
Left or right arrow keys	Steps back or advances one frame
Enter or spacebar	Plays if paused; pauses if playing
Double-click movie image	Plays
Single-click playing movie image	Stops playing
[Ctrl] right arrow key	Plays
[Ctrl] left arrow key	Plays the movie backward
[Shift] double-click movie image	Plays the movie backward
[Shift] Volume Control button	Overdrives audio
[Shift] pointer over image in VR movie	Zooms in
[Ctrl] pointer over image in VR movie	Zooms out

Volume Control button

Right Step button

Left Step button

Figure A.4 QuickTime Standard Controller elements used in mouse and keyboard shortcuts and enhancements.

Configuring QuickTime

When you install QuickTime, it's configured according to some default settings, which usually work just fine. However, you can—if you need to—change your configuration via the QuickTime Settings control panel or the QuickTime Plug-in Settings dialog box. We discuss both of these in this appendix.

Using the QuickTime Settings Control Panel

The QuickTime Settings control panel (which we introduced in Chapter 1 and mentioned elsewhere in the book) includes a number of panels, which we summarize below. Most do not affect QuickTime Player and thus do not need to be changed.

Autoplay (Mac OS only)

This panel (**Figure B.1**) specifies what happens when certain volumes or discs appear on your desktop.

We recommend that you leave the Enable CD-ROM AutoPlay option unchecked because a virus (the AutoStart virus) can infect your system when this is checked.

Connection Speed

This is where you choose your Internet connection speed (**Figure B.2**). The speed you select will be used when you come across a page that includes a reference movie (see Chapter 17). If you choose a connection speed of 56K Modem/ISDN or slower, the Allow Multiple Simultaneous Streams buttons becomes enabled. If you check this, QuickTime will split the available bandwidth between multiple movies, potentially degrading performance. (For connections faster than 56Kbps, Allow Multiple Simultaneous Streams is always checked.)

File Type Associations (Windows Only)

You use this panel (**Figure B.3**) to indicate whether you want QuickTime applications (for example, QuickTime Player, the QuickTime Plug-in, or PictureViewer) to open various types of file types.

— Select this checkbox if you want your audio CDs to play from start to finish when inserted

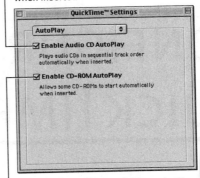

— Select this checkbox only if you don't mind if programs on certain CDs (designated as auto-play by their creators) start automatically

Figure B.1 AutoPlay panel.

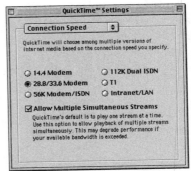

Figure B.2 Connection Speed panel.

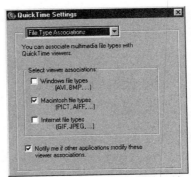

Figure B.3 File Type Associations panel.

Click here to enter an assigned access key

Figure B.4 Media Keys panel.

Select a synthesizer in this list

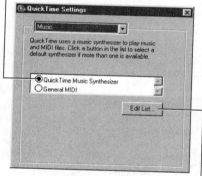

Click here to change the choices available in the list above. For example, to add your hardware synthesizer.

Figure B.5 Music panel.

Click here if you want your Mac OS machine to use DOS file extensions to determine what application should be used to open a file

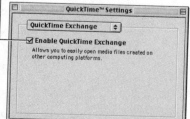

Figure B.6 QuickTime Exchange panel.

Media Keys

Some movies can be encrypted: To play back such movies, you need an access key, which you enter in this panel (**Figure B.4**).

Music

If you have a hardware MIDI synthesizer, register it on this panel (**Figure B.5**). (See Chapter 13 for more details.)

QuickTime Exchange (Mac OS Only)

The Mac OS usually recognizes files by *filetype* (data stored with the file). QuickTime Exchange (**Figure B.6**) enables the Mac OS to recognize standard DOS file-name extensions (for example, .bmp and .wav) even if there's no file type.

USING THE QUICKTIME SETTINGS CONTROL PANEL

Registration

This panel (**Figure B.7**) can be used to enable QuickTime Pro (see Chapter 1).

Sound In (Windows Only)

Use this panel (**Figure B.8**) when you have more than one audio input and you need to specify which to use when you're capturing audio for QuickTime movies.

Click here if you've already purchased QuickTime Pro and need to enter registration information

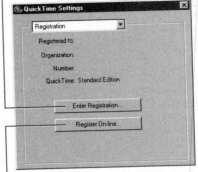

Click here if you want to load a Web page that contains information about purchasing QuickTime Pro

Figure B.7 Registration panel.

Select the audio input you want QuickTime to "listen to" when recording audio

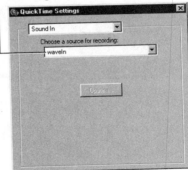

Figure B.8 Sound In panel.

Windows computers may have multiple devices for playing back sound. If your system is DirectSound compatible, choose DirectSound. WaveOut is the lowest common denominator.

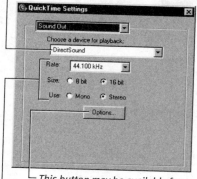

This button may be available for certain audio playback devices. Click it to change additional settings specific to the device.

Click here if you want to load a Web page that contains information about purchasing QuickTime Pro

Figure B.9 Sound Out panel.

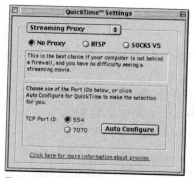

Figure B.10 Streaming Proxy panel.

Sound Out (Windows Only)

Use this panel (**Figure B.9**) to specify sound playback characteristics.

Streaming Proxy

You'll only need to change the No Proxy radio button selection on this panel (**Figure B.10**) if firewalls are preventing you from receiving QuickTime streams. (Firewalls control data flow by allowing only certain types of data to come through.) If you're behind a firewall, you'll need to contact your network administrator to get the numbers you'll need to enter after clicking RTSP or SOCKSv5. If you're not behind a firewall but are still having trouble receiving streams, experiment with the TCP Port ID numbers; start by clicking the Auto Configure button.

USING THE QUICKTIME SETTINGS CONTROL PANEL

Video Settings (Windows Only)

These settings **(Figure B.11)** determine how QuickTime works with your video display system.

✔ Tip

■ For the best QuickTime playback performance under Windows, you'll need the current version of DirectX. You can get this at http://www.microsoft.com/directx/download.asp. You'll also want to get the current drivers for your video and sound cards. (You can find these at http://www.download.com/. Choose Drivers from the Categories list. To locate a sound driver, choose Sound & Multimedia in the Subcategories list. To locate a video driver, choose Display & Video in the Subcategories list.)

This is the slowest method for Windows to draw graphics on your screen, but compatible with the majority of video cards

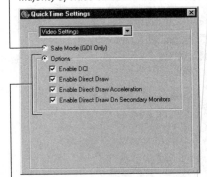

These options will provide better playback performance. Only deselect them if you believe they're not compatible with your graphics card.

Figure B.11 Video Settings panel.

Specifying Connection Speed in Location Manager (Mac OS Only)

Useful for portable computers, Location Manager is a Macintosh control panel that allows you to specify various settings for each location at which you run your computer. With QuickTime 4, one of the settings you can edit for each location is QuickTime Speed. This enables you to specify the same settings as you do in the Connection Speed panel of the QuickTime Settings control panel.

Using the QuickTime Plug-in Settings Dialog Box

Movies on Web pages have an extra button in the controller—a down-pointing triangle at the far right side. Clicking and holding this button reveals a drop-down menu. Choose Plug-in Settings to open the QuickTime Plug-in Settings dialog box **(Figure B.12)**.

If this is checked, movies are saved in cache space on your local hard disk along with other documents (as long as there's room); when you revisit the page with the movie, it will play from the cache (if it's still there) rather than downloading again.

If this is checked, movies on Web pages will start playing automatically when enough data has been downloaded—regardless of what the Web page author has specified. If this is not checked, only movies designated "AUTOPLAY=true" will play automatically.

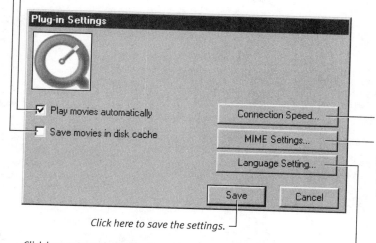

Click here to indicate your connection speed. Changes you make here alter the Connection Speed panel of the QuickTime Settings control panel (and vice-versa).

Click here to set the MIME types that you want the plug-in to handle. You can let QuickTime automatically configure these settings if you prefer.

Click here to save the settings.

Click here to specify your preferred language (Spanish, French, and so on) so that for Reference movies in which different languages are specified, you get the correct alternate movie. (If you don't specify a language the default is the same as your operating system language.)

Figure B.12 The QuickTime Plug-in Settings dialog box.

RESOURCES

In this appendix we list vendors and products mentioned in this book (along with URLs), followed by a select group of informational Web resources.

Vendors and Products

Abvent

Katabounga
http://www.abvent.com/intl/katabounga.html

Adobe Systems

GoLive
http://www.adobe.com/prodindex/golive/
main.html

Photoshop
http://www.adobe.com/prodindex/
photoshop/main.html

Premiere
http://www.adobe.com/prodindex/premiere/
main.html

Apple Computer

Apple MIDI manager (unsupported)
ftp://ftp.info.apple.com/Apple_Support_Area/
Apple_Software_Updates/US/Macintosh/Misc/
MIDI_Management_Tools_2.0.2.sea.bin

Final Cut Pro
http://www.apple.com/finalcutpro/

HyperCard
http://www.apple.com/hypercard/

Indeo 3 Mac
http://asu.info.apple.com/swupdates.nsf/
artnum/n11266

Indeo 4 Mac
http://asu.info.apple.com/swupdates.nsf/
artnum/n11265

Indeo 5 Mac
http://asu.info.apple.com/swupdates.nsf/
artnum/n11430

Indeo 5 Win
http://asu.info.apple.com/swupdates.nsf/
artnum/n11431/

QuickTime and QuickTime Player
(888) 295-0648 (to order QuickTime Pro)
http://www.apple.com/quicktime/

**Sprite Export Xtra, Plug-In Helper,
MakeRefMovie, QTVR Flattener, QTVR
PanoToThumbnail, QuickDraw 3D
Movie Maker, others**
http://www.apple.com/quicktime/developers/
tools.html

Asymetrix

ToolBook
http://www.asymetrix.com/

Digital Origin

MotoDV
http://www.digitalorigin.com/products/
MotoDV.html

Duck

TrueMotion
http://www.duck.com/

Eidos Technologies

Eidos Escape
http://www.eidostechnologies.com/

Electric Cafe

ModelShop
http://www.eleccafe.com/modshop/
modshop.html

Electrifier

Electrifier Pro
http://www.electrifier.com/Products/
ElectrifierStudio/

Equilibrium

DeBabelizer
http://www.debabelizer.com/

Inklination

FineArt 3D
http://www.inklination.com/Pages/Products/
Q3D-Renderer/overview.shtml

IncWell

SuperCard
http://www.incwell.com/SuperCard/
SuperCard.html

Interactive Media

Special Delivery
http://www.imcinfo.com/MasterSD.html

Interactive Solutions

MovieWorks
http://www.movieworks.com/

Macromedia

Authorware
http://www.macromedia.com/software/
authorware/

Director
http://www.macromedia.com/software/
director/

Flash
http://www.macromedia.com/software/flash/

MacSourcery

BarbaBatch
http://www.macsourcery.com/web/
BarbaBatch/barbabatch.html

Mark of the Unicorn

Free MIDI
http://www.motu.com/english/software/
freemidi/fmdist.html

David McGavran

Spritz
http://home.earthlink.net/~dmcgavran/spritz/

MetaCard

MetaCard
http://www.metacard.com

Microsoft

PowerPoint
http://www.microsoft.com/powerpoint

Opcode/Gibson

OMS (Open Music System)
http://www.opcode.com/products/oms/

Paceworks

ObjectDancer
http://www.paceworks.com/products/
objectdancer.html

Pangea Software

3DMF Optimizer
http://www.pangeasoft.net/

Pitango

ClickWorks
http://www.pitango.com/

QDesign

**QDesign Music Codec
Professional Edition**
http://www.qdesign.com/

Roger Wagner Publishing

HyperStudio
http://www.hyperstudio.com/

Sorenson Vision

Sorenson Broadcaster
http://www.s-vision.com/products/
SorensonBroadcaster/

Sorenson Video Developer Edition
http://www.s-vision.com/products/
SorensonVideo/

Strata

Strata VideoShop 4.5
http://strata.com/html/videoshop.html

Terran Interactive

Media Cleaner Pro
*(Can also purchase Sorenson Video Developer
Edition, QDesign Music Codec Professional
Edition, and Fraunhofer MP3 Encoder here.)*
http://www.terran.com/

Totally Hip Software

LiveStage
http://www.totallyhip.com/Link/
ProductsLiveStage.html

Tribeworks

iShell
http://www.tribeworks.com/

Uni Software Plus

easy beat
http://www.unisoft.co.at/products/
easybeat.html

Informational Resources

Channel QuickTime
Frequently Asked Questions about
QuickTime.

http://www.quicktimefaq.org/

Codec Central
Lots of info on compressors.

http://www.codeccentral.com/

**Judy and Robert's
Little QuickTime Page**
A weekly information page by the authors of
this book.

http://www.bmug.org/quicktime/

QuickTime Pro 4
Visual QuickStart Guide Companion Web
site to this book.

http://www.peachpit.com/vqs/quicktime/

INDEX

INDEX